T0295635

The Flow of Management Ideas

The widespread promotion of management ideas, their regular inclusion in textbooks and business school curricula and their use in organisational change programmes, has engendered debates about the impact of these ideas on management and organisational practice. Based on analyses of managerial audience members' activities and related meaning-making prior to, during and after guru events with leading management thinkers, this book sheds new light on how management practitioners come to use management ideas in the different relevant contexts of their working lives. The authors argue that a broader, more differentiated and more dynamic view of managerial audiences is essential in understanding the impact of management ideas as well as the nature of contemporary managerial work. For scholars and students in organisation studies, knowledge management and management consultancy, as well as reflective management practitioners.

Stefan Heusinkveld is an associate professor at the Vrije Universiteit Amsterdam. His research concentrates on the production and consumption of management ideas, and professions. He has published widely on these topics and has edited special issues in various academic journals. He is co-editor of *The Oxford Handbook of Management Ideas* (2019).

Marlieke van Grinsven is an assistant professor at the Vrije Universiteit Amsterdam. Her research focuses on narrative constructions of organisational realities in processes of change. She is particularly interested in the uptake and translation of management knowledge and the identity processes involved. She has published in various organisation and management journals.

Claudia Groß is an assistant professor at the Radboud University, Nijmegen. Her research focuses on the flow of management ideas and how to design organisations that support ethical behaviours. She has published in various journals and communicates her academic insights to the wider public via TV, newspaper and internet contributions.

David Greatbatch is Honorary Visiting Professor in the York Management School at the University of York. His research focuses on the use of oratory by management gurus and corporate executives. He has published widely in leading international journals and co-authored *Management Speak: Why We Listen to What Management Gurus Tell Us* (with Timothy Clark, 2005).

Timothy Clark is Provost and Professor at Singapore Management University. His research focuses on oratory in management guru lectures and the nature of consultancy work. The publications emanating from this work include *Management Speak* (with David Greatbatch, 2005), and *The Oxford Handbook of Management Consulting* (with Matthias Kipping, 2012).

The Flow of Management Ideas

Rethinking Managerial Audiences

Stefan Heusinkveld

Vrije Universiteit Amsterdam

Marlieke van Grinsven

Vrije Universiteit Amsterdam

Claudia Groß

Radboud University, Nijmegen

David Greatbatch

University of York

Timothy Clark

Singapore Management University

CAMBRIDGE
UNIVERSITY PRESS

University Printing House, Cambridge CB2 8BS, United Kingdom

One Liberty Plaza, 20th Floor, New York, NY 10006, USA

477 Williamstown Road, Port Melbourne, VIC 3207, Australia

314–321, 3rd Floor, Plot 3, Splendor Forum, Jasola District Centre, New Delhi – 110025, India

79 Anson Road, #06–04/06, Singapore 079906

Cambridge University Press is part of the University of Cambridge.

It furthers the University's mission by disseminating knowledge in the pursuit of education, learning, and research at the highest international levels of excellence.

www.cambridge.org
Information on this title: www.cambridge.org/9781107182912
DOI: 10.1017/9781316863473

First published 2021

A catalogue record for this publication is available from the British Library.

Library of Congress Cataloging-in-Publication Data
Names: Heusinkveld, Stefan, author.
Title: The flow of management ideas : rethinking managerial audiences / Stefan Heusinkveld, VU University of Amsterdam [and four others].
Description: Cambridge, United Kingdom ; New York, NY : Cambridge University Press, 2021. | Includes bibliographical references and index.
Identifiers: LCCN 2020050810 (print) | LCCN 2020050811 (ebook) | ISBN 9781107182912 (hardback) | ISBN 9781316863473 (ebook)
Subjects: LCSH: Management. | Management – Study and teaching.
Classification: LCC HD31.2 .H48 2021 (print) | LCC HD31.2 (ebook) | DDC 658–dc23
LC record available at https://lccn.loc.gov/2020050810
LC ebook record available at https://lccn.loc.gov/2020050811

ISBN 978-1-107-18291-2 Hardback

Contents

Figures

Tables

Acknowledgements

We would like to thank all the research participants including Guru A and Guru B for their time, commitment and for sharing their valuable experiences. In addition, we are indebted to Erik Lazeroms, Hans Janssen and Lex Baggerman for their crucial help in securing research access.

Portions of this book are reproduced by permission of SAGE Publications Ltd., London, Los Angeles, New Delhi, Singapore and Washington DC, from Greatbatch, D. and Clark, T. Displaying group cohesion: Humour and laughter in the public lectures of management gurus. *Human Relations* (Copyright Sage Publications, 2003).

Portions of this book are reproduced by permission of INFORMA UK Ltd., Abingdon, from Greatbatch, D. and Clark, T. (2005). *Management Speak: Why We Listen to What Management Gurus Tell Us* (Copyright INFORMA, 2005).

Portions of this book are reproduced by permission of Edward Elgar Publishing Ltd., Cheltenham, from Clark, T., Bhatanacharoen, P. and Greatbatch, D. Conveying the adaptation of management panaceas: The case of management gurus. In A. Örtenblad (ed), *Handbook of Research on Management Ideas and Panaceas* (Copyright Edward Elgar Publishing, 2015).

Portions of this book are reproduced by permission of John Wiley & Sons Inc., from Groß, C., Heusinkveld, S. and Clark, T. (2015). The active audience? Gurus, management ideas and consumer variability. *British Journal of Management* (Copyright John Wiley & Sons, 2015).

Portions of this book are reproduced by permission of SAGE Publications Ltd., London, Los Angeles, New Delhi, Singapore and Washington DC, from Greatbatch, D. and Clark, T. *Using Conversation Analysis for Business and Management Students.* (Copyright Sage Publications, 2018).

1 The Flow of Management Ideas

Management ideas such as Balanced Scorecard (BSC), Core Competences, Lean Management, Total Quality Management (TQM), Corporate Social Responsibility (CSR), Big Data and Agile have received widespread interest from management practitioners and academics alike (Sturdy et al., 2019). This interest may be related to the expansion of management as an ideology and practice in contemporary society, and the important role of a range of traditional management intellectuals (Guillén, 1994) or knowledge entrepreneurs (Clark, 2004a) – which include management gurus, management consultants, business schools and mass media organisations (Abrahamson, 1996; Engwall et al., 2016; Kieser, 1997; Piazza and Abrahamson, 2020; Sahlin-Andersson and Engwall, 2002).

Management ideas are generally presented – mainly via these knowledge entrepreneurs – as an essential guide to management practitioners in performing their tasks, and promote and legitimate the management occupation in general as important for the functioning of contemporary organisations (Sturdy et al., 2019). At the same time, the widespread promotion of these management ideas has led to important questions related to whether these can be considered beneficial or not. Indeed, many of these ideas have been heavily criticised for lacking an adequate scientific basis as well as for possible unfavourable consequences for organisations and their members such as inducing a 'permanent need for organizational change' (Sorge and van Witteloostuijn, 2004: 1209), enhancing the likelihood of 'organizational forgetfulness' (Brunsson and Olsen, 1997: 41; see also Lammers, 1988) and creating 'more stressful and intensive' working conditions (Knights and McCabe, 1998: 163).

In spite of these critiques, management ideas have become widely associated with many, and oftentimes substantial, organisational change programmes (Abrahamson and Fairchild, 1999; Strang, 2010), and have a taken-for-granted presence in many textbooks and business school curricula. In their recent overview, Piazza and Abrahamson recognised that: 'managers rely on such practices to improve their organizations' effectiveness [. . .] students of management learn about these techniques in business schools, corporate universities, training programs, industry associations, and the management press' (2020: 17). Some management ideas have even become generally accepted ways of thinking and talking about management and organisation in general (Clark and Salaman, 1998). For example, Sturdy and Gabriel noted that: 'reading Michael Porter or Tom Peters or at least "knowing" their ideas is considered a *sine qua non* for today's practicing manager or business-person' (2000: 983). This has fed the general assumption of knowledge entrepreneurs' success in gaining widespread attention for their ideas, but has also given rise to long-standing debates concerning their influence on the nature of managerial work and organisational life (Sturdy, 2011). For instance, Clark emphasised that these knowledge entrepreneurs can be assumed to have a major impact on the conceptualisation and practice of strategy, yet also recognised that 'how they impact on and influence strategy is presently little understood' (2004b: 105).

Although the literature on management ideas has expanded substantially over the last few decades, and has significantly advanced both empirically and theoretically (Sturdy et al., 2019), *a primary focus on the potential impact of these ideas on management and organisational practice remains*. As Clark explained in his review, the increased research interest in popular management ideas: 'may be partly motivated by a desire to understand the factors which account for the success and impact of a number of leading fashion setters' (2004a: 298), yet offering limited detail on 'the way in which different domains select and then process management ideas and how these then impact on managers' (2004a: 304). In a similar vein some years later, Sturdy and colleagues considered the possible impact as 'a persistent theme in the study of management ideas' (2019: 510), and relate this to the general preoccupation with outcomes and effects in the field of management, and to widely shared concerns about difficulties in realising the potential effects as well as the nature of potential (unintended) effects. Recently, Piazza and Abrahamson emphasised the need to see questions related to the diffusion and use of management ideas as non-trivial particularly 'given the role that management practices play in the management of organizations nationally and globally' (2020: 18).

In addressing concerns about impact, this now large and established literature has developed in different productive directions, focusing primarily on the (macro-level) diffusion of these ideas and on their (micro-level) organisational implementation (e.g. Ansari et al., 2010; Huising,

2016; Reay et al., 2013). Yet, although these individually long-standing, broad and varied approaches have established strong theoretical and empirical bases, they consider only parts of the broader flow of management ideas as they move between different contexts (Sahlin-Andersson and Engwall, 2002), thereby allowing a largely fragmented and incomplete view of their possible impact. As Huising (2016) has succinctly put it: 'Between macro patterns of diffusion and micro processes of organizational change *lies a no-mans land*' (p. 384, emphasis added). In other words, studies on *management idea diffusion* generally do not consider where these ideas go, beyond the broad assumption that some of them receive widespread attention amongst management practitioners and organisations. Adoption here is generally considered a proxy for impact given that 'full use' is typically assumed (cf. Rogers, 1995). At the same time, studies on *management idea implementation* lack a systematic understanding of where these ideas come from beyond the assumption that various pressures may enhance formal adoption. Here, adoption is merely considered a necessary but not sufficient condition for – mainly organisational – impact as it is seen as largely 'unrealised' or undefined. These issues in understanding the impact of management ideas may not only stem from different scholarly traditions (Gray et al., 2015; Sturdy et al., 2019), but may also be an artefact of the increased academic emphasis on research papers or 'experimental reports' (Strang and Siler, 2017: 533) as a dominant genre which may encourage limited foci compared to other genres such as essays and books (Gabriel, 2016; Suddaby, 2019), and may constrain possibilities of addressing the conceptual complexities inherent to studying flow.

In this book we seek to address this lacuna in researching the impact of ideas by considering how *management ideas flow between relevant contexts* (cf. Sahlin-Andersson and Engwall, 2002). A focus on flow contributes to further bridging and extending the broad but largely disconnected literatures of *diffusion and implementation* as it allows us to reveal some of the complexities critical to understanding the impact of management ideas that are currently obscured from view (cf. Sturdy, 2011). For this purpose, our research focuses on management practitioners as audience members that various management knowledge entrepreneurs aim to reach through different media channels such as their books, columns, radio and television appearances, live lectures or via social media and the Internet (Barros and Ruling, 2019). Given the apparent popularity of these traditional and new business media, as well as management education such as MBA programmes, being an audience member can be seen as particularly significant to contemporary management practitioners. After all, managerial audiences are likely to play a critical role in how ideas flow between different contexts. Indeed, in their role as audience members, management practitioners are not only involved in contexts typically related to management idea diffusion, but also in the implementation of these ideas within and beyond their organisational contexts (Hancock and Tyler, 2019). Theoretically, an audience perspective offers vital possibilities to develop a more comprehensive view on mass communication processes: 'from the structure of the production of the message at one end to audience perceptions and use at the other' (Hall, 1980: 1; see also McQuail, 2010). This is in line with Strang (2010) who emphasises the need for combining a 'greater diversity' (p. 11) of research approaches to studying the impact of ideas.

In sum, rather than understanding the potential impact of a single management idea in terms of its possible widespread diffusion *or* organisational implementation, we seek to explore how these foci can be bridged and extended via studying management practitioners who, as audience members, are considered central actors in the broader flow of ideas between these and other relevant contexts. Therefore, we propose that central to studying the impact of management ideas is the question: *How do management practitioners come to use management ideas in contexts of their working lives?*

Our empirical interest then is in examining how practitioners come to use these ideas in relation to the context of management guru lectures, management and organisational practice, and beyond by analysing managerial audience members' activities and related meaning making prior to, during and after a lecture. We focus on management gurus because they are widely considered as the most high-profile communicators of management ideas (Greatbatch and Clark, 2005). Within the group of knowledge entrepreneurs, management gurus are viewed as having a particularly critical role in the development and communication of these ideas. As Suddaby and Greenwood emphasise, the creation and communication of new ideas by management gurus is a 'starting point for the cycle of knowledge production and consumption' (2001: 249). Management gurus are therefore often viewed as figureheads and leaders of a particular idea movement that in turn influences the activities of the other knowledge entrepreneurs (Bodrozic and Adler, 2018; Huczynski, 1993; Kieser, 1997; Sahlin-Andersson and Engwall, 2002). In addition, their live lectures constitute an important moment of relatively unmediated and bounded consumption that may occur prior to organisational implementation (Carlone, 2006; Clark and Salaman, 1998; Collins, 2012; Grint and Case, 1998; Micklethwait and Wooldridge, 1996). As Greatbatch and Clark (2003) note, these are critical events that 'create the conditions necessary to win and retain converts' (p. 1539) and thus build the momentum necessary for an idea to become popular and be used in management and organisational practice (see Suddaby and Greenwood, 2001; McCabe, 2011).

A primary focus on managerial audiences is important because it offers vital insights into the complexities concerning how the impact of management ideas becomes apparent and is mediated throughout different relevant contexts (cf. Sturdy, 2011). Shedding more light on managerial audiences both within and beyond mass communication settings may thus permit a better approach to bridging and extending the currently disconnected approaches to researching the impact of ideas. Developing a critical understanding of what it means to be an audience member in the context of management not only constitutes an important basis to further develop our understanding of the broader impact of different management knowledge entrepreneurs and their ideas in different contexts, but also helps expand our view of management occupations and the nature of contemporary managerial work (e.g. Clark and Salaman, 1998; du Gay, 1996; Grey, 1999; Sturdy et al., 2006).

Based on the data, approaches and findings of research on speaker-audience interaction in guru lectures (Greatbatch and Clark, 2003, 2005, 2010, 2017), and audience members' experiences of guru events (Groß et al., 2015) involving a range of leading management thinkers from the USA and Europe (see Chapters 3 and 5, and Appendices 1 and 2 for further details), this book argues that a broader, more differentiated and more dynamic view of managerial audiences is essential to shed more light on important complexities in understanding the broader impact of management ideas as well as on the nature of contemporary managerial work. In this way the book provides an account that foregrounds management practitioners' activities and related meaning making in their role as audience members with regard to contemporary management media which, given the omnipresence of these media, can be assumed as essential in management practitioners' present-day working lives (cf. Barros and Ruling, 2019; Piazza and Abrahamson, 2020). By revealing how individual audience members resolve tensions and ambiguities prior to, during and after a guru lecture which may or may not ultimately result in the organisational adoption of an idea and beyond, the book not only contributes to developing a fertile ground for advancing the flow of management ideas as a critical perspective in researching their broader impact, but also develops a better understanding of management practitioners in their role as audience member. In the following sections we discuss the key streams in the study of the impact of ideas, prior to outlining our audience perspective and providing a general overview of the structure of the book.

Researching the Impact of Management Ideas

During the last few decades, there has been a growing research interest in the potential impact of management ideas (Abrahamson, 1996; Huczynski, 1993; Piazza and Abrahamson, 2020; Sahlin-Andersson and Engwall, 2002; Strang, 2010; Sturdy, 2004). This now large and established field of research (Sturdy et al., 2019) has taken two broad, but largely dispersed directions – one focusing mainly on diffusion and another on implementation. These comprise diverging conceptualisations of adoption and impact that are rooted in their specific application of what they see as relevant *scope* and related attention to *agentic meaning making* (see Table 1.1 for an overview). Again, whilst both research approaches have essential merits individually, they have focused on specific parts of the broader flow of management ideas, thereby allowing

Table 1.1 *Main approaches to researching the impact of management ideas (MIs)*

Key dimensions	Diffusion of MIs	Implementation of MIs
Key research question	How do MIs obtain widespread attention?	How do MIs translate into practice?
Adoption decision	End point	Starting point
Impact	• Full use assumed • Derived from adoption – 'proxy' for impact	• Largely unrealised and undefined • Preceded by adoption – necessary, but not sufficient condition for impact
Scope and agency		
• Level of analysis	Mainly macro: potential adopters in relation to various settings within the context of a broad management-knowledge market, some micro analyses	Mainly micro: adopters in relation to different settings in an (intra-) organisational context, some macro analyses
• Nature of agency	Concerted efforts aimed at obtaining widespread attention amongst management practitioners	Concerted efforts aimed at translating (abstract) ideas into management and organisational practice
• Focal agents	Knowledge entrepreneurs as key *initiators*, organisations and management practitioners in *recipients'* positions, mainly driven by socio-psychological and legitimacy motives	Higher-level managers as key *initiators*, organisational members in *recipients* positions mainly driven by own specific interests

a largely fragmented and incomplete view of their possible impact (cf. Huising, 2016).

Diffusion Approaches

Studies of management idea diffusion focus typically on explaining how ideas are able to obtain widespread attention in the context of a broad management knowledge market (cf. Piazza and Abrahamson, 2020). Here, particular research attention has been given to the processes and conditions that enhance the likelihood of widespread (formal) adoption of these ideas by managers and organisations (e.g. Sturdy, 2004). In line with Strang (2010), the formal adoption of management ideas is widely considered as: 'the end point of most diffusion studies' (p. 10), thereby assuming 'a decision to make full use of an innovation' (Rogers, 1995: 21). In this approach, the impact of management ideas is generally considered as directly derived from adoption. In this way adoption is, arguably, more or less explicitly regarded as a proxy for impact, particularly given that 'full use' tends to be assumed. This influential approach to researching management ideas can be seen as rooted in a specific view on scope and agency.

First, in terms of *level of analysis*, the extant diffusion literature provides a number of mainly macro-level explanations that account for the adoption of management ideas amongst a large population of managers and organisations. The general focus is on a wide variety of different settings in the general context of a broad management knowledge market which may signal acts of 'adoption' of these ideas, such as book sales, business media attention, guru lecture attendances, formal consulting service offerings, formal accreditations and use of change programme labels (Abrahamson and Fairchild, 1999; David and Strang, 2006; Furusten, 1999; Westphal et al., 1997; Kieser, 1997; Mazza and Alvarez, 2000; Zeitz et al., 1999). In addition to these macro-level analyses of diffusion, a number of studies have provided detailed analyses of the managerial responses to particular ideas in the micro-level interactions between gurus and their audiences (e.g. Greatbatch and Clark, 2003) and between consultants and their clients (e.g. Sturdy et al., 2009). Overall, this substantial and evolving body of work has explanatory value with regard to understanding the widespread attention to particular ideas amongst an audience of mainly managers and organisations. It provides important evidence that the potential influence of these ideas is driven by multiple forces and signals that, at least for some ideas, the population-level impact can be substantial. Studies of management idea diffusion have particularly contributed to our insight into mainly macro-level processes of 'adoption' in the context of knowledge market exchange.

Second, a substantial number of studies in this influential stream of research have furthered our conceptualisation of the *nature and direction of agency* in relation to processes of diffusion. In particular, a set of mainly macro-level explanations have focused on the way in which management ideas are actively shaped as part of various knowledge products and services so that they are intrinsically attractive to a large group of managers (Clark and Salaman, 1998; Sturdy, 2004; ten Bos and Heusinkveld, 2007). For instance, one group of studies has focused on best-selling management books and highlighted the importance of a focus on a single concept, pithy sentences, promises of significant performance improvement, references to well-known and highly reputable organisations, examples of concrete and successful implementation, interpretive space and a set of shared editorial practices (Furusten, 1999; Giroux, 2006; Grint, 1994; Kieser, 1997; Lischinsky, 2008; Røvik, 2002). Related studies have examined the importance of rhetorical practices and persuasive strategies deployed by different management knowledge entrepreneurs. When deployed effectively, these practices and strategies have been shown to enhance the prominence of their messages and increase audience attentiveness, thus creating the conditions necessary for a managerial audience to empathise with those communicating the ideas (Cullen, 2009; Greatbatch and Clark, 2003, 2005; Jackson, 1996, 2001; Sims, Huxham and Beech, 2009).

Other explanations of management idea diffusion also relate the attractiveness of certain management ideas to the extent in which these have framed their analyses of contemporary management problems and solutions so that they resonate, and are in harmony, with the expectations of their target mass audience, but have downplayed the role of agency (e.g. Abrahamson and Fairchild, 1999; Abrahamson and Eisenman, 2008; Barley and Kunda, 1992). Management ideas are unlikely to gain traction with target audiences if they fail to convince them of their plausibility by apprehending the zeitgeist or 'spirit of the times' (Grint, 1994: 193; see also Abrahamson, 1996; Kieser, 1997). The point here is that popular management ideas are assumed to have articulated persuasively both how they address key managerial problems and priorities (e.g. efficiency, performance enhancements, creating effective change), and why they offer the best means to do so at a certain point in time. However, although this particular notion draws on economic approaches to explaining why management ideas may generate a mass appeal (Bikchandani, Hirshleifer and Welch, 1998; Bloom and van Reenen, 2007; Bodrozic and Adler, 2018), in line with Grint (1994) the benefits of particular ideas in terms of means-ends relationships are likely discursively constructed via the zeitgeist – thereby suggesting the role and significance of agency.

Third, concerning the *position and positioning of the key agents*, diffusion studies tend to take different knowledge entrepreneurs as the main focal point and primary setting to understand the impact of management ideas (Abrahamson, 1996; Clark, 2004a; Kieser, 1997; Suddaby and Greenwood, 2001). Sturdy and colleagues observed that within the field, 'most studies focus primarily on one key actor such as management gurus, management consultants, business schools, multinationals, and the business and social media' (2019: 10). Whilst all these actors are considered relevant in understanding the adoption of ideas amongst managers and organisations, they are expected to perform different interdependent roles in the context of a broader management knowledge market or system of management ideas (Mol et al., 2019; Suddaby and Greenwood, 2001). Indeed, in this context, business schools are generally considered to educate the potential consumers of ideas, consultants are associated with processes of knowledge commodification and management gurus are seen as essential in legitimating management knowledge in a particular field (Suddaby and Greenwood, 2001). For instance, drawing primarily on analyses of these books and lectures, a significant body of prior work has helped us understand complex issues concerning the way management gurus, as an important group of knowledge entrepreneurs, use media to build their personal reputations with managerial audiences, and promote their ideas. In particular, this stream of research has significantly advanced our knowledge about gurus' ability to shape their ideas in ways that widely appeal to a mass audience (Clark and Salaman, 1996, 1998; Furusten, 1999; Huczynski, 1993; Jackson, 2001).

In research on diffusion, actors in 'adopter' positions generally receive a 'subordinate and predetermined or highly structured status' (Heusinkveld et al., 2011: 142). On the basis of acts of adoption in these settings – signalling attention to management ideas – theorists have also developed assumptions about the nature and main drivers of actors in these roles (Bort and Kieser, 2019; Wilhelm and Bort, 2013). An important stream of literature suggests that managers and organisations use these ideas primarily in response to legitimacy pressures. In this way organisations seek to *externally* display their conformity to generally accepted norms of how organisations should be governed (e.g. Abrahamson, 1996; Fiss and Zajac, 2006; Peters and Heusinkveld, 2010; Wilhelm and Bort, 2013). In line with this assumption, various diffusion studies have shown that managers' signalling of having adopted a relatively 'new' idea relates to how firms are valued within a society in general and by experts such as stock market analysts in particular (Nicolai et al., 2010; Nijholt et al., 2016; Staw and Epstein, 2000). Such a favourable reputation can have significant consequences for the viability of an organisation (Benders, 1999). Another explanation for the desirability of popular management ideas amongst those in 'adopter' positions relates to the 'intra-psychic' tensions and search for control and certainty that are generally associated with enacting the managerial task in a world that appears messy, capricious and unstable (Abrahamson, 1996; Gill and Whittle, 1993; Huczynski, 1993; Jackson, 1996; Sturdy, 2004; Wilhelm and Bort, 2013). Thus, these ideas are viewed as attractive to and build dependence from management practitioners, because they help 'satiate individuals' [managers'] *psychological* needs' (Abrahamson, 1996: 271; see also Ernst and Kieser, 2002; Jackall, 1988; Piazza and Abrahamson, 2020). Exemplifying this approach, Watson writes, these ideas are attractive because they help managers to 'create a sense of order in the face of the potential chaos of human existence' (1994: 904).

Implementation Approaches

In relative parallel to this body of work on macro-level diffusion, there is a growing research interest in the mostly micro-level implementation of management ideas (e.g. Benders, 1999; Benders and Verlaar, 2003; Huising, 2016; Kelemen, 2000; Knights and McCabe, 1998; McCabe and Russell, 2017; McCann et al., 2015; Mueller and Carter, 2005; Strang, 2010; van Grinsven et al., 2020). Here studies focus primarily on explaining how these ideas, once formally adopted within organisational contexts, are subsequently transformed or 'translated' into management and organisational practice (e.g. Ansari et al., 2014; Reay et al., 2013; van Grinsven et al., 2016). Thus, adoption is not seen as an end point but as an essential point of departure for a series of concerted efforts within specific, organisational contexts. Viewed in this way, adoption is a necessary condition but no guarantee for impact. Rather studies of implementation typically consider the impact of management ideas – habitually within organisations – as largely unrealised and undefined. This growing stream of research can also be related to a specific view on scope and agency.

First, in terms of *level of analysis*, whilst some analyses have connected to macro-level explanations by showing how organisational experiences may shape the wider evolving reputation of a specific management idea (e.g. Benders et al., 2019; Scarbrough et al., 2015; Zbaracki, 1998), implementation studies typically focus on explaining how abstract ideas, formally adopted at the organisational level, are translated and institutionalised into management and organisational practice (e.g. Ansari et al., 2014; Mueller and Whittle, 2011; Nicolai and Dautwiz, 2010; Reay et al., 2013). The primary focus of most studies is on the efforts of a selected group of higher-level managers whilst other organisational members are habitually positioned in recipient roles in relation to these initiatives. Although the perceived 'success' of these management-led efforts may vary (McCabe, 2011; Reay et al., 2013; Zbaracki, 1998), studies often suggest major (un)intended organisation-level implications.

Second, prior studies have significantly advanced our conceptualisation of the *nature and direction of agency* in the way concepts get translated in the local interaction of the organisational context. Much emphasis is on the concerted efforts and conscious micro-level actions of relevant actors to promote the value of an idea, facilitate the development of meanings and support its overall institutionalisation (for an overview, see Radaelli and Sitton-Kent, 2016). For instance, using an activity-based view, Reay and colleagues relate organisational implementation of management ideas to the managers' engagement in 'micro-level theorizing, encouraging people at the front line to try the new practice and facilitating meaning-making' (2013: 985–6). Theorists have also emphasised that activities aimed at gaining widespread intra-organisational support for particular ideas are certainly not sufficient for, and even potentially at odds with, the likelihood of institutionalisation (Gondo and Amis, 2013; Reay et al., 2013). Moreover, extant research on implementation indicates that agency is primarily aimed at enhancing the translation of ideas from 'the broad policy level into a set of specific practices' (Morris and Lancaster, 2006: 207). In other words, a central concern in most studies is on how and why 'higher-level meanings are continually refined and modified as they are moved to lower levels' (Reay et al., 2013: 983; see also Zilber, 2006). This may be a consequence of, or a reason for, the primary focus on the micro-level activities in relation to more systemic change programmes that are generally associated with 'mobilizing change at the level of the firm' (Morris and Lancaster, 2006: 215).

Third, and related to the previous point, research on management ideas has also shed important light on the *position and positioning of the key agents* in terms of their responses towards particular ideas in processes of organisational implementation (van Grinsven et al., 2020). Although research varies in the agency that is attributed to different relevant actors (van Grinsven et al., 2016), the primary focus of most studies of implementation is on actors at the managerial level as the assumed main starting point for the organisational use of management ideas (Ansari et al., 2014; Canato and Ravasi, 2013; Huising, 2016; Reay et al., 2013; Spyridonidis and Currie, 2016). Higher-level managers are generally portrayed as key initiators of processes of organisational use of these ideas which then – to various degrees – cascade downwards to other members in an organisation (see Heyden et al., 2017; Knight and Paroutis, 2016; Thomas et al., 2011).

Whilst those in managerial roles are generally considered to be supportive of formally adopting particular management ideas, others often receive a 'recipient' status. Organisational research has emphasised various implementation dynamics as these managerial actors may be confronted with large varieties of attitudes and related responses from other organisational members (Kelemen, 2000; McCabe, 2011; McDermott et al., 2013; Sturdy, 1997, 1998). Indeed, other initiatives to use management ideas, particularly from people in subordinate positions, tend to be less visible in extant studies (Cassell et al., 2017), or, particularly from managerialist perspectives, are easily considered as illegitimate because they do not 'fit' the official managerial interpretation of the idea (e.g. Ansari et al., 2014). For instance, Fiss and colleagues suggested that in the implementation of ideas, the (senior) management of an organisation tends to be: 'promoting wanted variation on the one hand and suppressing unwanted variation on the other' (2012: 1095). In particular, studies of organisational implementation tend to classify these responses by organisational members into relatively stable recipient categories according to their congruency with, or deviation from, the managerial interpretation, including: (1) positive responses (e.g. 'embracement', 'commitment', 'enthusiasm', 'full and true adoption', 'outspoken proponent' and 'adding to initiatives'), (2) unfavourable or negative responses (e.g. 'rejection', 'resistance', 'avoidance' and 'detachment'), and (3) various partial, or even contradictory, forms of conformity (e.g. 'behavioral compliance', 'assent adoption', 'lip service', 'low-dosage adaptation', 'ambivalence' and 'ceremonial integration') (terms in parentheses used within the studies of Ansari, Fiss and Zajac, 2010; Boiral, 2003; Jackall, 1988; Kelemen, 2000; Kostova and Roth, 2002; McCabe, 2011; McDermott, Fitzgerald and Buchanan, 2013; Peccei and Rosenthal, 2000; Sturdy, 1997, 1998; Watson, 1994).

Rethinking Scope and Agency in Researching Impact: A Critique

Prior work in these two broad areas of study provided powerful explanations of the attractiveness and popularisation of certain management ideas amongst managers and organisations, and has shed important light on how these ideas are translated into management and organisational practice. Yet, we still know little about *how management practitioners come to use management ideas in different relevant contexts in their working lives*. Rather, most studies on diffusion end their analysis with the organisational adoption of a new idea (e.g. Strang, 2010), whereas studies on the organisational implementation have more or less treated the widespread attraction and (organisational) adoption of these ideas as a given, and as a starting point for exploring how these are translated into practice (e.g. Morris and Lancaster, 2006; Mueller and Whittle, 2011; van Grinsven et al., 2020).

Given that (macro-level) analyses of diffusion tend to 'end' with adoption, and those on (micro-level) implementation take this as their starting point, the literature on the impact of management ideas may leave critical aspects related to adoption largely obscured from view. In line with this, Huising concluded that: 'The managerial work of adoption requires being a part of and moving between macro and micro realms to transform universal prescriptions into activities that can be implemented in a particular organisation. This work has been given short shrift in organizational theory' (2016: 384). As indicated by Figure 1.1, adoption can thus be seen as a 'hinge' – a pivot point of potential exchange between research on diffusion and implementation and, as such, as a starting point to unfold their currently fragmented and incomplete views on the impact of management ideas.

The lack of connection between these broad streams on diffusion and implementation and the limited understanding of processes of adoption is a critical shortcoming in the extant literature. As such, it may not only stand in the way of a fruitful dialogue, but may, in the light of the broader

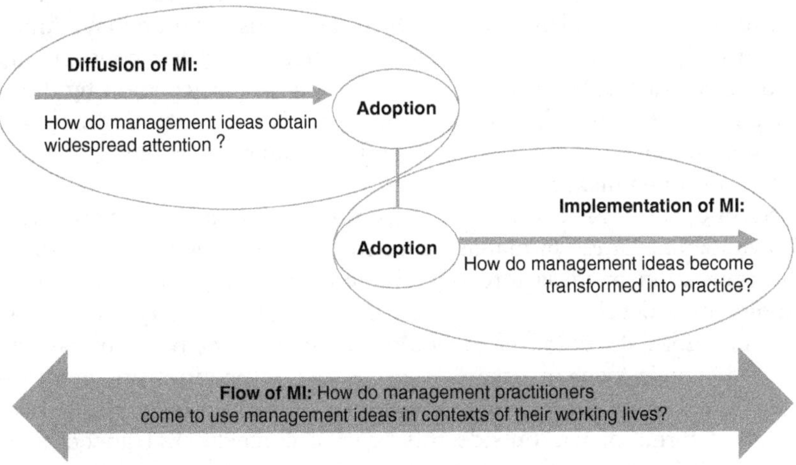

Figure 1.1 Main areas of research

flow of ideas, also leave critical aspects concerning scope and agentic meaning making under-conceptualised.

First, by its main focus on the population-level adoption of management ideas there has been limited consideration of how meanings of potential adopters are shaped outside the specific realm of diffusion. In particular, responses are generally put in terms of adoption and non-adoption, with limited consideration of the adoption decision as this is generally where analyses end. Adoption tends to be seen and measured as the decision to fully use an idea and non-adoption is framed as rejection altogether (e.g. David and Strang, 2006). As such, the prior diffusion literature provides little detail on the agentic meaning making of relevant actors in their adoption of ideas. Given the inter-organisational focus of most diffusion research, the potential variety of responses towards ideas and those who are promoting them – a central element in studies of organisational implementation – is remarkably absent. As Strang noted in his elaborate study on benchmarking: 'the sophistication of diffusion research, in short, often comes at the price of limited contact with the *actions* that the models are supposed to represent' (2010: 11, emphasis added). Rather, the relatively mechanistic or reactive portrayal of managers and organisations that willingly adopt management ideas to resolve common and apparently pressing problems is at variance with their image of being *active agents* in research focusing on the organisational implementation of these ideas. Furthermore, the primary emphasis on the promotion of management ideas in studies of diffusion is also notable given that studies of implementation have conceptualised these processes not as sufficient conditions or even at odds with conditions that enhance the likelihood of implementation. Or in the words of Gondo and Amis: 'the discourse required for effective implementation is less conceptually and more practically oriented and requires wide participation by those affected' (2013: 240). Building on this, there is a need to view management practitioners in the context of diffusion more as 'independent and active' meaning makers.

Second, and in contrast, by focusing primarily on those with a favourable attitude in management roles and their agency in shaping the translation of ideas into organisational practice, prior micro-level studies may develop a limited view on the use of management ideas beyond formal management-induced implementation initiatives. Indeed, a main focus on organisations as 'the' setting for using management ideas avoids essential understandings of relevant relationships and different forms of use outside this specific context (cf. Hancock and Tyler, 2019), which may ultimately feed back and shape processes of diffusion and use. For instance, from their review of the literature,

Radaelli and Sitton-Kent concluded a lack of adequate theorising of how management practitioners may act as carriers of management ideas and 'assimilate and organize these inputs' (2016: 317). Rather, most implementation studies relate the organisational adoption of ideas only to some conformity pressures without developing a detailed view on the wide variety of settings in which processes of management idea 'adoption' may occur. Given the organisational focus of most implementation research, the widespread attraction and subsequent decisions for organisational adoption – central elements in studies of diffusion – are considered as a given, and taken as a starting point for exploring how these are translated into practice. In doing so, this stream of literature has also offered little detail on the agentic meaning making of relevant actors in relevant contexts beyond the point of formal organisational adoption of ideas. As Huising concluded: 'Beyond observing managers as change agents in particular organizations, we need to understand their relationship to extra-local communities. Membership in these communities influences the meanings that managers attach to their work, thereby affecting how they do this work' (2016: 387).

In addition, a primary focus on (top) management activities in the literature on implementation is highly remarkable given the likely exposure of a multitude of organisational members to the macro-level promotion of management ideas. Indeed, Clark and Greatbatch (2004) have emphasised that management gurus' lectures attract an essentially differentiated audience of practitioners. In addition, given the ubiquity of new forms of mass media, it can be assumed that more management practitioners have access to the ideas of these gurus (cf. Piazza and Abrahamson, 2020). However, in the current literature on implementation most of these practitioners are obscured from view or receive only a secondary role as recipients of ideas from top managers, viewing their responses in terms of their adherence or deviance from a managerial interpretation.

Overall, we find that, in the light of the broader flow of management ideas, the extant streams of literature on diffusion and implementation both apply relatively narrow scopes with respect to the local-extra-local relationships involved in the adoption decision, and have each paid limited attention to the agentic meaning making related to the adoption dynamics. In other words, prior work on the impact of management ideas has considered only parts of the broader flow of these ideas, leaving under-conceptualised critical aspects concerning *scope and agency*. As such, this book argues that a broader, more differentiated and dynamic view of how management practitioners come to use management ideas throughout different relevant contexts of their working lives is necessary to deepen our understanding of the complexities concerning their impact on management and organisational practice and beyond (cf. Sturdy, 2011).

Management Practitioners as Audience Members

In response to these challenges in researching the impact of management ideas, our focus is on studying *management practitioners as audience members*. Managerial audience members are important, albeit largely unappreciated, carriers of management ideas (Sahlin-Andersson and Engwall, 2002; Suddaby and Greenwood, 2001). In particular, and as suggested above, they may not only bring particular ideas to their work environment, but may also shape other actors' attitudes to these ideas during processes of organisational implementation, and may enhance or impede receptivity to ideas when these are being 'sold' by other knowledge entrepreneurs such as consultants (e.g. Sturdy, 1997). For instance, Engwall and Wedlin posited that if business graduates are put in a role as consultants they might become 'significant missionaries of management ideas, both those learnt during their business studies and those they have picked up from their employers and clients' (2019: 163). Yet, such a potentially far-reaching, albeit complex area of influence has received little detailed analysis in the present literature on management ideas. We argue in this section that, in the light of the broader flow of ideas, there are important reasons for advancing a conceptualisation of managerial audiences not the least because it offers important possibilities for studying the complexities concerning how the impact of management ideas becomes apparent and is mediated throughout different relevant contexts (cf. Sturdy, 2011).

First, as explained below, the growth in MBA programmes and other forms of management education (Engwall et al., 2016), the increased sales of management books and the emergence of social media platforms particularly targeted at management practitioners provides concrete evidence of managers increasingly being put in the role of *audience member* (Barros and Ruling, 2019; Piazza and Abrahamson, 2020). Indeed, a substantial proportion of today's managers have received some form of management education either by following a regular (under)graduate programme in management and/or organisation studies at a business school, or by following executive programmes within a university or a private training institution (Engwall and Wedlin, 2019). Also, it has become much more common for management practitioners to attend lectures or watch videos of management thinkers that may or may not have obtained a guru status (Greatbatch and Clark, 2005; Sahlin-Andersson and

Engwall, 2002; Sturdy et al., 2019). For instance, Radaelli and Sitton-Kent (2016) found that processes of idea acquisition by management practitioners also entailed: 'formal and extended occasions such as meetings, workshops or seminars to informal chats, gossiping and rumors with peers [...] or brief contacts with top management' (p. 316).

Moreover, we learn from Pagel and Westerfelhaus (2005) that the sales of management books – traditionally one of the most recognised carriers of management ideas – has shown a substantial growth during the last thirty years or so. They refer to statistics that show that in the early 1990s 1,421 books in the category 'Business and Economics' were published representing a turnover of about 500 million dollars. Only ten years later the number of new titles increased to 5,023 and the turnover to almost a billion dollars. Such an increase in market size would suggest that the managerial ideas carried by these books continue to appeal to a large managerial audience. Also, recent figures from the *Library and Book Trade Almanac*, published in the years 1998, 2005, 2008, 2010, 2013, 2015 and 2018 indicate a relatively stable – after substantial growth in the first decade of this millennium – and large market (see Table 1.2), which is generally consistent with developments in overall US book production. Out of fifty-one categories, 'Business and Economics' is ranked fourth in terms of yearly US book title output (after the categories 'Children', 'Family and Relationships' and 'Health and Fitness') (Bogart, 2018: 395). Also indicative of the current size of the market for management knowledge is that the number of North American (US and Canada) academic textbooks, published or distributed in the year 2017, the category 'Business and Economics' is even ranked second (after the category 'Medicine') (Bogart, 2018: 366–7).

Relatedly, Barros and Rüling signal that management practitioners are increasingly attracted to internet-driven social media platforms such as LinkedIn, Facebook and YouTube that allow for the creation of sites

Table 1.2 *US book title output in the category 'Business and Economics'*

		Including	
Year	Number of all titles	audiobooks	e-books
1997 (Bogart, 1998: 522)	1,788	-	-
2002 (Bogart, 2005: 521)	5,028	-	-
2007 (Bogart, 2008: 536; Bogart, 2010: 494)	12,815	295	-
2012 (Bogart, 2013: 446–8; Bogart, 2015: 455)	13,811	465	11.296
2017 (Bogart, 2018: 395–406)	12,103	870	6.463

'where management ideas and practices can be presented, debated, and disseminated' (2019: 208). This may include guru and management thinkers' lectures – both whole lectures and clips from lectures such as organised via YouTube or the TED Talks channel. For instance, amongst the most popular TED Talks on management and leadership (August 2020) are Simon Sinek – more than 51 million views (TED, 2009), Rosaline Torres – more than 5.3 million views (TED, 2013), and Tim Harford – more than 2 million views (TED, 2011). Some management thinkers have their own YouTube channel and website including links to training videos, presentation slides, blogs and columns (see for example tompeters.com). Theorists note that these 'new' media tend to give a potentially larger group of management practitioners immediate access to a variety of ideas from different sources. In addition, these media may respond quicker to 'new' developments, and better allow for different forms of interaction (cf. Piazza and Abrahamson, 2020). Madsen even emphasised that: 'the new digital era that is upon us has many implications for the study of management ideas' (2020: 3). Thus, prior work has shown that *management practitioners are audience members in a large number of different contexts*. Arguably, given the presence and apparent popularity of different forms of new mass media primarily targeted at management practitioners, *being an audience member is an essential part of the contemporary managerial role*. As such, developing an adequate understanding of the role of managerial audiences in the flow of management ideas is not only of significance for organisations and the broader society, but also for the field of management as a whole as it requires us to rethink the conceptualisation of management occupations and managerial work to one that includes a role as audience member both within and beyond mass communication settings.

Second, theoretically, mass communication research emphasises the importance of accounting for the complexities of audiences in discussions on the impact of media messages. As Abercrombie and Longhurst have stressed in their overview, despite the omnipresence of mass media in contemporary societies, many of the approaches that are apparent in discussions of the possible impact of mass media tend to be 'seriously misplaced' (1998: 1), and require at least a much more nuanced and critical understanding of audiences particularly as a temporal and situated role (see also Butsch, 2008; Sullivan, 2013). In the context of management ideas, research on media audiences offers critical insight into how messages are mediated in different stages of the communication process. Central to the media research tradition that we follow in our analysis is the individual audience members' own activities and related meaning making of mass media prior to, during and after exposure (Rubin, 2009). In other words, to understand the possible impact of management ideas, we focus primarily on what audience members do with mass media in terms of their motives for using particular media in relation to different relevant contexts.

In the light of the broader flow of ideas across different contexts (Sahlin-Andersson and Engwall, 2002), the concept of managerial audience contributes to our understanding of the complexities related to studying the impact of management ideas. In particular, viewing management practitioners as audience members allows us to address our research question as it contributes to further exploring:

- why managerial audience members are open to particular management ideas in the contexts of mass communication events,
- how these ideas are filtered and critically appraised via a primarily differentiated audience and
- how this filtering may subsequently become apparent in the use of ideas in different social and situational contexts.

Structure of the Book

This book can be placed against the background of longstanding debates on the potential impact of management ideas on management and organisational practice. It is particularly concerned with the need to develop a more advanced understanding of *management practitioners as audience members* given their critical role in the flow of these ideas between different contexts (cf. Sahlin-Andersson and Engwall, 2002). For this purpose, it examines how these managerial audience members come to use management ideas in relation to different relevant contexts of their working lives. Based on analyses of audiences in relation to management guru lectures, the book argues that a more informed view of the managerial audience's activities and related meaning making of ideas is necessary if we want to further our insight into important complexities in understanding the broader impact of management ideas as well as on the nature of contemporary managerial work. The book is organised as follows.

Chapter 2 develops an integrated conception of audiences by drawing on three central approaches to audiences in the social sciences. In particular, we will consider: (1) research in the field of conversation analysis which is concerned with understanding the way lectures and speeches may influence and transform audiences and in turn, how audience responses may affect speakers' oratorical performances, (2) the 'uses and gratification' approach to studying media audiences which focuses primarily on the reasons and motivations for selecting specific media options and the way various audience activities relate to the nature of audience orientations, (3) more critical traditions of media research focusing on how audience members' interpretations of media messages relate to their social backgrounds and (4) literature on fans and fandom which provides an important lens to advance understanding of how and to what extent audience members take the ideas beyond a mass communication setting and may even become producers themselves. This provides the basis for a more detailed and nuanced conceptualisation of the managerial audience and how they perceive and use the mass communication events.

Chapters 3 and 4 examine the way the interactions between speaker and members of the audience may enhance or inhibit the flow of ideas beyond a mass communication setting. In particular, we look at the way gurus seek to create a *positive atmosphere* by promoting affiliative responses and limiting disaffiliative responses (Chapter 3). We also analyse how gurus present their ideas in ways which convincingly demonstrate that these ideas are potentially applicable to the variety of working lives of those who attend (Chapter 4). As such, these chapters shed more light on the conditions that may enhance the possibility that the management ideas that are promoted during the lectures leave the auditorium with audience members that are willing to use them in an organisational context or in other instances.

Chapters 5 and 6 analyse specific differences that exist between audience members in their orientations towards the ideas that have been conveyed beyond mass communication settings. Drawing on our study of management practitioners attending guru events we identify four *central audience orientations* (devoted, engaged, non-committal and critical) and explain their key characteristics, related audience activities and underlying rationales (Chapter 5). In addition, we consider how and why the development of these orientations may vary by elaborating on three forms of *shifts of consumption* (involvement-induced, utility-induced and alternating) that occur amongst audience members (Chapter 6). Overall, we stress that the identification of various shifts in individual consumption orientation indicates the need for a more fluid, conditional and variable understanding of management practitioners' responses towards management ideas.

Chapters 7 and 8 move our study beyond the mass communication setting within which management ideas are conveyed as we focus on the critical social and situational contexts of idea use. We consider how, within an organisational context, the flow of management ideas is related to the recursive deployment and reconstitution of three different forms of power (influence, force and domination), and how different directions of agency may relate to the relative power positions individual audience members may hold towards their assumed targets as they address subordinates (downward), peers (lateral) and superiors (upward) (Chapter 7). Also, we look at the different ways in which management practitioners *extend* their involvement with mass media and communicate management ideas. In particular we explore how audience members may engage in different forms of fan involvement (i.e. exaltation, socialisation and marketisation), each having a specific bearing on the way they construct themselves, the management ideas and related artefacts associated with a guru event. As such we further our insight into the way audience members can become 'productive' in various analytically distinct ways, and how these are associated with specific imaginary communities that act as points of reference beyond the scope of a specific organisation (Chapter 8). These two chapters are particularly focused on understanding how and to what extent audience members can be considered co-producers in and of themselves.

In Chapter 9 we conclude our analysis with an overview of our findings and implications for future research on the impact of management ideas as well as on the nature of contemporary managerial work.

2 Studying Audiences

In Chapter 1 we identified a number of critical deficiencies in the extant literature on management ideas, and stressed that a more advanced understanding of management practitioners as audience members is essential to shed more light on the potential impact of these ideas on organisations as well as on managers themselves. We found that such an understanding of managerial audiences needed to be grounded in a more comprehensive and coherent view on the mass communication process that is able to make connections to relevant social contexts that shape their appreciation and use of media contents (cf. Hall, 1980).

To address this need, the present chapter explores a number of important perspectives in the extant research on (1) live speaker-audience interaction and (2) mass media audiences. These perspectives to audiences constitute the main conceptual basis for the empirical chapters of this book (see Table 2.1 at the end of this chapter). The focus on live audiences is important given that gurus use their public lectures as a key means for communicating their ideas to management audiences both directly and through video recordings of the lectures. Previous research on speaker-audience interaction is particularly valuable because it provides a basis for understanding why gurus are often depicted as powerful charismatic orators whose public speaking skills account in part for the appeal of their ideas among managers. The focus on mass media audiences is of particular significance given the omnipresence of mass media (and mass marketing) in contemporary society, as well as the related audience roles as a key component of its members including those in management roles. The use of mass media perspectives on audience is also valuable given the recurrent societal debates on the potential negative impact of media messages on individuals and society as a whole as well as the role of new media on management practitioners (cf. Piazza and Abrahamson, 2020).

Overall, and in line with Abercrombie and Longhurst's (1998) view, our use of multiple perspectives on audiences is essential to deal with the inherent complexities of conceptualising audiences. Generally, audiences are too large to observe each member directly, and in its totality. Moreover, given that individuals cannot be considered audience members on a continuous basis (Butsch, 2008), their experiences not only relate to media exposure alone. The remainder of the chapter will first provide an outline of the relevant research on live speaker-audience interaction and mass media audiences and then explain how these perspectives may generate a number of critical questions that allow advancing our conceptualisation of the management practitioner as audience member and the flow of management ideas throughout different mass communication contexts.

Interactive Audience: Conversation Analysis

Conversation analysis (CA) emerged in the 1960s as part of the broader programme of sociological research known as ethnomethodology, which aims to document the tacit common-sense knowledge and practices that people use to navigate their daily lives and tasks (Garfinkel, 1967). Conversation analysis focuses on the social organisation of verbal and non-verbal aspects of spoken interaction through fine-grained analysis of audio and video recordings of naturally occurring social encounters and transcripts thereof. The transcripts capture not only what is said ('the verbal part of the talk'), but also various details of speech production (such as overlapping talk, pauses within and between utterances, pitch and volume) and visual conduct (such as gaze direction and gestures) (Psathas, 1995).

The approach is qualitative, but generally involves analysis of numerous instances in a collection of examples in order to describe generic dimensions of the interactional practices that people use to manage their social encounters in an orderly fashion. Although CA was initially primarily focused on the study of casual conversations, it has subsequently been applied to social interaction in a wide range of organisational settings and has led to the emergence of a growing body of studies in the field of business and management research that offers distinctive theoretical contributions in areas such as leadership and influencing (e.g. Clifton, 2006; Larsson and Lundholm, 2013; Svennevig, 2008), decision-making (e.g. Asmuß and Svennevig, 2009; Barnes, 2007; Clifton, 2009; Huisman, 2001; Nielsen, 2009; Svennevig, 2008, 2012), emotion (e.g. Kangasharju and Nikko, 2009), performance appraisal (e.g. Asmuß, 2008, 2013; Kikoski, 1998; Kikoski and

Litterer, 1983; Scheuer, 2014) and sales and service work (Llewelyn and Hindmarsh, 2013; Oshima, 2014.

Conversation analysis research on political oratory in the United Kingdom and the United States (e.g. Atkinson, 1984a, 1984b; Clayman, 1993; Heritage and Greatbatch 1986) constitutes the main conceptual basis for the analysis of the managerial audiences in guru lectures in Chapters 3 and 4 of this book (see Table 2.1). This stream of research has demonstrated that, while oratory has traditionally been regarded as monologic, it should be conceptualised as a form of interaction between speaker and live audience, thereby drawing on the premise that audience members are not powerless or passive (Atkinson, 1984a, 1984b; Heritage and Greatbatch, 1986). The adoption of this perspective has led to a number of new insights into the ways in which audience responses such as applause, laughter, cheering, booing and heckling are evoked and co-ordinated in real time speaker-audience interaction.

First, CA research shows that collective audience responses to political speeches, do not generally comprise spontaneous reactions to the messages that evoke them (e.g. Atkinson, 1984a, 1984b; Clayman, 1993; Heritage and Greatbatch, 1986). As collective actions, their production is informed by the basic sociological principle that individuals usual prefer to act like those around them so as to avoid social isolation (Asch, 1951). Thus, for example, individual audience members will generally only applaud/clap in response to public speakers' remarks in circumstances in which they are confident that other audience members will do the same.

In addition, CA research contends that audience responses are facilitated by two methods, (a) independent decision-making in the context of a specific media event and (b) mutual monitoring, which may in some cases co-occur. Independent decision-making involves audience members acting independently of one another but nonetheless managing to co-ordinate their actions, whereas mutual monitoring involves individual response decisions being guided, at least in part, by audience members monitoring each other's aural and visual actions (Clayman, 1992, 1993). These two scenarios result in distinct forms of live audience responses. Responses that are mainly facilitated by independent decision-making begin with a 'burst' and rapidly grow in intensity as numerous audience members respond in concert by co-ordinating their actions around a common reference point. Responses that are primarily organised by mutual monitoring are characterised by 'staggered' onsets as the reactions of a handful of audience members prompt other individuals to join in (Clayman, 1992, 1993).

Also, CA research demonstrates that the onset of applause during political speeches is organised primarily by independent decision-making (Atkinson, 1984a, 1984b). Generally, applause begins with a 'burst' immediately after or just before message completion. Individual audience members are able to respond in concert because political speakers indicate clearly to them that and when applause is relevant. Atkinson shows that political speakers often accomplish this not only by marking out messages from a background of other speech material but also emphasising then and providing them with clearly projectable message completion points around which individual audience members can co-ordinate their actions (see also Heritage and Greatbatch, 1986; Brodine, 1986; Clayman, 1993; Grady and Potter, 1985; McIlvenny, 1996). Clayman (1992, 1993) found that, in contrast to applause, audience booing and other disaffiliative responses are primarily co-ordinated through mutual monitoring – their onset is usually delayed and is co-ordinated mainly by audience members monitoring each other's conduct so as to respond together.

Greatbatch and Clark's previous studies (e.g. Clark, Bhatanacharoen and Greatbatch, 2015; Greatbatch and Clark, 2003, 2005, 2010) have shown that this approach provides a basis for developing a more advanced understanding of how gurus communicate their ideas to live managerial audiences at their lectures. In Chapters 3 and 4 we build on these studies to develop a framework for understanding how gurus seek to (1) create a positive atmosphere amongst their audiences at their live lectures by inviting audience laughter and avoiding direct criticism of their live audiences and (2) convey the adaptability and plasticity of their ideas, thereby maximising the chances of individual audience members subsequently using their ideas in different contexts.

Mass Media Audiences

In the next sections, we focus on an influential approach in contemporary media audience research which, similar to CA research, starts from the premise that audience members are not powerless or passive but active agents that have the possibilities for relatively independent decision-making between different media and for developing their own interpretations of media contents (see Webster, 1998 for an overview). Rather than a typical focus on elite concerns about possible negative 'effects' of media messages on people's cognition and behaviour or measuring the degree of attention they pay to different media, the primary question that underlies many of these studies involves: 'what do people do with media?' (Webster, 1998: 194). Whilst mass media communication is intimately connected to management and organisation (e.g. Vaara and Monin,

2010; Vaara et al., 2006), and various studies have furthered our understanding of mass media in relation to the flow of management ideas (Barros and Rüling, 2019), approaches to mass media audiences have received little attention in the field of business and management research.

With regard to this more agentic approach to audiences that is central in Chapters 5, 6, 7 and 8, we will further elaborate on three influential streams or paradigms of mass media research, and the way they relate to each other. In particular, we focus on: (1) the uses and gratification paradigm, its main theoretical developments (audience activities, shifts and the role of (domestic) contexts) as well as its critiques from (2) the research grafted in more critical traditions emanating from an incorporation/resistance paradigm and (3) studies that draw on a spectacle/performance paradigm that view audiences mainly as producers. Overall, the approaches share common ground, in particular with regard to the assumed agency of individual audience members, yet also have important differences, for instance, in their assumptions about the role of media and the nature of activity of audiences. Despite these differences, these approaches may complement each other in developing a more advanced understanding of managerial audiences and the potential impact of management ideas on management and organisational practice.

Active Audiences – Uses and Gratification Paradigm

The uses and gratification approach is often traced back to a number of theorists who signalled the emergence of studies of media audiences around the 1940s that differed significantly from those that prevailed in mass media research around that time (Gunter, 2000; McQuail, 2010; Rubin, 2009; Ruggiero, 2000; Sullivan, 2013). It was noted that in these studies, the traditional 'effects approach' to mass media messages was replaced by what is considered more 'functional inquiry' focusing on analysing the audience members' motives for using different forms of mass media. This entails that neither the communicator nor mass media were central in this line of research, but the variety of functions of this media to their potential audience members in relation to their underlying needs. For instance, in his ground-breaking 1959 paper, Katz considers this line of research as highly promising particularly in addressing the question as to why (relatively short-term) 'media campaigns' were generally less effective than expected: 'The "uses approach" – as I shall call it – begins with the assumption that the message of even the most potent of the media cannot ordinarily influence an individual who has no "use" for it in the social and psychological context in which he lives' (1959: 2).

Overall, the early uses and gratification theorists emphasised that media may have specific effects, but these are not direct and unmediated, and particularly relate to the agency of audience members. Such a view on audiences as essentially purposive has been considered as significantly at variance with the relatively mechanistic view traditionally drawn upon in media effects research (Rubin, 2009). Whilst these emerging audience-focused studies were also aimed at explaining possible outcomes of mass communication, they direct attention to the significance of analysing the main motives and underlying needs to understand audience members' choices for particular media or related contents. Given this focus, it is suggested that mass media need to be studied as one, albeit distinguished, source of influence amongst and in relation to many others in the audience members' life. Or in the words of Klapper: 'Whatever it be called, it is a shift away from the tendency to regard mass communication as a necessary and sufficient cause of audience effects, toward a view of the media as influences, working amid other influences, in a total situation' (1960: 5).

According to Blumler, 'there is no such thing as the uses and gratifications theory, although there are plenty of theories about uses and gratifications phenomena' (1979: 11). Whilst acknowledging the variety of different uses and gratification studies, and the need for further development, this approach to media audiences has been widely seen as valuable and distinctive. In his overview of the historical development of the approach since the 1940s, for example, Liu concluded: 'U&G has been gradually developed as one of the most influential audience theories' (2015: 76). The uses and gratification studies have been widely associated with a number of key theoretical, methodological and value-related assumptions (Katz et al., 1974) that have constituted a key basis for research conducted over the last few decades (cf. McQuail, 2010; Rubin, 2009; Ruggiero, 2000).

First, theoretically, studies in the uses and gratification tradition tend to share a view of mass media use as primarily driven by individual need satisfaction. In other words, the 'functions' of media or media contents to its potential consumers are seen as critical to understand its possible effects. Relatedly, it is also assumed that audience members are not only conceived of as goal-oriented and active in seeing gratifications from media use, but also as having substantial agency in making various media-related choices. For instance, according to Gunter (2000), uses and gratification studies generally see audience members as: 'being able to determine which media they use and media content they choose to consume' (p. 15). As such, theorists typically position their research against a view of audiences as relatively passive victims of mass media messages. Another central theoretical assumption typically shared by uses and gratification studies relates to the availability of alternatives to mass media. In particular, this stream of research tends to reframe the theoretical focus in mass media studies beyond the potential 'effects' of one particular programme to include why audience members may or may not use particular programmes to satisfy their needs. This assumes that mass media is not the only way to gratify particular needs, thereby signalling that it needs to be considered as only one part of people's broader lives.

Second, in terms of methods, uses and gratification theorists have persistently shared an interest in explaining media uses and effects by focusing on individual users' own experiences in mass communication processes and the main motives that underpin their choices with regard to media and media contents in particular (Cooper and Tang, 2009; Godlewski and Perse, 2010; Ruggiero, 2000). This implies that generally the empirical focus is on understanding individual audience members' own perceptions of media and media use rather than on analysing their responses in terms of the media contents. As Gunter succinctly states: 'these effects must be measured among audience members themselves ... they cannot be inferred though guesswork, no matter how detailed or sophisticated the media content assessment happens to be' (1988: 124).

Third, the position that uses and gratification researchers typical adopt with regard to their object of research are considered to be at variance with traditional media effects research. Indeed, beyond a general desire to gain more insight into media use and effects, theorists have signalled an important agenda that underlies much uses and gratification research is to give voice to audience members thereby providing a counterbalance to the broad emphasis on media messages over the individuals that may or may not 'consume' them. This not only involves putting audience members' viewpoints as much as possible 'in their own terms' (Katz et al., 1974), but also refraining from judgement as a researcher of the choices audience members make, whatever they may be. As Blumler stated:

> it is the distinctive mission of uses and gratification research to get to grips with the nature of audience experience itself which is ever in danger of being ignored or misread by (a) elitists who cannot partake of it, and (b) grand theoreticians who believe they understand the significance of such experience better than do the poor benighted receivers themselves. (1979: 12)

This brief discussion of the background and main characteristics of studies that draw on a uses and gratification approach shows that it has a long-standing tradition in mass media research. Whilst there is an ongoing debate about its limitations, the approach has undergone continuous theoretical development and continues to be widely regarded as an important approach not least due to its potential for enhancing understanding of new media use (Liu, 2015; McQuail, 2010; Rubin, 2009; Ruggiero, 2000). This is consistent with Ruggiero's conclusion at the turn of the century that: 'any attempt to speculate on the future direction of mass communication theory must seriously include the uses and gratification approach' (2000: 3). In the next sections, we will further detail a number of important theoretical developments in the uses and gratification approach that contribute to the main purpose of this book in better understanding the attraction of management ideas for an audience of management practitioners.

Audience Activities, Orientations and Variability

In his seminal work Blumler (1979) pointed out that, although the concept of an active audience constituted a critical basis of early uses and gratification research, it had been inadequately conceptualised. In particular, he found that in the early uses and gratification studies the concept of 'activity' in the context of mass media audiences was associated with a variety of different things, whilst at the same time it was treated as a dichotomy (audience are active or not), and did not account for differences in mass communication situations. Whilst recognising that early uses and gratification theorists primarily used 'active audience' to signal audience members' agency in making decisions about media use, he argued for understanding audience activity as a critical intervening variable (cf. Biocca, 1988). Building on Blumler's work, a substantial and still growing literature has focused on how various audience activities relate to the nature of audience experiences and, ultimately, to media effects (e.g. Cooper and Tang, 2009; Kim and Rubin, 1997; Levy and Windahl, 1984; Rubin, 2009; Tefertiller and Shehan, 2019; Valenzuela et al., 2019). According to Godlewski and Perse, this research has developed a more advanced 'multidimensional' view in which audience members are conceptualised as 'variably active along several dimensions and at different times in the media use process' (2010: 150). We first discuss the nature of these activities and then outline *how* individuals may vary in their active agency.

First, uses and gratification theorists suggest that audience activity becomes apparent in audience members 'selectivity', 'involvement' and 'utility' orientations in relation to a mass communication process. Selectivity involves activities associated with the making of choices about media and media contents: for example, deciding to watch television and choosing a particular programme from a number of alternatives

(Blumler, 1979; Davis, 2005; Perse, 1990). Activities of involvement entail the assignment of meaning and related mental and/or emotional states of anticipation with media content, such as being fascinated or feeling turned-off by certain media content or characters (Fiske, 1992a; McQuail, Blumler and Brown, 1972). Utility refers to activities related to the way in which audience members actually experience use, ignorance and even rejection of particular forms of media and media content for various social and psychological purposes (Bauer, 1964; Biocca, 1988; Levy and Windahl, 1985). Watching the news, for example, may allow audience members to 'express and perhaps share some set of political or social sentiments' (Levy and Windahl, 1984: 56).

Various studies indicate that audience members may vary in the way they perceive these activities, resulting in differing orientations towards the media and the specific contents these media convey (Blumler, 1979; Levy and Windahl, 1984; Perse, 1990; Rubin and Perse, 1987). In the words of Levy and Windahl: 'audience activity clearly is best conceptualised as a range of possible orientations to the communication process, a range that varies across phases of the communication sequence' (1984: 73). They submit that the variety in orientations indicates the way audience activities are associated with the specific gratifications that audience members seek and obtain from mass media: 'there is a demonstrable association between their activeness and the uses and gratifications they associate with media exposure' (Levy and Windahl, 1984: 74). Other studies have related audience members' perceptions of their activities during and around media exposure more directly to impact (Rubin, 2009). For instance, Kim and Rubin indicated how some audience activities are experienced as encouraging media effects whilst others are systematically associated with inhibiting some form of media influence on audience members. In other words, their study suggests that media effect is less likely when audience members perceive distraction during media exposure or deliberate avoidance of particular messages. Overall, these findings indicate that beyond the assumption of audience activity as a variable, 'differences in audience activity have important implications for media effects' (Rubin, 2009: 173).

Second, the uses and gratification literature has also related the nature of audience activity to different stages of media use. The findings of different studies suggest that individual audience members' level of activity is 'not consistently high or low at all times' (Levy and Windahl, 1984: 57). Rather, it is emphasised that each audience member is likely to be variably active along the communication process (Biocca, 1988; Blumler, 1979; Godlewski and Perse, 2010; Gunter, 1988; Levy and Windahl, 1984). For instance, building on Gunter's understanding of media usage as comprising both active and passive elements, Cooper and Tang found that: 'an individual is likely to be (at varying degrees) passive and active at different points, at times actively choosing the medium (or another technology), and at other times choosing the medium because it is accessible or a habit' (2009: 403). In sum, uses and gratification theorists stress the need to account for the highly dynamic character of the consumption process and the complex role of audience activity in this.

Audience Activity and Gratifications Sought versus Obtained

A notable theoretical advancement in the uses and gratification paradigm to media audiences is based on an expectancy-value perspective. This relates particularly to the widely recognised research work by Palmgreen and colleagues (1980) (see also Palmgreen and Rayburn, 1982; Rayburn and Palmgreen, 1984). In seeking to explore audience members' experiences of particular evening news programmes in relation to their perceived expectations, these theorists took issue with a number of problems related to the conceptualisation of gratifications in prior uses and gratification studies. In particular, they emphasised the need to better understand the audience members' reports about how they value particular media as well as the role of actual media exposure. For instance, in developing their critique, Palmgreen and colleagues quoted Greenberg (1974) who noted that prior research approaches: 'cannot distinguish whether the response obtained from the viewer of the medium, or a fan of some specific content, is an accurate statement of what he wanted, or what he thinks he got' (1980: 162). Another key concern that constitutes a starting point for their research stems from the relatively ill-defined conceptualisation of the notion of 'audience expectations' and its antecedents despite this being widely considered as 'essential to the uses and gratifications assumption of an active audience' (Rayburn and Palmgreen, 1984: 538).

To address these concerns, studies have focused on exploring the possible discrepancy between the gratifications sought by an individual audience member, and their gratifications obtained from a specific media experience in explaining their experiences of viewing programmes. In particular, in their expectancy-value model of uses and gratifications, Rayburn and Palmgreen (1984) sought to (1) develop an advanced conceptualisation of the main elements shaping individual audience members' gratifications sought, and (2) better explain how gratifications sought are connected to gratifications obtained.

First, Rayburn and Palmgreen argue that an expectancy-value model of uses and gratifications sees the gratifications sought as shaped by two primary components, namely (1) the beliefs of an audience member or their expectation that 'a media object possesses a particular attribute in a general sense' (Rayburn and Palmgreen, 1984: 540), and (2) the individual audience member's evaluation whether or not they would actually value the media attribute concerned. In other words, it is posited that 'gratifications sought' systematically relates to the general expectation that a particular medium will fulfil a specific audience need, and the individual appreciation of that medium. However, whereas the evaluation component is considered as relatively invariant and personal, audience members' beliefs are seen as emanating from various sources and primarily based on 'the sum of an individual's experience (direct and indirect) with a particular media object (Palmgreen and Rayburn, 1982: 575).

Based on Fishbein and Ajzen's (1975) expectancy value theory, Palmgreen and Rayburn's (1982) research conceptualised three distinct sources that constitute the main basis of belief formation in relation to media audiences. They hypothesised that audience members may form or modify their beliefs of whether particular media will gratify particular needs on the basis of their direct experiences of that media. Audience members' beliefs may also be shaped by particular characteristics that are attributed to media by habit whilst not directly or indirectly experienced. Finally, it is assumed that the basis for belief formation about media relates to information that stems from targeted advertising campaigns or an audience member's network such as friends and peers. In particular, given the difficulties of notifying, let alone actually experiencing, potentially relevant media and media output, the latter is considered to 'constitute a large proportion of our total media belief system' (1982: 576).

Second, the model indicates how the gratifications audience members seek and the gratifications that they report obtaining (1980: 183) are connected via two main processes. One is that the pursuit of particular gratifications is expected to result in and shape processes of media consumption which, in turn, may define audience members' perceptions of 'gratifications obtained'. The other key process relates to the assumption that the gratifications obtained from media exposure likely influence audience members' belief that particular media contribute to need gratification. Or as Palmgreen and colleagues stated: 'Perceived gratifications obtained are not totally based on preconceptions but are sensitive to actual content or media characteristics; thus, they will feed back to influence gratifications sought' (1980: 164).

The expectancy-value model also signals that feedback processes can shape gratifications sought in two analytically distinct ways. In particular, audience members' experiences either reinforce or modify extant beliefs dependent on whether or not these experiences are in line with their expectations. In case of the latter, gratifications obtained from media exposure may be lower than expected but can also exceed expectations (Rayburn and Palmgreen, 1984). Whatever the case, a lack of consistency between gratifications sought and obtained is hypothesised to result in changes in audience members' motivations to pursue particular gratifications with regard to a particular medium. The relation between gratifications sought and gratifications obtained may not only be strengthened by recurring feedback processes, but also by audience members' limited awareness of alternative media channels. In particular, Palmgreen and colleagues' (1980) study of the relationship between gratifications sought from television news and gratifications obtained from network evening news programmes suggested that: 'viewers who watch more than one program obtain gratifications from a wider variety of sources, and thus any single program would likely be inadequate in providing all the TV news-related gratifications these individuals are seeking' (p. 184). As such, the model thus not only signals the role of time, but also the audience members' broader consumption patterns – the accumulated prior audience activities – in understanding possible (in)consistencies in audience members' need gratification.

Levy and Windahl (1984) sought to develop a more comprehensive conceptualisation by incorporating the insights from the expectancy-value perspective in a model that connects gratifications to audience activities and media exposure. In particular, their model suggests that gratifications sought are primarily related to audience activities performed *before* actual media exposure. In other words, gratifications sought do not directly lead to exposure, but increase the likelihood of audience members' engagement in 'pre-activity' which is seen as an essential condition for the occurrence and nature of media exposure. Perceptions of gratifications obtained, in contrast, are not only associated with expectations and activities *during* media exposure ('duractivity'), but also to what Levy and Windahl termed as 'post-activity'. This means that a notable part of the satisfaction derived from media exposure is related to audience activities that are performed long *after* this exposure. As such audience members may experience consistency between gratifications sought and obtained with regard to 'duractivity', but feel inconsistencies concerning 'post-activity'.

Audiences in Domestic Contexts

Another important development within the uses and gratification paradigm involves studies of mass media use in everyday life and within the spatial context of the home in particular. In essence, this stream of research has concentrated on the role of specific relevant social environment at the moment mass media is actually being used to better understand media need gratification. Focusing primarily on analyses of television viewing in relation to family social interactions, various theorists have emphasised that (1) quantitative approaches to mass media research are not well suited to understanding the processes of meaning making by audience members, and in particular (2) there is a need to further develop the uses and gratification research beyond a primary focus on generic individual motives of mass media use.

First, various media theorists have shared a concern about the dominance of survey-based research traditions in conceptualising media uses and television in particular (e.g. Lull, 2014; Moores, 1993; Morley, 2003; Silverstone, 1994). It is argued that, in these traditions, conceptualisations of the social uses of mass media are primarily based on quantitative analyses of the amount and variety of people watching particular television programmes and the extent to which they find these programmes enjoyable. As such, what is dubbed the 'head counting tradition of industry audience measurement' (Gunter, 2000: 128) was considered as being unable to actually 'measure' what audience members actually do during the act of TV viewing, or uncover other motives for watching particular TV programmes rather than merely the assumed content-related interest of audience members (Silverstone, 1994; Sullivan, 2013; Morley, 2003). In addition, Morley also noted that survey-based studies of television audiences primarily focus on individual decisions by audience members to view a particular TV programme, and tend to consider what watching television may actually mean to these people in a largely undifferentiated fashion. In his words: 'much audience research assumes that "watching television" is a one-dimensional activity which has equivalent meaning for all who perform it' (2003: 176).

Second, researchers have also criticised prior work in the uses and gratification tradition for treating individual audience members as largely disconnected from the specific social context of media use (Lull, 2014; Moores, 1993; Silverstone, 1994; Sullivan, 2013). This may be the result of the limited possibilities offered by prior audience studies to develop a view of the 'natural setting' (Morley, 2003: 177) in which people tend to interpret media messages. Indeed, building on Silverstone (1994), Gunter considers media use as one element in a broad range of other social activities audience members are habitually engaged in. For example, he argues that: 'Television watching is a very complex activity which is enmeshed with a range of other domestic practices and can only be understood with that context' (Gunter, 2000: 127). The underlying assumption is that audience members' mass media use cannot be understood as an isolated activity and therefore an understanding of the sociocultural environment in which it naturally occurs is seen as an essential basis for theorising how and why individual members may use it (Lull, 2014; Morley, 2003).

In other words, whilst offering an essential basis for understanding media audiences, an important limitation of many uses and gratification studies lies in their primary focus on general audience members' needs that could be satisfied by media use, and the lack of systematic attention to the specific social environment 'within which readings of [TV] programs are ordinarily made' (Morley, 2005: 14). For instance, with regard to watching television, Morley noted that: 'much viewing is, in fact, done in groups where power is unequally distributed and choices must be negotiated – so that much viewing is, for many viewers, "enforced"' (2003: 175). Thus, a number of theorists have stressed the need for extending the uses and gratification approach by developing a deeper analysis of the various interpersonal communication processes in the context of a group to explain possible variations in individual media need gratification. As such, this has been expected to offer a more complex theorisation of media use as an important and habitualised element in domestic context.

In seeking to extend the uses and gratification approach to better account for the social aspects around media use, various studies have considered the family as 'the' natural setting of watching television thereby offering important possibilities to better understand how media need gratification is connected to social interactions and relationships (Lull, 1980, 1982; Morley, 2003). Particularly the seminal studies by Lull and later Morley gave rise to an important stream of research that has focused on the use of television or other technologies within a specific '*rule-governed social environment*' (Silverstone 1994: 38; see also Kortti, 2011; Morley and Silverstone, 1990). Whilst prior uses and gratification studies have used various qualitative methods in studying audiences, Lull's work has become well-known for pioneering an ethnographic approach to analyse viewers' choices, motives and modes of media use. In particular, by studying media use at the moment that it occurs, this approach allowed him not only to directly observe the influence of the broader social context, but also to avoid relying solely on self-reports, a data source that constituted an important basis for much uses and gratification research (Sullivan, 2013). To date, Lull's research is not only seen as a 'touchstone' (Silverstone, 1994: 38) for understanding the role of television in family life, but the family has also become widely considered 'a natural unit in ethnographic audience research' (Kortti 2011: 298).

An essential finding from this pioneering research analysing the 'politics of the sitting room' (Moores, 1993: 31) was that the main needs being gratified do not relate to television as a medium per se, but rather are strongly connected to the specific social relationships around the medium. In particular, analyses indicated how media use is systematically related to family members' social position and the specific interpersonal objectives concerning power and influence. For instance, Morley concluded that 'to consider the ways in which viewing is performed within the social relations of the family is also, inevitably, to consider the ways in which viewing is performed within the context of *power relations* and the differential power afforded to members of the family in different roles' (2005: 36, emphasis added). As such, a key implication is that media, like any technology, can be seen as an important social resource (see also Jensen, 1988; Morley and Silverstone, 1990; Silverstone, 1994) to reinforce or modify extant power positions, whist at the same time media use is also being constrained by the specific family roles and related institutionalised expectations and structures (Lull, 2014).

Lull's pioneering research (1980, 1982) identified a number of different ways in which family members use television as a social resource in shaping and maintaining interpersonal relations and indicated how these relate to the relative power position. Overall, this research examines the processes of need gratification in the specific social context by considering how family members in more powerful positions, relatively equal positions and less powerful positions use mass media to serve their needs.

Direction 1: Downward. Lull discussed various instances in which television is used in a downward fashion, and in particular for the purpose of establishing or maintaining a dominant position in the family vis-à-vis other members. For instance, the recurrent possibility to grant access to TV or a particular programme to others can be seen as a confirmation of the gatekeeping role – and thus dominant role – of parents. At the same time, parents may also deploy their relative power position towards other family members by commenting on programmes from their point of view or selectively referring to particular programmes that promote specific roles that are in line with the parents' ideology or extant role enactment: 'programs are used by the parents to educate their children about topics being presented in accord with their own view of the world' (Lull, 1980: 205). In this way, dominant actors (i.e. those in parent roles) use television in seeking to influence others' perceptions of 'acceptable role behavior' but also to signal their own alignment with these ideal roles.

Direction 2: Lateral. The research by Lull revealed various uses of television in interpersonal relations of a more lateral kind, that is, amongst those in relatively equal positions in a domestic context. For instance, television is appreciated as a useful resource for family members and friends to share experiences, emotions and information about programmes that may relate to others' interests. As such this mass medium is not only used to maintain a feeling of togetherness, solidarity – thereby re-emphasising equality in the current positions – but also seen as a key resource to influence other members for instance about the 'appropriateness of certain male and female behavior' (Lull, 1980: 206) amongst adolescent family members by vocalising negative feelings or in developing an 'esteemed position in the eyes of peers' by presenting oneself as expert or signalling an expert status on certain issues. In this way, interpersonally clarifying attitudes amongst peers can be seen as a way of developing common ground (welcome visitors/guests and feeling as one of them while at the same time expressing feelings can be seen as demonstrating competence in interpersonal relations or vocalise negative feelings and thereby influence them.

Direction 3: Upward. Lull's empirical evidence has also shed important light on how family members in less powerful positions use mass media to serve their specific needs, particularly in their – upward – communication with other members. For instance, an important social use of television for children relates to the possibility to better explain and justify their emotions, views and beliefs towards parents and older family members. Referring to television programmes is expected to not only facilitate communication and understanding in general but also helps children to convince others in more dominant positions of their particular views. In addition, children may also use media to strengthen their position in the household, for instance by using the opportunities of physical proximity typically related to watching television: 'the proxemic nature of audience positioning in front of the television is often used to advantage by young children who desire to engage physically or verbally their admired older siblings' (Lull 1980: 203). Thus, proximity during watching television increases opportunities for interpersonal contact with those in powerful positions and, as such, enables gaining access to adult conversations children may be otherwise excluded from.

In this section we have elaborated on some key conceptual and empirical developments in what is called the 'uses and gratification' paradigm, a highly influential approach in media audiences research. In the next section we seek to outline another central paradigm in the study of media audiences – often dubbed the critical or incorporation/resistance paradigm – that runs partly in parallel to the uses and gratification paradigm, but differs in a number of essential ways.

Constrained Audiences: Critical Paradigm

Whereas uses and gratification research tends to focus on generally understanding how media and its contents may serve the needs of individual audience members, studies in the critical paradigm share an interest in understanding why and how audience members may interpret messages that are communicated via mass media (Abercrombie and Longhurst, 1998; Sullivan, 2013). In particular, critical theorists have stressed the significance of analysing whether or not people may accept or reject the 'preferred understandings' of particular topics that are designed and built into mass media messages, and how this relates to audience members' social backgrounds (Hall, 1980; Moores, 1993; Morley, 2003). So, for instance, a central concern in critical studies is how audience members' backgrounds – including class, gender and race – relate to their interpretation of media contents.

Similar to uses and gratification studies, critical theorists tend to conceptualise audience members as essentially active in their engagement with media. As such, both traditions share a critique on positivistic 'effects' research on media audiences as being limited in its understanding of the possible meanings attributed to mass media consumption and the agency attributed to audience members – elements they consider as essential in understanding communication processes (Abercrombie and Longhurst, 1998; Morley, 2003). Studies in both traditions also share a preference for qualitative studies and especially ethnographic analyses of audiences (Sullivan, 2013). However, there are also a number of more or less fundamental differences. First, a more subtle difference lies in the motivation for the preferred methodology in studying audiences. For critical theorists, an ethnographic approach may not only serve the need to better understand the social context of media use but also signals their more fundamental emancipatory intent to give voice to specific audience members and their variety of interpretations which may otherwise be easily overlooked or ignored. For instance Morley stressed that one of the major limitations of 'effects' research is that audience interpretations are only put in terms of conformance with the assumed meaning of the message producer, or as he puts it: 'the problems of the effects of communication can now be reformulated, as that of the extent to which decodings take place within the limits of the preferred (or dominant) manner in which the message has been initially encoded' (2003: 86).

Second, theorists in the critical tradition also took issue with the seemingly unconstrained individualistic responses to media messages as suggested in much of the uses and gratification studies. In particular, critical media theorists questioned the assumed autonomy of audience members in their engagement with media, and criticised the uses and gratification approach for its lack of attention to the actual message that is communicated to media audiences. Morley formulates this as follows: 'here we part company with the uses and gratification approach, which treats the message simply as if it were an empty box, a stimulus, which the decoder [i.e. audience member] is free to use as he or she wishes' (2003: 83). As such, critical theorists not only stressed the need to bring back the contents of media messages into the analysis of media audiences, but also highlighted the importance of gaining more insight into the possibilities for audience members' agency in their use of mass media with reference to wider social structures.

For instance, with regard to the latter, Moores (1993) noted that although the renowned ethnographic work by Lull on mass media in a family context (discussed in the previous section) also considered the influence of social relationships on audiences' media utilisation, it still needs to be seen as a typical exponent of the uses and gratification tradition (see also Sullivan, 2013). Moores recognises that the notion of power is a central theme in Lull's conceptualisation of media use. However, compared to the work in the critical paradigm, Lull's analyses focus primarily on audiences' individual psychological motivations related to the home situation as the key context of media use, and hardly connect to larger sociological explanations related to cultural and societal structures that play a role in interpreting media messages.

To a large extent, the critical tradition of media audiences research builds on the theoretical work by Hall (1980) whose essay on encoding/decoding is widely considered as a 'catalyst' (Moores, 1993: 16) for what many theorists see as a highly influential stream of research work on media audiences (Abercrombie and Longhurst, 1998; Gunter, 2000; Kim, 2004; Morley, 2003; Sullivan, 2013). Partly in response to studies in the uses and gratification tradition that tend to be not particularly concerned with media contents, Hall developed a comprehensive conceptualisation of the media communication process that included both the production of media programmes and the audience consumption of them (Busse and Gray, 2014). Drawing on both semiotics and sociological traditions, he recognised the potential of a media message to limit the variety of interpretations amongst an audience whilst also emphasising the agency of the audience member to develop their own reading including the possibility that this may vary significantly or even be oppositional to the message as intended. At the same time, Hall recognised the limits of audience agency by relating the range of possible interpretations to individual audience members' social position. As such, Hall's work views media communication not as a transmission of neutral messages to different audience members, but essentially as 'a struggle over meanings; different social groups aim to give their own meaning to events or ideas that receive public discussion' (Abercrombie and Longhurst, 1998: 13).

Central in Hall's conceptualisation of audience reception of media messages are the processes of *encoding* and *decoding*, which are connected to what he sees as the critical stages in a media communication process, particularly because they entail important occasions where people may actually shape or reshape a message in line with their own specific interest or beliefs. For instance, drawing on Hall's research, Sullivan defines these processes as: 'moments in which the meaning of a message or text was subject to human intervention and therefore involved power relations' (2013: 140). Hall argues that an understanding of communication processes in terms of encoding and decoding has a number of key implications.

First, he emphasises that media messages cannot be seen as some way of reflecting reality, or as Morley put it: 'there is, in television, no such thing as an innocent text' (2003: 82). Rather, events or experiences are 'encoded' into a message form by producers in their efforts to communicate 'effectively' to their targeted audiences. Hall considers this process of encoding as essential for a message to enhance the likelihood of becoming transmitted: 'Television producers or encoders, who find their message failing to get across, are frequently concerned to straighten out the kinks in the communicative chain, and thus to facilitate the effectiveness of their messages' (1980: 15). However, putting things in terms of a media language is not a neutral process, but unavoidably involves the inclusion of more or less latent ideological assumptions in the message. This implies that, as a result of symbolic work, messages are 'imprinted' with codes that promote or reinforce a particular ideology. Media messages thus tend to provide a particular way of representing reality, most likely a view of reality that is held by the encoders. As Gunter states: 'content is structured in a way that produces a *preferred reading* or the meaning the producers of the text intend the receiver to accept' (2000: 85, emphasis added).

Critical media theorists tend to emphasise that media messages primarily promote the ideologies of the powerful, and thus require profound knowledge of their 'codes' to get full access to messages and enhance appreciation. In other words, media messages are unavoidably encoded 'from within the dominant frame or dominant global ideology by media personnel who operated professionally from within the hegemonic order, often reproducing messages associated with political and economic elites' (Abercrombie and Longhurst, 1998: 14). Thus, in the view of Hall, the ideological position of the elites in a society tends to underlie the dominant interpretation of any media message. Therefore, an understanding of the possible audience responses to a media message should account for the use of specific codes in these messages that may promote a particular 'preferred reading'.

Second, by pointing at their engagement in processes of *decoding*, critical approaches to media audiences have also emphasised the agency of audience members in shaping the meaning of a message. In his seminal work Hall stressed that, similar to encoding, decoding needs to be considered as a form of symbolic work. Thus in understanding media communication, the concept of decoding highlights the significance of considering the audience members' activities to interpret media messages in relation to their specific contexts and backgrounds. As a result, critical theorists have emphasised the possibility and even likelihood that audience members may interpret a message in a different way than the producers' intentions, or in Hall's words: 'The degrees of symmetry – that is, the degrees of "understanding" and "misunderstanding" in the communicative exchange depend both on the degrees of symmetry/asymmetry between the position of encoder-producer and that of the decoder-receiver' (1980: 4).

In his work on media audiences, Moores (1993) suggests that the reasons for the potential asymmetry between encoded and decoded meanings are twofold. One reason is connected to the nature of the texts to be decoded. It is argued that, in spite of the likelihood of a preferred reading unavoidably 'imprinted' in a media message, there will always be a possibility of multiple interpretations. Hall stated, for instance, that: 'There can never be only one, single, univocal and determined meaning for such a lexical item' (1980: 9) and Morley even referred to the 'impossibility of a total closure' (1992: 86) in the interpretation of media messages. Another reason relates to the broader context within which decoding may take place. In line with Hall's work, Moores (1993) conceptualises processes of decoding not as activities performed by isolated individuals, but as primarily a social practice. This refers to the importance of considering audience members' interpretations of media messages in relation to established discourses and social processes they are engaged in. Thus, in understanding the reception of a media message, not only the preferred reading of the message may play a role but also the social position of the audience members, which may: 'set the parameters to the range of potential readings through the structure of access to different codes' (Morley, 2003: 87). Seen from this critical perspective, the study of media impact becomes a question of whether or not audience members buy into, or tend to 'incorporate', a dominant ideology as promoted by the media, and why.

One of the most influential empirical studies in this critical tradition (Kim, 2004; Sullivan, 2013) is Morley's work on audience responses to media messages. In what is generally referred to as the Nationwide Television Studies, Morley (2003) set out to analyse how audiences' interpretations of television programmes relate to their social backgrounds and related cultural frameworks. Here, in line with Hall's conceptual work, Morley considered the messages broadcasted by mass media as a 'complex sign in which a preferred reading has been inscribed, but which retains the potential, if decoded in a manner different from the way it has been encoded, of communicating a different meaning' (2003: 86). In understanding audience responses to mass media messages, he studied the reception of two different episodes of a widely known UK news and current affairs television programme – Nationwide – amongst people from distinct occupational groups. The research focused on eliciting responses from small groups consisting of people from particular social, economic and cultural backgrounds (managers, students, apprentices and trade unionists).

In his analysis, Morley identified three different typical interpretive positions towards the Nationwide programme (dominant, negotiated and oppositional), and explained how these may relate to individuals' social backgrounds. In line with Hall's work, these positions towards the TV programme can be seen as different 'patterns of decoding', and as such, represent the extent to which different audience members may (partially) accept or reject the preferred reading of the media messages.

Position 1: Dominant Reading. The study indicated that some groups generally interpret the programme within what is called the *dominant reading.* In Morley's analyses, particularly the bank managers and apprentices were found to generally accept the messages and the underlying view on reality as they were presented in Nationwide, albeit for slightly different reasons. Indeed, whereas audience members in a management role talked about the programme's contents in terms of being generally aligned with their specific interests, the apprentices (mainly consisting of young-adult white males) experienced the messages established by the programme as simply 'common sense'. Whilst being critical about the old-fashioned form in which the messages were presented, this latter group perceived possible alternative readings of the contents as more or less unthinkable.

Position 2: Negotiated Reading. A *negotiated reading* of Nationwide was found mainly amongst some of the student groups investigated (university arts students) and amongst trade union officials. Such a decoding position can be broadly understood as audience members' 'general acceptance of the dominant definitions and a rejection of their local implications' (Moores, 1993: 19). Interpreting a programme in terms of a negotiated decoding typically involves audience responses that include seemingly contradictory elements, that is, show signs of both acceptance and rejection of the message. In Hall's view this position primarily becomes apparent through an emphasis on interpreting media messages in terms of 'exceptions to the rule' (1980: 17) thereby generally putting themselves in a subordinate position whilst at the same time allowing themselves to significantly adapt the message to context.

Position 3: Oppositional Reading. The analysis also revealed *oppositional readings* of Nationwide, which were primarily found amongst trade union members (shop stewards) and students (further education) with a relatively recent migration background. Interestingly, whilst different groups apparently share a similar oppositional interpretation of the programme, the main motivation for the underlying decoding position varies significantly. The trade union members actively resisted the dominant classical economic encoding of issues as promoted in the programme, and stressed the need to replace this with a perspective based on 'the labour theory of value' (Morley, 2003: 117). At the same time, the oppositional reading of the further education students is more characterised by silencing thereby signalling that they found nothing of relevance in the programme that motivated them to pay attention to it at all. Based on Hall's work, Morley explained the latter response in terms of the lack of connection between the cultural codes used by Nationwide to make 'descriptions' of the world and the cultural codes of the community these students identify with. Or in his words: 'they fail, or refuse to engage with the discourse of the programme enough to deconstruct or re-define it. There is simply a disjunction between the set of representations with which the programme works and those generated by the students' sub-cultural milieux' (2003: 114).

The elaborate re-analyses of the data from the Nationwide study by Kim (2004) confirmed the significance of audiences' social position in understanding their interpretation of mass media messages. Kim's study re-emphasised that interpretations of media texts cannot be considered a purely individual matter. In addition, in his re-analysis he was not only able to show how class, race and gender relate to different decoding positions, but also revealed how a social group's decoding position may vary because of the specific presentation of the issues in a programme. In this way he refocused attention to the role of the encoding process in understanding audiences' responses to media messages: 'these cases illuminate how textual characteristics as the outcome of encoding practices can affect the decoding process' (Kim, 2004: 96). Overall, these critical studies emphasise the significance of understanding media messages as 'structured polysemy' (Morley, 2003: 86), that is, open to different interpretations, but constrained by a preferred reading imprinted by its producers and the social context of the audience members.

Up to this point, we have focused on two influential approaches in the study of media audiences, that is, the uses and gratification approach and the critical approach. We have indicated that studies in both traditions share an understanding of audience members as essentially active, but these traditions typically differ in their primary empirical focus and related assumptions of the exact nature of audience agency. The next section will elaborate on a third, more recent, research tradition in the study of media audiences which is grounded in what is referred to as a spectacle/performance paradigm (Abercrombie and Longhurst, 1998).

Diffused Audiences: Spectacle/Performance Paradigm

Studies within the spectacle/performance paradigm also draw on the premise of audience members as active agents in the consumption of media messages, but seek to develop a more advanced understanding of audiences beyond the context of production. This allows for a conceptualisation of audience members as more than 'simply' consumers of media messages and can gain more insight into how and why audiences may 'extend their media experiences beyond the reception of the original text' (Sullivan, 2013: 191), while at the same time explaining how it is intimately connected with it. Hill even emphasised that the spectacle/performance paradigm is 'remarkably relevant for digital media environments' (2018: 3).

One of the key pillars of the spectacle/performance approach to media audiences is the research on fans and fandom. In the last few decades, academic studies on fandom have become an established and recognised element of audience theory. Since the early 1990s, a growing number of studies have stressed the significance of exploring audiences in relation to fans and fandom. In particular, these analyses tend to focus on the audience members' role in the development of different forms of 'interpretive communities' or sub-cultures around particular media and cultural material (e.g. Fiske, 1992b; Harrington and Bielby, 1995; Sandvoss, 2005), and their related textual (re)production of media contents (Busse and Gray, 2014). These studies have provided important possibilities for shedding an alternative light on how and to what extent audience members should be seen as (co-)producers in themselves thereby providing more insight into the generally assumed boundaries between media production and consumption. For instance, in his theoretical overview Sandvoss considers the position of fandom in contemporary societies as something 'that do[es] now allow for simple bipolar oppositions between media and audiences' (2005: 43).

Whilst acknowledging the merits of the uses and gratification and critical tradition in studying mass media audiences, various spectacle/performance scholars have highlighted a number of key limitations of these earlier traditions, in particular related to (1) the assumed limits of audience responses and interpretations of media messages, (2) the potential role of mass media in people's personal lives and (3) the conceptualisation of the relation between producers and consumers of media contents, and the role of power that follows from the first two central points of critique.

First, whilst studies in the spectacle/performance tradition may agree with others on audience members' latitude in developing their own orientation towards mass media and interpretation of its contents, they also challenge the assumed limits of audience responses. In particular by showing how audience members have become 'textually productive' (Abercrombie and Longhurst, 1998: 147) with regard to media contents, it is shown that these audience responses may not necessarily be confined by or even related to the mass media as a potential source. As a result, audience reception of media text needs to be considered much more diverse and open-ended and at least studied beyond the consumption of the original text. For instance, in their study of soap-fan culture, Harrington and Bielby (1995) emphasised that only focusing on audiences' viewing practices of soaps would provide a limited view which easily excludes the ways audience members would translate this into a variety of cultural activities. In addition, rather than relating possible interpretations to social backgrounds, this stream of research emphasises the audience members' skills and competencies to produce their own contents and use media contents as a resource in relation to their own specific purposes and relevant cultural communities that primarily exist outside the domestic sphere (Abercrombie and Longhurst, 1998).

Second, the spectacle/performance approach provides an important base for a critique of many established assumptions about the nature of the audience in relation to the media. Whereas most approaches to media audiences see mass media as just one relatively separate element of peoples' lives, exponents of the spectacle/performance tradition consider media more as constitutive to audience members. In this view, media is primarily seen as a critical part of people's lives, and as something that plays an important role in constructing who they are. Spectacle/performance theorists thereby refer in particular to the omnipresence of different forms of media in contemporary society as well as the general acceptance of showing some form of structural enthusiasm for it (e.g. Busse and Gray, 2014). Sandvoss referred to a study by Tulloch and Jenkins indicating that at a particular moment in time more than half of the US population did not refrain from identifying themself as being a *Star Trek* fan (2005: 4). Or as Sandvoss and colleagues (2017) have succinctly put it: 'most people are fans of something' (2017: 1). Media is conceptualised as constitutive of audience members' identity, not least because it offers important opportunities and incentives to construct themselves: 'since people are simultaneously performers and audience members, cultural consumers become cultural producers' (Abercrombie and Longhurst, 1998: 75).

Third, and following from the previous points, the conceptualisation of power in studies drawing on a spectacle/performance tradition shows notable differences from the other approaches. In particular, both the centrality of power in the analyses as well as the understanding of the nature of power differ substantially. Whereas the possibility for domination has been central to the critical approach, conceptualisations of power remain more implicit in the spectacle/performance tradition and follow from the general assumptions about the nature of media and their role in audience members' lives. One point is that the omnipresence of different forms of media and a substantial involvement of audiences in producing media contents assumes a more diffused distribution of power. As Abercrombie and Longhurst concluded: 'if power is indeed diffused and not exercised in a unitary way on behalf of a dominant power bloc, then it makes less sense to see the culture of a society as driven by the twin forces of dominance and resistance' (1998: 36). It also assumes an enlarged ability of audience members to challenge the authority of the traditional cultural producers, thereby engaging in various forms of 'cultural subversion' (Sandvoss, 2005: 13) which may not be particularly appreciated by these producers. For instance, Sandvoss indicates how sub-groups are able to reconstruct and transform the initial meaning of cultural items relatively independent from the original producers: 'Popular texts and icons such as Madonna may be commodities and means of capital accumulation to the media industry, yet they are appropriated by fans as meaningful resources in their everyday lives' (2005: 13).

As noted above, research on fans and fandom lies at the heart of the spectacle/performance approach to media audiences. For instance, Abercrombie and Longhurst stated that: 'ordinary audience members are more like fans and enthusiasts than might initially be thought' (1998: 122). This field of research can be traced back to the work of Jenkins, Jolie and Fiske published in the early 1990s. In this, what is now often referred to as first wave of fan studies, theorists sought to challenge the mainly negative understanding of fans and fandom. Instead they have stressed that fans are of particular significance in viewing audiences and need to be considered as a common and widely accepted aspect of media consumption and of contemporary societies as a whole. In his seminal study of how dedicated audience members have become textually productive in their interpretation of and engagement with their favourite media text, Jenkins (2013) presented a view of audience members as skilful authors who are engaged in textual production and showed how they use original media contents only as raw material for their own specific purposes. Scardaville characterised this research as mainly focused on analysing 'the interplay between the show and the products fans produce' (2005: 881).

Research on fans and fandom allows for the development of a much more advanced and nuanced view on the often-used separation between readers and writers of media contents. First, by focusing on fandom, theorists stressed the significance of a *sphere beyond production* that is at the same time closely connected to it. For instance, in one of the foundational pieces on fans, Fiske stressed that fandom resembles a 'shadow cultural economy' (1992b: 30). As he explains: 'on the one hand it is an intensification of popular culture which is formed outside and often against official culture, on the other it expropriates and reworks certain values and characteristics of that official culture to which it is opposed' (1992b: 34). Thus, whereas this stream of research also draws on an assumption of audience members as active agents, it stresses the need to go beyond only studying people as more or less active in their experiences of media.

Second, research on fans and fandom has also advanced our understating of how and why being a fan can take a *variety of different forms*. Rather than a sole focus on the general characteristics of fans and fan culture, this stream of research has shed important light on individual-level considerations. In particular, whereas much of early research on media fandom focused on macro-level fan consumption, later studies focus much more on individual fans as members of fan communities thereby emphasising the importance of fandom as an identity resource in contemporary society. This growing stream of research distinguishes fans as actors with high levels of passion and involvement, but at the same time recognises that the degree and nature of their passion and involvement may vary substantially. Theorists have indicated that this variation not only applies to different audience members, but also relates to one person over time. For instance Sandvoss' definition of fandom as 'the regular, emotionally involved consumption of a given popular narrative or text' (2005: 8) not only allows for a variety of different objects of fandom and media genres (from popular books, television shows to texts on sports and sports events), but also different levels of involvement from dedicated/die-hard fans to more casual fans (e.g. Scardaville, 2005). Moreover, such micro-level studies not only reveal more of the variety in audiences but also illuminate attributes of fandom that are considered important to the individual fan such as who they are and what they do.

Overall, the growing body of research on media fans and fandom has expanded from debunking stereotypes and negative meanings that are associated with fan activities to a more comprehensive and advanced conceptualisation of the social and interpretative elements of fandom (see Fiske, 1992b; Gray et al., 2017; Sandvoss, 2005). This includes a general recognition of different levels of fandom and more detailed analyses of the main characteristics of fan activities and fan subcultures (see Beaven and Laws, 2007; Harrington and Bielby, 1995; Thorne and Bruner, 2006). For instance, Abercrombie and Longhurst (1998) have distinguished between categories of media fans (consumer, fan cultist, enthusiast and petty producer) that vary in their degree of involvement. They show how these categories also typically differ significantly in (1) the skills that are required to perform the roles associated with these categories, but also (2) the forms of textual production and (3) the identities that relate to these roles.

Abercrombie and Longhurst define *consumers* as audience members whose patterns of media use show little systematic attachment to particular contents or media. As a result of limited occasions for experiencing media contents or interest in obtaining 'inside information' about it, they are typically less explicit and less able to define 'good taste' on particular cultural products or cultural fields. Consumers are typically characterised by little textual production beyond occasional talk about cultural products in relation to their everyday life.

In relative contrast, *fans* are conceptualised as intensive media users who are much more explicitly attached to particular cultural products or tastes. Similar to consumers, they tend to produce talk about particular media contents in the context of their personal life, but they also engage in

Table 2.1 *Overview of theoretical perspectives on audiences used in this book*

Perspective on audience	Underlying paradigm	Main empirical focus	Representative studies	This study
Interactive audience: Audience actively contributes to, and shapes oratorical performances	Conversation analysis	Audience responses and the ways in which speeches, lectures and presentations unfold on a moment-by-moment basis through speaker-audience interaction	Atkinson (1984a, 1984b) Clayman (1992, 1993) Heritage and Greatbatch (1986) Greatbatch and Clark (2003, 2005, 2010)	How do the rhetorical practices and persuasive strategies deployed by gurus potentially enhance receptivity towards their management ideas? (Chapter 3)
			Clark, Bhatanacharoen and Greatbatch (2015) Greatbatch and Clark (2010)	How do gurus present their ideas as being generally applicable, significant and potentially relevant to individual audience members? (Chapter 4)
Active audience: Individuals actively choose media in relation to their expected need gratification	Uses and gratification	Central motives of individuals to use media (messages)	Levy and Windahl (1984)	How and why do audience members vary in the way they are attracted to a guru and the management ideas they are promoting? (Chapter 5)
			Lull (1980, 1982) Morley (2005)	How is the social use of management ideas in organisational contexts

Table 2.1 *(cont.)*

Perspective on audience	Underlying paradigm	Main empirical focus	Representative studies	This study
			Rayburn and Palmgreen (1984)	related to the relative power positions of individual audience members? (Chapter 7)
Constrained audience: Individuals structured by preferred reading of text and social position	Encoding/ decoding	Factors shaping likelihood of incorporation or resistance of dominant ideology promoted in media messages	Hall (1980) Kim (2004) Morley (2003)	How and why do audience members' consumption orientations shift throughout the communication process? (Chapter 6)
Diffused audience: Individuals who become simultaneously perform-ers and audience	Spectacle/ performance	Textual practices and related capabilities and identities of audience members	Abercrombie and Longhurst (1998) Harrington and Bielby (1995)	How and why do audience members become involved in using management ideas in their wider social contexts? (Chapter 8)

textual production, particularly in relation to 'informally or formally structured groups' (Sullivan, 2013: 195), primarily to exchange experiences and align interpretations about particular media. This may become apparent in their more advanced skills in developing 'fuller and more reasoned technical judgements' (Abercrombie and Longhurst, 1998: 143) about particular cultural products as well as the process of producing them.

Enthusiasts and *cultists* are typified on the one hand as more extreme in their engagement with media and its contents – as they are generally considered as heavy users – but at the same time they are also engaged in challenging the interpretive authority of media industries. Media use is assumed to be subordinate to and serving their own interests and activities related to cultural production and community building on a rather specialised terrain. Their textual production is particularly geared towards exchange in their network relations, and thus they are: 'produced by enthusiasts for enthusiasts' (Abercrombie and Longhurst, 1998: 139).

Finally, *petty producers* are understood as audience members that have translated their enthusiasm into an occupation as 'full-time producer' (Abercrombie and Longhurst, 1998: 140). In contrast to the previous types, they do not target their cultural production to groups of peers, but to potential clients in a market. Their abilities to connect their cultural production to markets are primarily drawn upon for the purpose of capital accumulation.

Conclusion

In the context of this book, different literatures on audiences critically emphasise the inherent complexities of conceptualising the audience phenomenon. The overview suggests that to better understand the attraction of management ideas for an audience of management practitioners as well as their possible impact on management and organisational practice, it is essential to draw on multiple perspectives as well as account for their possibilities and limitations. For instance, based on his broad overview of the uses and gratification approach within mass media research, Rubin has stressed the need for combining multiple conceptual foci (see also Chapter 1): 'Single-variable explanations continue to have appeal to some researchers and policymakers. However, such explanations distract us from the conceptual complexity of media effects' (Rubin, 2009: 178).

In this chapter we have discussed a number of broad and influential perspectives to studying audiences, explained differences and similarities in background as well as explored their main possibilities in understanding the flow of management ideas. As indicated above, these perspectives provide the conceptual backdrop and guiding research questions that are used as starting points for our analyses in the following chapters (Table 2.1). In particular, the CA literature on oratory provides the basis for our analyses, in Chapters 3 and 4, of how gurus deliver their ideas during lectures and how these ideas are received by live audiences of managers. Drawing on this approach, Chapter 4 identifies the rhetorical practices that gurus use to evoke displays of audience affiliation and to minimise the likelihood of negative audience reactions. This chapter also considers the rhetorical practices that gurus use in their lectures to convey the significance and adaptability of their ideas. The uses and gratification approach constitutes the main basis for our analyses of audience motives for using guru seminars and ideas in Chapter 5, 6 and 7. For the purpose of addressing the issue of how and why audience members may vary in their attraction to gurus in Chapter 5 the uses and gratification perspective is complemented by a critical approach mainly to explore the role of audience members' background in more depth. In better understanding the possible shifts in consumer orientations, the analysis in Chapter 6 will not only build on the categories identified in Chapter 5, but also draw primarily on an expectancy-value perspective on uses and gratifications. In a similar way, the analysis in Chapter 7 will take the stream of research in uses and gratification studies that focus on media use in domestic contexts as its main conceptual lens in order to gain an advanced conceptualisation of audience members' use of guru ideas in management and organisational practice. Finally, in gaining more insight into how audience members may extend this involvement beyond the habitual contexts of diffusion and organisational implementation, the analysis in Chapter 8 will particularly draw on a spectacle/performance perspective.

3 Creating a Positive Atmosphere among the Audience

The Chapter 2 explored a number of perspectives on audiences in CA and mass media research that may further our understanding of management practitioners as audience members and the flow of management ideas throughout different mass communication settings. We suggested that to better understand how management gurus make their ideas attractive to audiences of management practitioners and how they come to use these ideas in different contexts, it is essential to start by focusing on how they interact with such audiences during their live lectures. In particular, we need to explore how gurus tailor their messages to accommodate diverse audiences of managers.

This is the first of two sequential chapters that explore how management ideas flow from management gurus to audiences of managers during gurus' lectures. Drawing on detailed analyses of video recordings of real-time management guru-audience interaction, the chapter asks: *How do the rhetorical practices and persuasive strategies deployed by gurus potentially enhance receptivity towards their management ideas?* Subsequently, in Chapter 4, we extend our focus to consider how gurus present their ideas in ways that are designed to convincingly demonstrate they are potentially applicable across a broad range of circumstances. Together the two chapters[1] shed light on the conditions that may increase the possibility of audience members leaving the auditorium with an enthusiasm for and a willingness and intention to use management ideas promoted by the gurus in their own organisations.

Management Guru Lectures and Management Ideas

Management gurus have developed some of the most influential management ideas of the past forty years (Abrahamson, 1996; Kieser, 1997; Spell, 1999, 2001) and, as noted in Chapter 1, are often regarded as the figurehead

[1] These chapters draw in part on material published in Clark and colleagues (2015) and Greatbatch and Clark (2003, 2005, 2010, 2018).

and leader of a particular idea movement (Abrahamson, 1996; Huczynski, 1993). Despite the recent attention to new forms of management media (e.g. Piazza and Abrahamson, 2020), their relationship with followers is built through writing best-selling management books. Few write more than one best-selling management book (Furusten, 1999; Huczynski, 1993; Jackson, 2001) and, after their initial success, some management gurus cease writing books altogether (Clark and Greatbatch, 2003). As sales of their books start to decline, they seek to maintain a direct relationship with managerial audiences by giving talks on the international lecture circuit. They use their lectures to build their personal reputations with managers and consultants in order to generate a continuous stream of speaking engagements. Many gain reputations as powerful public speakers as they build and sustain a mass live following over a long period of time. Their reputations and reach are further enhanced by their talks being uploaded onto the Internet by conference organisers then watched by many millions of times (see examples in Chapter 1).

During the 1990s and early 2000s, the relatively small body of literature on management guru lectures largely depicted them as quasi-religious events. Guru lectures were therefore regarded as exercises in persuasive communication where the main purpose is to transform the consciousness of the audience to the guru's way of thinking (e.g. Clark and Salaman, 1996, 1998; Huczynski, 1993; Jackson, 2001, 2002). The idea that guru lectures are episodes of persuasive speaking and opportunities for conversion was first explored in Huczynski's (1993) seminal study of management gurus. He wrote that:

> it is in their interest to make a convert . . . How can a speaker persuade members of his audience to his way of thinking if they are not already predisposed to it? A realistic aim of the guru's persuasive communication is not that his ideas should necessarily and immediately modify the *actions* of his audience, but that they should alter their *beliefs*, *attitudes* and *feelings* towards his suggestions. (Huczynski, 1993: 245)

Huczynski's (1993) characterisation of gurus' lectures and the reasons for the assumed impact of their management ideas on audiences has been very influential. Indeed, as Guthey, Clark and Jackson (2009) observe, it has become a widely accepted caricature with many descriptions of these events equating the gurus' presentational style with the high-energy performances of evangelical preachers at Pentecostal and Charismatic Church meetings. For example, an article in *The Economist* (1994a: 90) draws parallels between management gurus and the influential American evangelist Billy Graham who preached to people in stadium events for more than sixty years: 'management gurus are not so much latter-day

Buddhas as would-be Billy Grahams. They deal in tub-thumping certainties rather than calm reflection; and think nothing of ranting and raving, shouting and imploring, in order to ram their point home'. In a further article *The Economist* (1994b: 101) characterised the management guru Tom Peters as a 'performance artist' in that 'Every year thousands of middle managers gape in awe as Mr. Peters, arms flailing, brow sweating, voice horse, urges them to nuke hierarchy and thrive on chaos'. Similarly, Caulkin describes Peters' style of lecturing as follows: 'He rants, sweats, stomps up and down and manipulates the emotions of his middle-management audience with the skill of an old-time evangelist' (1997: 14). Baur (1994) depicts gurus in general as 'management evangelists' and 'corporate hot gospellers' with a talent for phrase making. Krohe writes that gurus on the international lecture circuit 'Like any successful preacher . . . need to find new sins, new sinners, new paths to salvation to keep their message fresh and their audiences awake' (2004: 34). Greatbatch and Clark summarise this broad characterisation of the gurus' style of lecturing as follows: 'Gurus' live lectures are repeatedly portrayed as equivalent to evangelical religious revivalist meetings. They are evangelists who pass among their flock. Their talks are replete with parables about companies and individuals that saw the light and were saved. They are presented as whipping their "congregations" into a state of hysterical compliance with their message by engaging in hellfire preaching' (2005: 21–2).

In summary, the initial body of literature on management gurus viewed their lectures as occurring within an evangelical frame that creates an emotional arousal to soften and seduce the audience members so that they are open to the messages delivered by the gurus. Once converted, they are assumed to return to their organisations as active advocates for implementing the gurus' ideas (Groß et al., 2015).

Given that the literature focuses on the notion that gurus are powerful charismatic orators, guru lectures are characteristically portrayed as 'episodes of one-way communication in which the gurus dazzle passive managerial audiences with their commanding and persuasive performances' (Clark, Bhatanacharoen and Greatbatch, 2015). In this respect audience members are depicted as supplicants who attend guru lectures to learn the latest teaching of a guru. Their attendance is motivated by their devotion to the guru, in the same way fans of a popular music act attend one of their concerts. However, as we indicated in the Chapter 2, Greatbatch and Clark (2003, 2005, 2010, 2018) have attempted to develop a more nuanced understanding of the gurus' lectures and oratorical styles through fine-grained analyses of video recordings of their live perfomances. Greatbatch and Clark's research demonstrates that gurus' live lectures are never single-person-dominated, unidirectional events in which ideas on management are transmitted by the speaker to the audience. Rather, they unfold out of interactions between the speaker and audience members and, as they deliver their lectures, the gurus adjust their rendition of their management ideas in accordance with the reactions of the audience (Greatbatch and Clark, 2003, 2005, 2010). Their lectures are thus a jointly negotiated endeavour in which the delivery of the content changes from event to event depending on how different audiences respond to the gurus' messages (Greatbatch and Clark, 2010).

Management gurus' lectures are characterised and shaped by both individual and collective responses from audience members, which are overwhelmingly positive. Audience members rarely, if ever, produce disaffiliative responses, such as booing or heckling, hissing, head shaking or ironic laughter. When audience members produce displays of approval during gurus' presentations they do so by, inter alia, clapping, laughing, nodding their heads in agreement and smiling. In some cases, one or two individuals produce these responses. In others, however, they involve multiple audience members acting in concert with each other by producing *collective* displays of affiliation. When audience members do this, they do so predominantly by laughing at actions and remarks that are perceived as humorous. With rare exceptions, applause is confined to the beginning and end of the gurus' presentations (Greatbatch and Clark, 2003, 2005). In contrast to political speeches, it is very unusual to find instances of audiences applauding statements with each they agree. Moreover, in contrast with stand-up comedy routines, they rarely use applause alongside laughter as a means of registering their appreciation of a speaker's humour. In these respects, the gurus' lectures are akin to various forms of public speaking, including university lectures and training seminars, in which applause is usually not treated as a relevant activity *either* on its own *or* in conjunction with laughter. This suggests that the widespread characterisation of management guru's lectures as being equivalent to religious revivalist meetings and managers as devoted followers, should not be taken at face value. Rather, to better understand the possible impact of their ideas, it is of particular significance to develop a much more advanced conceptualisation of how gurus interact with their audiences during their lectures.

Why are guru's presentations characterised by positive displays of approval from audiences? Why are negative reactions so rare? These are intriguing questions given that the gurus' audiences are diverse and generally are not composed purely of followers and acolytes who have already been converted to their way of thinking. Audiences and their members can differ significantly from one another in ways that are relevant to the performance they are witnessing. These differences partly relate to the national diversity of their audiences. Guru lectures are not confined to one country. Typically, they talk to audiences in a range of countries, which include among others America, Australia, Brazil, Canada, Germany, the United Kingdom, Mexico, New Zealand, Singapore and Switzerland. In addition, these lectures are to different groups including governmental and non-governmental organisations, private sector organisations, industry associations and conferences on a wide range of topics. The events at which they speak often involve a number of presentations over a day or two given by different people. The audience may therefore be attending not to hear their talk but that of another contributor. Members of the audience are not only numerous but also highly differentiated in terms of the levels of affiliation to the gurus' ideas that they bring to the lectures. For instance, a survey of audiences attending four gurus' lectures in the early 1990s indicated that the great majority of the audience (83 per cent) attended not because of a personal commitment to the guru but because it was a corporate perk. Only 9 per cent of the audience attended because of a strong commitment to the guru. The remaining members of the audience were guests of either the sponsors or the guru (Guerrier and Gilbert, 1995).

A key problem for management gurus, if they are to effectively communicate their management ideas, is to deliver a lecture that, whilst it advocates a particular course of action, does not alienate sections of the audience. The fact that many management gurus are able to attract large audiences, and maintain their reputations as highly effective public speakers over a long period of time, suggests that they package their messages in ways which do not result in adverse reactions from their audiences, and so undermine their reputations. Indeed, they tend to create a positive dynamic that ensures their longevity as an international public speaker. This has to be achieved within a context of not knowing in advance the extent to which members of the audience are sympathetic to the specific ideas they express.

To shed more light on how gurus deal with these critical challenges, as noted in Chapter 2, our analysis in this chapter and Chapter 4 draws on the approach and findings of conversation analytic research on speaker-audience interaction during public speaking engagements involving politicians (Atkinson, 1984a, 1984b; Heritage and Greatbatch, 1986) and management gurus (Clark et al., 2015; Greatbatch and Clark, 2003, 2005, 2010, 2018). In particular, we use excerpts from a corpus of twenty-three professionally produced video recordings of public lectures given by Tom Peters (eight), Rosabeth Moss Kanter (four), Gary Hamel (three), Charles Handy (three), Peter Senge (three) and Daniel Goleman (two):

- Tom Peters – Tom Peter's Experience 1 and 2, Thriving on Chaos 1–3, Service with Soul, Reimagine Business Excellence in a Disruptive Age and Key Note Speech at Drucker Day;
- Rosabeth Moss Kanter – Managing Change, Lessons in Leadership and The Great Corporate Balancing Act Part 1 and 2;
- Gary Hamel – Lessons in Leadership, Creating the Future and Leadership Alliance;
- Charles Handy – Trinity Horne 2012 Annual Lecture, Skoll World Forum and The Sigmoid Curve;
- Peter Senge – The Fifth Discipline and the Infrastructures of a Learning Organisation, The Knowledge-Building Process: The Important Role of Learning Communities and Creating Transformational Knowledge;
- Daniel Goleman – Emotional intelligence and Emotional Intelligence: A Cornerstone of Learning Communities.

These gurus were selected because they represent a range of popular ideas that have had a major impact on organisational life in the last thirty years. Although the selection of lectures was partly determined by their availability, each of the speeches elaborates their key ideas and so can be considered as 'pivotal' (Emrich et al., 2001). The video material contains approximately twenty hours of gurus lecturing to audiences of managers, consultants and trainers. Six of the videos involving Peters and three of those involving Moss Kanter combine footage of the two gurus lecturing with case studies and interviews concerning organisations that are mentioned in the gurus' lectures. The other videos include complete performances by the gurus.

The analysis of the lectures revealed that there are two core elements of the guru's messages that may help explain why affiliative responses from audiences are commonplace, while disaffiliative responses are rare. In particular, we found:

- Management gurus regularly package their ideas using practices that enable audience members to respond positively (either collectively or individually) without necessarily being seen as displaying their approval of the gurus' core ideas;
- Gurus use a range of practices in order to divert criticism of those who do not use the ideas they are advocating away from members of the audience.

In this chapter, we look at each of these sets of practices (i.e. practices to evoke affiliative responses and practices to minimise the likelihood of disaffiliative responses from audiences) in turn.

Practices that Gurus Use to Evoke Affiliative Responses from Their Audiences

Greatbatch and Clark (2003, 2005, 2018) demonstrate that in most cases, audience laughter during management gurus' lectures is not simply a spontaneous reaction to messages whose content is self-evidently humorous. Instead, gurus usually invite audience laughter through the use of a range of verbal and non-verbal practices, which establish its relevance and indicate when it will be appropriate for audience members to commence laughing. These practices can be summarised as follows:

- The gurus 'highlight' their messages in relation to surrounding speech matter, and supply the messages with clearly projectable completion points around which audience members can co-ordinate their responses, through the use of:
  - Rhetorical techniques associated with 'persuasive' talk, including antithesis (contrasts), three-part lists and puzzle-solution formats (Atkinson, 1984a, 1984b; Greatbatch and Clark, 2003, 2005; Heritage and Greatbatch, 1986).
  - Volume, pitch or stress variation; marked speeding up or other rhythmic shifts; and/or facial, hand and/or body gestures.
- Rather than relying on audience members to recognise their humorous intent from the content of their messages alone, the gurus establish the relevance of audience laughter by, for example, (1) announcing that they are about to say something humorous, (2) smiling or laughing and/or (3) using 'comedic' facial expressions, gestures and prosody – including, for example, displays of emotions such as disgust, disbelief, anger, horror and amazement by themselves or others to the actions, practices or issues that are being discussed.

The transcripts analysed in this chapter illustrate how these practices come together and contribute to the creation of a positive atmosphere within auditoriums that is conducive to the delivery of their management ideas. A glossary of the symbols used in the transcripts can be seen in Appendix B.

On occasion, gurus evoke laughter in response to messages that convey their management ideas. This is the case in Extract 3.1 in which Tom Peters is in the midst of recounting his experience of eating with his wife at a restaurant in Auckland in New Zealand called Vilario's, which he suggests provided him with insights into the importance of what he came to term as 'service with soul', one of his core management ideas.

Extract 3.1 – [Service with Soul: 0.05.50]

TP: =But it was it was.=But but but let me let me now tie that back to
what we are talking about here OK. Because words are important.
(1.0) VILARIO'S DID NOT SATISFY THE CUSTOMER. Or to
use that phenomenally stupid accountant engineering word 'IT DID
NOT EXCEED EXPECTATIONS'.
Audi: LLLLLLLLL LLLLLLLLL LL
TP: What Vilario's does was an event, it was a transformation. (0.2) It is
about a total redefinition about what is possible. (0.2) And I happen
to think that it applies to the making of plastics, the making of software
as well as the making of good tabbouleh

At lines 1–2, Peters establishes a puzzle in the minds of audience members ('But but but let me let me now extract tie that back to what we are talking about here OK'), namely what it is that he sees as being important in relation to his account of what he witnessed at the restaurant. Peters fashions the solution as a two-part contrast between what the restaurant did not do (simply satisfy the customer and exceed customer expectations) (lines 3–5) and what it did do (redefine what is possible) (lines 7–8). In the first part Peters presents a view on understanding the quality of service provision that has become commonplace, which he ridicules in a manner that evokes laughter from the audience. He thereby obtains a display of audience affiliation (line 6) for a negative characterisation of an alternative view of exceptional service before presenting his own perspective on exceptional service on a serious footing. In this way he provides positive emphasis for his own formulation of 'service with soul' and because he links this back to Vilario's at the same time he reinforces the insight he obtained from this experience.

Using humour in this particular way can be very effective because, if successful, it enables gurus to elicit collective displays of affiliation with their ideas about management. However, generally speaking it is a high-risk strategy due to the diverse nature of their audiences and the fact that gurus often will not know the levels of agreement with their ideas. In view of this, it is perhaps unsurprising that more often than not gurus adopt a more cautious approach. This involves them constructing their humorous remarks such that subsequent audience laughter is not open to interpretation as an expression of unvarnished support for their ideas about management practice.

An example can be seen in Extract 3.2, in which Daniel Goleman recounts a story about a bus driver that he has often used during his lectures to explain the idea of Emotional Intelligence, which he regards as a key leadership skill that distinguishes the best leaders from merely average ones. According to Goleman, the bus driver displays a key component of Emotional Intelligence in the manner in which he interacts empathetically and sociably with passengers on his bus.

Extract 3.2 – [Emotional Intelligence 1: 00.40.00]

DG: The (.) last element the fifth (0.9) part of emotional intelligence is social
skill which (.) in a sense means .hhh handling emotions in relationships.
.hhh Handling emotions in the other person. (1.2) Well if you're really
skilled that's what you're doing. .hh I was once waiting for a bus on a hot
(0.9) horrible August da:y in Manhattan. (0.7) The kind of da:y when
it's so humid and awful and yucky .hhh that everybody's going round in
a bubble like don't look at me:, don't talk to me,=don't touch me. .hhh
And I was standing there in my bubble waiting for the bus and the bus
pulled up and I (.) got o:n bubble intact. .h And the bus driver did
something (.) surprising. (.) He spoke to me.
Aud: l-[l-l
DG: [He actually spoke to me. He said hi how are you doing? .hh (0.8) I
was taken aback. .hh And I sat do:wn, (0.7) and I realised that this
bus driver was carrying on a dialogue with everyone on the bus.=.h
Oh you're looking for suits are yuh,=well you know there's a great sale
in this department store up here on the right, .hh and did you hear
about the movies in the cineplex here on the left,=the one in .hh
cinema one (0.2) isn't very good.=I know it got good reviews but
cinema three that's really good. .hh And did you hear about what's
opening up in this museum up here on the right. .hh On and on and
on like that. .hh And people would get off that bus (.) and he'd say
well so long it's been great having you.=And they'd say yea:h it's been
great being on this bus.
(.)
Aud: l-l[-l-l LLLL [l-l
DG: [That ma:n [was an urban saint.
[((Smile face by DG))
(.) ((DG smiles))
Aud: LLLLLLLLLL LLLLLLLLLL LLLLLLLLL –[-h-h
DG: [You see emotions
are contagious.
(1.4)
DG: There is a hidden emotional economy that passes (.) amongst us a:ll,
=it's part of every interaction

Goleman enlivens his telling of the story by mimicking the positivity of the bus driver and the positive reactions of the passengers as they got off the bus (lines 1–10 and 12–23). He then stresses the highly unusual nature of the bus driver's actions by characterising him as an urban saint (line 26), before moving to a serious footing as he further explains his idea of

Emotional Intelligence. Goleman evokes laughter following both the culmination of his story (line 25) and his post-story characterisation of the bus driver as an 'urban saint' (line 29). Although Goleman uses the story to illustrate the importance of the idea of Emotional Intelligence, audience members do not, by laughing, necessarily display affiliation with Goleman's ideas concerning Emotional Intelligence. The bus driver's and passengers' actions depart radically from everyday expectations and experiences of the ways in which bus drivers and passengers conventionally interact and, consequently, can be seen by audience members as incongruous and potentially humorous, irrespective of whether or not they agree with (or are indifferent to) Goleman's ideas about Emotional Intelligence.

Extract 3.3, from a lecture given by Charles Handy, provides another example. It involves Handy telling a story about an encounter with someone from whom he asked directions (lines 1–13). Handy has regularly used this story to illustrate the S-shaped curve or sigmoid curve, which he suggests provides a powerful metaphor for thinking about how individuals and organisations plan and implement transformational change. Knowing when to intervene before the curve plateaus and falls is critical. Handy uses this metaphor to support his idea that organisations and individuals should undertake transformational change when they are doing well (i.e. on the up-curve of their past creativity) rather than waiting for evidence of decline (in the plateauing or subsequently downward curve).

Extract 3.3 – [Sigmoid curve: 0:11:56]

CH: I mean I was traveling in the Wicklow Hills behind the city where I was
born Dublin (0.5) not so long ago. And I lost my way because the (.)
hills in those days anyway didn't have any signposts. But then of course
after a bit saw an Irishman at the roadside so I stopped and I said 'can
you tell me the way to Avoca'. And he said 'yes of course' he said.
=He said 'it's very easy. You go on straight up this hill mm and then
down the other side for about for for about a mile and a half (0.2) and
you will see a bridge over the river a little bridge and Davy's Bar on the
other side. (.) Its painted red you can't miss it. (.) Have you got
that?' And I said 'well yes up the hill down the hill bridge Davy's
Bar'. [He he said 'well' he said 'half a mile before you get there turn
[((CH smiles))
right up the hill'.
Aud: LLLLLLLLL LLLLLLLLL
CH: [And you see
[((CH smiles))

Aud: L[LLLLL[LLLLL l-l-l-l-l-l-l
CH: [this [this is the problem. You only know where you should
have turned r-h-h-ight up the hill (0.2) when you've passed it. (1.0)
And I've met many many, many firms many people at Davy's Bar
downing their drinks saying that was good while its lasted but you know
if only we'd listened, if saying that was good while its lasted but you
know if only we'd listened, if only we'd (0.2) etcetera. (.) So it is very
very difficult to know (0.2) and the only thing I can tell you is that when
you're feeling pretty pleased with yourself with business or with life (.)
that's the time to start thinking

As he approaches the conclusion of the story and delivers the punch line, Handy raises his voice, speeds up the pace of his speech and smiles (lines 9–13). The audience responds to the story by laughing collectively (line 14). Subsequently, as he starts to deliver the summary message emanating from the story, Handy continues to smile broadly (lines 15–16) and this evokes further audience laughter (line 17). Handy pauses slightly, acknowledging the initial burst of laughter, but then speaks over the laughter as it fades (line 18). In so doing, he maintains a humorous frame by speaking with a breathy voice and interpolating laughter tokens in the word 'right' (lines 18–19). However, following this, Handy adopts a serious frame when suggesting that what he saw in the encounter regarding Davy's Bar is more generally applicable ('I've met many, many firms many people at Davy's Bar') (lines 20–26).

Audience members' laughter does not unequivocally signal affiliation with Handy's management ideas about how to successfully plan and implement transformational change, even though he uses the story about Davy's Bar to illustrate and convey those ideas. Rather, it is linked to the bizarreness of the events in the story, which are recognisably incongruous and potentially humorous in their own right. The audience's laughter therefore establishes a positive atmosphere within which Handy goes on to introduce his management ideas but does not explicitly indicate that the audience members who laugh necessarily agree with those ideas.

A final example of gurus evoking laughter that does not involve audience members displaying unvarnished affiliation with their core ideas about management can be seen in Extract 3.4, which is drawn from a lecture given by Gary Hamel. Hamel's central argument during this lecture was that the commonly held idea that transformational change starts at the top of organisations, and that executives are best placed to judge when change is necessary, is wrong. In his view, there is therefore a need for a shift away from bureaucratic structures towards organisational structures that involve highly empowered and involved workforces in order to devolve the responsibility for initiating change across organisations.

Extract 3.4 [Creating the future: 00.45.00]

GH: The last point I throw out uh and I'm leaving many things out but just
a last little er thought maybe you think about and take away. (0.6) u:hm
(1.2) You will often hear people say something like (.) uhm) (0.8) you
know people are against change. Right. You've all heard that. (.) Or- or
worse you'll hear folks say change must start at the top
(0.2)
Aud: -l-l-l[-l
GH: [Well you know I've thought about this a bit and I've gone out and
I've looked at how change happens in large social systems. (.) And
guess what, (.) the revolution doesn't usually start with the monarchy,
(.) you know almost never, er I lived in Britain for ten years and
I never saw Queen Elizabeth out there you know er at the end of the
Mall there in front of Buckingham Palace with a big sign saying we
want a republic. Right.
[And down with the monarchy.
Aud: [-l-l LLLLLLLLL LLLLLLLLL [LLLLLLLLL l-l[-l
GH: [Uhm [But the
question
I want to think about is (.) do you understand how to create activists in
your company. Do you understand how to give them a share of voice
and share of influence. (0.2) Because the people who create change
are Nelson Mandela, Václav Havel, Mohandas Gandhi, Aung San Suu
Kyi and so on. (.) They are people whose ratio of passion to power is
infinite

Hamel illustrates his argument by stating that during his time living in London he never saw the queen of the UK standing in front of Buckingham Palace holding aloft a sign calling for a republic (lines 8–15). Hamel frames these remarks as humorous and they evoke the audience's collective laughter (line 16). Recognising the humour in Hamel's remarks and laughing does not indicate or require acceptance of his underlying idea that organisational change does not start at the top. You could, as an audience member, display that you find his imaginary image of the queen amusing by laughing together with others, even if you do not agree with his views about transformational change in organisations. Nonetheless, the audience's affiliative laughter creates a positive context within which Hamel goes on to elaborate on his ideas (lines 17–24).

In summary, gurus regularly evoke audience laughter and this contributes to the creation of a positive atmosphere amongst their audiences. Generally speaking, the likelihood of audience members laughing when invited to do so by gurus is increased by the fact that the gurus provide the opportunity for them to laugh regardless of whether they agree or disagree with the gurus' ideas about management practice. Gurus achieve this by using sources of humour that do not rest on agreement with these ideas.

Practices that Gurus Use to Minimise the Likelihood of Disaffiliative Responses from Their Audiences

Despite the potentially controversial nature of management gurus' ideas and the highly differentiated character of many of their audiences, audience members rarely, if ever, produce disaffiliative responses, such as booing or heckling, to the gurus' messages. The absence of disaffiliative responses from their audiences indicates that the gurus are able to project their messages in such a way that they receive either a neutral or publicly indicated positive response (i.e. laughter). This is not to imply that potentially controversial messages are expunged from their public presentations. These lectures are not about the neutral presentation of factual information. Rather the aim is to present the guru's understanding and ideas on management and organisational life and how it can be changed and improved. Consequently, in delivering their talks the gurus invariably extol the virtues of behaviours and practices that many members of the audience are unlikely to be using, or they disparage behaviours and practices that they are very likely to be employing since they are the conventional approach. When the gurus state these messages, they run the risk of alienating their audiences since they may feel that they are being criticised or characterised as inadequate in some way. The gurus are therefore presented with the delicate task of commending the virtues of particular practices and criticising others whilst avoiding alienating some or all of their differentiated audience.

So how do management gurus project their messages so as to minimise the likelihood of displays of audience disapproval? Most notably in delivering their messages, they avoid directly criticising members of the audience and thereby avoid creating an antagonistic relationship with their audiences. The practices they use to achieve this can be summarised as follows:

- When they criticise commonplace management practices, which many audience members are likely to be using, the gurus characteristically refrain from suggesting that managers in the audience may be using them and are naive or at fault for doing so.

- When the gurus praise organisational practices that audience members may not be using, they generally refrain from suggesting that audience members should have known about these practices (and be using them), even if the gurus have been writing and speaking about them for a number of years.

Both of these features can be seen in the Extract 3.5, in which Rosabeth Moss Kanter first criticises traditional corporate bureaucratic structures that involve people at the lower levels having very limited understandings of their work, and then advocates her idea on management, which involves workers understanding how their activities benefit their company and connects with the company's vision and strategic goals.

Extract 3.5 [Charlie Brown: 0.07.45]

RMK: Now there was a ti:me (.) when we didn't have to count o:n
(0.5) people at the (.) lowest levels, at the grass roots, at the street level,
at the production level to understand our policy or do anything about it.
Because all they di:d was a narrow routinised job in which they had no
decisions to make, (0.7) no autonomous actions, no power,=no influence,
they did what they were told. (1.4) In fa:ct (1.0) that was the essence of
bureaucracy, you don't have to know our strategy just do the job. (0.5)
One of my favourite stories about that kind of system (0.4) was told to
me by Charlie Bro:wn (0.7) the late chairman of AT&T, who was starting
to see the need for change and trying to produce it in the early nineteen
eighties.=And so he visited a lot of the AT&T factories. The telephone
factories, (0.2) Western Electric was the division name. (0.5) And he
talked about (0.5) chatting with a woman on the assembly line who
thought she was making iro:ns. (0.4) She thought she worked for General
Electric.

Aud: LLLLLLL

RMK: The thing that was (.) amazing to him was that people (.) in order to do
the jo:b people didn't have to know what product they made. (0.5) All
they had to do was follow instructions,=and do their piece of the process.
(0.5) Well toda:y (0.2) People need to know the connection between their
activities and the overall focus, skills of the fir:m.

Moss Kanter begins by asserting that lower level employees working in bureaucracies were once unaware of the strategy being pursued by the organisation for which they worked (lines 1–7). She then announces the telling of a story, originally told to her by Charlie Brown, the former Chairman of AT&T, which illustrates the problems that occur when production line employees are ignorant of an organisation's strategy (lines 8–11). The story is then articulated (lines 11–15) and at lines 17–21 she ends by emphasising the key point that she wishes the audience to draw from the story, in this case all employees, regardless of their position in the organisation, should be aware of its common values and goals. At no point during this episode does Moss Kanter indicate or hint that any audience members may either use or agree with the use of structures that could be deemed bureaucratic.

In criticising management practices that many of her audience members could well be using, Moss Kanter not only avoids drawing attention to this possibility but also directs her disparagement at a third-party organisation. This rhetorical practice is commonplace during guru lectures. In Extract 3.6, for example, Gary Hamel is developing an argument that companies should focus on becoming different and be the initiators of industry transformation.

Extract 3.6 [LinL: 00.26.01 – 'Famous car rental company']

Hamel: There is even a company that has enshrined peasantry in its mission statement. (0.2) There's a famous car rental company that likes to say 'we try (0.4) harder'. (0.6) Well I think that's pathetic in a way. (0.2) You know maybe somebody should tell them this time to try different and not just harder (0.2) because they are coming increasingly to the point of diminishing returns along the traditional trajectories for performance improvement.

Hamel does not explicitly raise the possibility that audience members are likely to be adopting/implementing organisational performance improvement strategies that he is criticising – although some may well be doing so. Instead, he criticises an unnamed (lines 1–3), apparently well-known rental car company's mission statement, which refers to 'trying harder' rather than 'being different'. In this way Hamel avoids directly confronting and possibly discomfiting the audience by deflecting criticism to unnamed third parties.

There are cases in which gurus directly criticise their audiences but when they do so, they generally include themselves amongst those being criticised and indicate that the practices are commonplace within the management community. The example in Extract 3.7, which is drawn from a Tom Peters lecture, occurs immediately after he has calculated that a Federal Express delivery person is managing a $15 million portfolio of business.

Extract 3.7 [TPE2: 00.16.50 – 'Attitude problem']

Peters: So my question as we begin this discussion of people is very crude and blunt. (0.2) Do you treat the average part-time hourly person in your company (0.6) like a person managing (0.6) a fifteen to forty million

dollar portfolio? (0.8) I think we have an attitude problem, (0.4) and
I think the attitude problem is us. (2.0) Because my suspicion is if we
started treating front-line people like fifteen million dollar people then
they wouldn't have that attitude problem that we say they have. (1.0)
The attitude problem is that we don't treat em like fifteen million
people

In lines 4–9 of this passage Peters candidly accuses his audience of failing to recognise the 'true' significance of their front-line staff. However, he mitigates the impact of this by identifying himself as someone who shares this attitude. In this respect, he portrays himself as being no different from members of the audience. Thus, whilst he directly criticises the audience, he does not create a distance between himself and the audience by insinuating that he is better than they are. Rather he implies that they are part of an 'in-group' of which he is also a member. In so doing, he implies that very few managers do not share the attitude to their front-line staff that he is referring to.

In summary, when they praise organisational practices, management gurus generally do not draw attention to the fact that the audience members may not be using them and when they criticise management practices, with rare exceptions (which are heavily mitigated), they do not direct their criticism at the audience members who are using them. By adopting this approach, the gurus are able to question common management ideas and practices without directly confronting, antagonising or discomfiting audience members who may be using them.

Conclusion

In this chapter, we have described how management gurus manage the delicate task of presenting ideas that many, if not all, of the members of their audiences do not use. On the one hand, gurus endeavor to create and maintain a positive atmosphere in the auditorium by providing audience members with opportunities to laugh collectively and engage in displays of group cohesiveness without having to unequivocally display agreement with their management ideas. In this way gurus are able to generate a positive atmosphere during their lectures regardless of the extent to which audience members agree or disagree with their ideas. Even though the audience members in cases such as these may not be demonstrating their unambiguous agreement with the gurus' management ideas, their collective laughter plays an important role with respect to the maintenance of rapport and group cohesion at these lectures: by laughing, they publicly constitute themselves at that moment as members of an in-group

(Greatbatch and Clark, 2003, 2005). Previous research into the functions of humour suggest that it can promote the emergence and maintenance of group cohesiveness by, inter alia, clarifying and reinforcing shared values and social norms; disciplining those who violate the rules of a social group, and unifying other group members against them; and dividing group members from other groups (those who would be expected to adopt a different perspective; e.g., see Meyer, 2000). It is generally unclear whether gurus and their audiences can be classified as members of distinctive social groups, whose boundaries are defined by reference to their members' affiliation with the gurus' management ideas. Nonetheless, by evoking and producing laughter, gurus and audience members participate in public displays of consensus and 'like-mindedness' (Glenn, 1989) and thereby *constitute* themselves as in-groups that share a common perspective in relation to the circumstances and events that the gurus describe. When gurus attack/disparage others (e.g,. Peters' attack on the concept of 'exceeding expectations' in Extract 3.1), the gurus and those audience members who laugh also publicly differentiate themselves from individuals or groups who purportedly do not share the ideas and underlying values or perspectives they are expressing. In these cases, then, humour and laughter serves to delineate group boundaries by acting as both a unifier and divider (Meyer, 2000). Whether these publicly displayed group affiliations actually reflect audience members' commitment to gurus' management ideas which may extend beyond the lifetime of the gurus' lectures is, of course, open to question and will be further elaborated in the remainder of the book. Nonetheless, even those cases of audience laughter that are not open to interpretation as unvarnished expressions of support for the gurus' core management ideas indicate a shared perspective and – like affiliative interactions in general (Goffman, 1983; Heritage, 1984) – contribute to a sense of cohesion and intimacy, which might make audiences more receptive to the gurus' recommendations. Greatbatch and Clark conclude by suggesting that '[g]iven that speakers are unlikely to persuade audiences to empathise with their positions unless they sustain the attentiveness of audience members, it seems likely that humor is one means through which gurus and other public speakers create the conditions necessary to win and retain converts to their ideas' (2003: 1539).

On the other hand, gurus also routinely seek to minimise the likelihood of a negative atmosphere emerging when they convey ideas that are likely to be at odds with the management practices used by many audience members. The gurus do this by avoiding directly confronting or criticising their audiences by using one or more of the following practices:

- Avoiding suggesting that audience members are at fault for not using the approaches they are recommending.
- Deflecting their criticisms of management practices away from audience members who may be using them to third parties.
- Including themselves amongst those people that use these ideas and practices.

The ability of gurus to effectively use the rhetorical practices described in this chapter to build a positive atmosphere in their audiences may operate to make their diverse audience members more receptive to their ideas on management. However, in order to convince audience members to take up their ideas, the gurus also need demonstrate that these ideas are applicable across a broad range of different organisations. In Chapter 4, we turn to consider how they seek to do this.

4 Conveying the Applicability of Ideas to Audience Members

Chapter 3 showed how gurus seek to enhance receptivity towards their potentially controversial ideas by deploying rhetorical practices and persuasive strategies that operate to build rapport and establish cohesion with their live audiences. Drawing on previous CA research on political oratory, the chapter explained how in developing a positive atmosphere at their lectures, gurus provide scope for audience members to collectively display their affiliation with them (in the form of laughter) irrespective of whether or not the audience members agree or disagree with the ideas the guru is promoting. It also considered how gurus minimise the likelihood of disaffiliative responses such as heckling, head shaking or booing by deflecting criticism away from their audiences or otherwise trying to avoid antagonising audience members when they either question common management practices that audience members may currently use or suggest alternatives that audience members could well view with scepticism. Overall, the findings from Chapter 3 shed important light on how gurus seek to create a positive atmosphere that is conducive to the promotion of their ideas.

If the gurus wish their ideas to be taken up by members of their live audiences, however, they need to go beyond developing a positive emotional connection with them. They also need to convincingly demonstrate that their ideas are potentially pertinent to the variety of working lives of those who attend. In this chapter we ask: *How do gurus present their ideas as being generally applicable, significant and potentially relevant to individual audience members?* The chapter shows how gurus use their lectures not only to convey the general applicability of their ideas across a wide range of contexts but also to construct an ambiguity that allows scope for managerial audience members to tailor the ideas to different contexts. In essence, the chapter shows how gurus deploy rhetorical practices that leave their ideas open to alternative interpretations and diverse courses of action in the diffusion and implementation process.

The Ambiguity of Gurus' Management Ideas

Previous literature has suggested that the widespread use of popular management ideas is due in part to the meaning of these ideas being ambiguous and therefore allowing room for them to be interpreted and implemented in different ways in diverse contexts (e.g. Astley and Zammuto, 1992; Benders and Van Veen, 2001; Giroux, 2006, 2019; Kieser, 1997; Örtenblad, 2007, 2015). This ambiguity has been identified in relation to a wide range of popular management ideas (Giroux, 2019) including Achieving Competitive Excellence (ACE) (Ansari et al., 2014), Business Process Re-engineering (BPR) (Benders and Verlaar, 2003), Core Competences (Nicolai and Dautwiz, 2010), Knowledge Management (Scarborough and Swan, 2001), Lean (Green and May, 2005), Learning Organisation (Örtenblad, 2007) and Total Quality Management (Boaden, 1997). Bort powerfully illustrates how the ambiguity of popular management ideas 'offers scope for multiple interpretations' by reference to TQM and the learning organisation: 'Boaden (1997) identified 40 definitions of TQM, but only 11 characteristics appeared in at least 10 per cent of the identified definitions, and none of the characteristics were present in more than 50 per cent of the definitions. Relatedly, Örtenblad (2007) identified 12 interpretations of Senge's conceptualisation of the "learning organisation"' (Bort, 2015: 40–1).

Although it is widely accepted that the ambiguity of management ideas is generally associated with their popularity amongst management practitioners, the extent to which ambiguity results from the diffusion and usage process, as these actors tailor the ideas to fit their requirements (cf. van Grinsven et al., 2016), or is built into novel ideas developed by gurus remains a matter of debate (Giroux, 2019). Giroux (2019), who introduced the concept of 'pragmatic ambiguity' to describe the condition of management ideas admitting more than one course of action, contends that it is a two-way relationship: '"(P)ragmatic ambiguity" is both the source and the result of adoption. Ideas become more general, ambiguous and vague as various stakeholders attempt to translate and align their interests, but this process is possible only if the label allows "interpretative viability" (Benders and Van Veen, 2001)' (2019: 312–13). Our analysis of the corpus of video recordings of live guru lectures, and research on speaker-audience interaction during public speaking engagements involving politicians (Atkinson, 1984a, 1984b; Heritage and Greatbatch, 1986) and management gurus (Clark et al., 2015; Greatbatch and Clark, 2003, 2005, 2010, 2018) which we described in Chapter 3 shows that:

- during their lectures, gurus routinely emphasise the general applicability of their ideas and define them in ways that allows space for multiple interpretations and courses of action during the diffusion and implementation process;
- in doing so, the gurus commonly use stories about change not only to provide entertaining illustrations of their ideas in action but also as precursors to statements that communicate the degree of adaptability of their ideas and their significance (Clark et al., 2015).

In the remainder of this chapter, we discuss how gurus juxtapose the particularities of stories about change with summary statements of their ideas that have high levels of ambiguity and allow scope for 'interpretative viability'.

Conveying the Adaptability of Ideas through Stories about Change

In their lectures and books gurus use stories as a key mechanism for framing and projecting messages about their ideas (Clark and Salaman, 1998; Collins, 2012; Greatbatch and Clark, 2010). However, not all stories are of equal importance in conveying their ideas to live audiences (Bhatanacharoen et al., 2013; Clark and Greatbatch, 2011; Clark et al., 2015). Stories about change are particularly significant since gurus use them disproportionately as a preface to summary messages concerning their management ideas.

Gurus' stories about change involve a central character (the guru or someone else) experiencing a moment of unanticipated personal realisation regarding the significance of a management idea that they are promoting (Bhatanacharoen et al., 2013). Following the stories gurus present a summary message that conveys the generic importance of practices identified in the story by providing a substantive assertion about the core idea on management that they are seeking to convey to their audience. This involves a transition from the specific to the general, with the gurus drawing attention to the broad applicability of their ideas. It also involves the gurus endowing their ideas with pragmatic ambiguity by offering high-level definitions that are vague and therefore open to multiple interpretations and uses in different contexts.

Our analysis of gurus' stories about change reveals that they fall into two groups, which we term epiphanic and non-epiphanic. Again, Appendix B provides a glossary of the symbols used in the transcripts.

Epiphanic Stories

Epiphanic stories present the central character as experiencing a sudden, discontinuous and personal transformation (Miller and C'de Baca, 2001). In this respect the gurus' stories convey a sudden and striking visionary moment that represents a turning point for the central character in that an ostensibly mundane event led to a complete reconsideration of how they thought about some aspect of the world (Clark et al., 2015). In Extract 4.1, for example, Tom Peters begins by announcing that he is about to describe an epiphany concerning the nature of exceptional service that he experienced whilst shopping in a delicatessen in San Francisco (lines 1–2).

Extract 4.1 [TP: SWS: 0.2.17: 2760 Octavia Street]

Peters: My epiphany came to be very precise at twenty-seven sixty Octavia Street in San Francisco. (0.2) I had screwed up my schedule in a wonderfully delightful way a few weeks ago and was going to spend an hour wandering down San Francisco Union Street (.) and I saw this little Deli. (0.2) Now its fair to say whether the topic is Chicago, Miami, Detroit, San Francisco, or any place else its fair to say a Deli is a dime a dozen is a great over elevation of the average Deli, (.) but this one, you know were all grown ups here, (.) I don't have to define to you what "sticks out" means. (0.2) There was something about this place that that made you want to go in (.) so I went in and it was a kick. (0.3) This place was just fabulous. (0.2) This place is called Curry's Deli café. (.) I walk in to this place. (.) I had moderate munches not main munches. (0.3) This guy overwhelms me with food. He's giving me the tabbouleh, he's giving me hummus, he's giving me everything in the world, (.) and every single one of them is like being to Anita Roddick's Body Shop. (0.2) This is the story of about 700 years ago, it started out and was developed (.) this is the way I cook and now my mother she's in the back cooks it slightly different. If you come back tomorrow that's her batch, (0.2) on and on this guy goes. (0.2) It was beautiful. (0.2) We only got into a fight at one point, (.) and the fight we got into was when I said 'You my friend are one hell (.) of (.) a (.) salesman'. 'I am NOT a salesman,

Audience: l-l-l-[l

Peters: [I LOVE MY FOOD AND I AM TRYING TO CONVEY THE ESSENCE OF IT TO YOU' he said.=What I saw at Curry's Delicatessen was something that I'm now calling service with soul. (0.2) You know, (0.2) and the definition of service with soul in part is something that grabs you (.) you don't know why but it's there no issue about it and you can leave the electron microscope at home.

At the beginning of his story, Peters emphasises the extraordinariness of what he is about to tell the audience by not only characterising the story as being about him experiencing an epiphany but also recalling the exact location at which it occurred (2760 Octavia Street in San Francisco) (lines 1–2). When people recall epiphanic events they often specify the date, time and location of the events (Miller and C'de Baca, 2001, pp. 13–14). By stating the address of the delicatessen where this epiphany took place, Peters conveys the enduring vividness of the events he is going to describe. From the outset Peters therefore alerts audience members that he is about to disclose something very significant and personal (the moment from which the ideas that are the subject of his lecture originated) and establishes a puzzle in their minds (what are the events that resulted in this epiphany?). In this way Peters focuses the audience's attention on his unfolding remarks by heightening their curiosity from the outset.

This example clearly illustrates the typical two-part structure associated with gurus' stories about change – namely, a story (lines 2–25) followed by a summary message that changes the focus from the particular to general (lines 25–30). The story is about something Peters experiences in a particular setting (his conversation with the proprietor of the delicatessen) whereas in his post-story summary he turns this into the general idea of his lecture – 'service with soul'.

The transition from story to post-story summary message involves a shift from a humorous to a serious footing. Peters concludes the story by describing a disagreement that he had with the person who served him in the delicatessen (possibly the owner) (lines 20–22). This evokes laughter from some members of the audience (line 23). Then Peters links his assessment of the actions of the person who served him with a revelatory insight into the generic importance of extraordinary service that he terms 'service with soul' (lines 25–30). Audience attention is funnelled to this post-story summary message which conveys a substantive assertion about the core idea he is seeking to convey in his lecture. The contrast between the light-heartedness of the story and the seriousness of the post-story conclusion provides emphasis to the message being delivered – the nature and meaning of 'service with soul' – as well as the transition from the specific to the general. The use of humour underscores the incongruity of the events described in the story whereas the serious frame accentuates the gravity of his generic point.

In transforming the story about events that happened at 2760 Octavia Street in San Francisco from being about something specific he observed and experienced in a particular setting to being an example of something generic and therefore potentially relevant to all those involved in service delivery, Peters' definition of 'service with soul' is left vague. Peters defines the idea of 'service with soul' as something that 'grabs you [and] you don't know why' (lines 27–30). In other words, it cannot be precisely defined. 'Service with soul' is tacit knowledge that is difficult to express but is immediately recognisable when it is experienced. In defining it in this way Peters creates a puzzle in the minds of audience members. He encourages them to ask themselves: 'Have I experienced service like that described in the story?' Peters both generalises the concept and encourages the audience members to apply it to their experience in order to solve the puzzle as to what it means. Moreover, he leaves the notion of 'service with soul' open to multiple interpretations and allows for pragmatic ambiguity if and when audience members – those in formal management functions and consultants in particular – come to apply it in different contexts.

A transition from the particularities of an epiphanic story to a general point that is broadly applicable can also be seen in Extract 4.2. In this extract Peter Senge, a member of faculty at MIT and author of *The Fifth Discipline* (1990), tells a story about an erstwhile economist named Fred Kaufman who experienced a moment of self-doubt followed by a sudden personal realisation that led him to leave the field of economics. Senge uses the story to exemplify his point that education does not necessarily tell you everything about how the world works.

Extract 4.2 [PS: Fifth Discipline: 00.04.40]

PS: If we've grown up in America (0.2) or we've grown up in probably
any industrial culture (0.2) we've bought into a notion that more
or less goes along the following lines.=There's a couple of different
variations to this notion. (0.3) It's like a (.) a little message that's
been whispered in our ears since we were very very young. (0.7)
And the message goes sort of like this. (0.5) To be effective you
must first understand. (1.1) You must figure it out. You must
know how the world works.=After all why would you be going
to school? (You're going to learn in school how everything
works).=Right?
(1.4)
Right. hhehehehmm
(1.2)

.hh Fred Kaufmann (.) used to tell a funny story about that. He said
you know. I went to school in Argentina and I- I grew up in a society
in a- in a perpetual state of disaster. (0.2) I knew that what I really
had to do was to figure out what was really going on and so I would
become an economist. (0.4) Because clearly (0.2) that was the most
pressing set of issues in my country. (0.2) So I became an economist.
.hh I went to graduate in economics. (0.2) I went to Berkeley which
is one of the best economics departments in theoretical economics,
=he said I really wanted to be absolutely world class (0.4) in- in er
theoretical economics understand the theories of how economies
work. (0.2) And I was somewhere about a year or two away from
getting my Ph.D .h and an odd thing happened.=I started to get
invited to give presentations. (0.3) He never used to say this but
Fred was identified as one of the (0.2) three top young economists in
the world. .hh One of the world's leading experts in a field called
game theory. .hhh He said suddenly I realised .hh people were
coming to listen to me:: talk about economic theory .hh and he said
realised (.) my Go::d (0.7) they're listening to me:? (1.1) And I don't
have a clue:?
Audience: LLLLLLLLLLLLLLLL[LLL
PS: [He then left the field of economics.
Audience: LLLLLL
(0.8)
PS: Because he'd suddenly realised that all the quote experts (0.2) really
didn't have a clue.> (1.6) Because he was one. (2.0) So somewhere
along the way we all kinda bought into the notion that life is about
figuring things out so that we can be in (1.0) – thank you – (1.2) the
gentleman in the front said control. (2.3) And our institutions are
based on this notion.

As with the story told by Peters in Extract 4.1, Senge's story is about the specific experiences of an individual and a general point is developed in a post-story summary message. As the story ends and the coda is articulated, there is a switch from a humorous to a serious footing (lines 37–42). This emphasises the shift from the specific to the general. Thus, Senge completes the story by asserting that Kaufman gave up his career in economics because he came to question the competency of so-called experts and being depicted as an expert therefore troubled him (lines 26–32). Senge's characterisation of Kaufman's realisation that, despite being portrayed as one of the leading young economists in the world, he did not 'have a clue' (lines 31–32) evokes a burst of collective audience laughter (line 33). Having confirmed the relevance of this laughter by remaining silent and ceding the floor, Senge starts to relate the final part of the story as the laughter begins to wane, stating that as a result of this realisation Kaufman left the field of economics (line 34). This evokes a second, shorter episode of audience laughter (line 35). On this occasion Senge sanctions the appropriateness of laughter by remaining silent throughout and immediately following (line 36) the audience's response.

Senge then delivers his post-story summary message in a serious frame, broadening the applicability of his point from a particular individual first by saying that 'all the quote experts really didn't have a clue' and then reinforcing this by stating that 'we all kinda bought into the notion' (of being in control) and that institutions are based on this notion (lines 37–42).[1] This story is therefore used to evidence the general point that thinking we are in control is highly questionable. As in the case of Peter's definition of 'service with soul' in Extract 4.1, Senge's general point remains vague in that it is never defined precisely and is open to the possibility of multiple acceptable interpretations and courses of action in the diffusion and implementation process.

Non-Epiphanic Stories

Non-epiphanic stories about change involve gurus presenting the change in their (or someone else's) thinking as a more cumulative, incremental and slow-burn change as individuals consider the implications of a single event or series of events and gradually make sense of them (Clark et al., 2015). As noted in the previous section, non-epiphanic stories exhibit the same two-part structure as epiphanic stories (a story about a single or series of events followed by a summary message, which highlights a generic lesson learnt). In Extract 4.3, for example, Rosabeth Moss Kanter tells the final story in a series of humorous tales about animals in organisational settings, which she ultimately reveals resulted in her coming to recognise the idea that in order to improve organisational performance it is necessary to challenge the past and question prevailing assumptions.

[1] Like Tom Peters in Extract 4.1, then, Senge first underlines the extraordinary nature of the events recounted in his story through the use of humour and then subsequently shifts from a humorous to a serious mode as he distills the general idea from the specifics of the story.

Extract 4.3 [Managing Change: 00.06.19]

Audience: LLLLLLLLLL LL[LLL (1.5)

RMK: [Well you'll see my point in a minute, I'm no(h)t ju(h)st try(h)ing to entertain you. (.) Because one more round of the elephant,=I then thought this was very very funny so added it to my repertoire,=and I told this story out in the valley (0.2) at a big meeting, and a man came up to me from Intel. (.) And he said on his first day on the job at Intel (.) he came in and there was a Lama in the lobby. (.) So said perfect straight person I said why a Lama? (0.2) And he said because they couldn't get an elephant though the doo::r.

Audience: LLLLLLLL[LL

RMK: [I should have kno:wn.

Audience: LLLL[L

RMK: [But why am I spending all this time telling silly animal stories. (.) What was I seeing, I was seeing that in that part of the country that at that time this was the early eighties, (.) it was the hot bed of creativity and innovation. (.) More change was happening there, more change was starting there,=they were the source of our surprises. (0.2) Or our new opportunities (.) as the case may be. But in that environment I was seeing a culture of pla::y and irreverence, (.) a culture where people had fun, had a sense of humour (.) and did silly things. (.) And when I put that together with the scientific (.) evidence on creativity (.) I realised that that was exactly right, because what is creativity (.) but play and irreverence.=It's playing with ideas, challenging old assumptions and it's irreverence (.) against somebody's tradition. (0.4) And so they were studying an environment (.) where people were freer (.) to come forth with new technological ideas,=new serious ideas, because they were also freer (.) to express other kinds of silly or crazy or wild ideas.

The audience responds to Moss Kanter's story by laughing collectively immediately after the punchline (line 11). Having confirmed the relevance of audience laughter by ceding the floor, Moss Kanter resumes speaking as the audience laughter starts to wane in order to humorously comment on her having unintentionally acted as a 'perfect straight person' in the story (line 12). This generates further audience laughter (line 13). As the laughter dies way, Moss Kanter shifts to a serious tone as she starts to deliver a post-story summary (line 14). This summary conveys a general idea about creativity and innovation that underpinned what she had witnessed, which she claims is more widely applicable (lines 15–30) – in order to improve the performance of organisations, it is necessary to challenge prevailing assumptions and act irreverently (lines 15–30).[2] This idea is presented as the outcome of her reflecting on the significance of what she had witnessed and putting this together with the available scientific evidence. Like Tom Peters and Peter Senge in the previous examples, Moss Kanter expresses her idea at a high level that allows for multiple interpretations and courses of action that could be used to encourage creativity in different contexts.

Whilst the summary messages that follow stories about change in this example and the previous two extracts involving epiphanic stories are expressed with absolute certainty, in some cases gurus' messages are stated more equivocally. In our dataset this occurs solely in the context of non-epiphanic stories.[3] An example is observable in Extract 4.4, which is drawn from the same lecture as Extract 4.1 and involves Tom Peters describing a set of events that occurred at a restaurant in Auckland called Vilario's that led him to conclude that the idea of 'service with soul' involves a 'total redefinition about what is possible' (a segment of the passage of Peters' lecture was considered in Chapter 3, see Extract 3.1). Prior to the beginning of the extract, Peters has described how the restaurant initially intrigued him because there was a sign on the menu board stating that they had not bothered to display a menu but had a great atmosphere, good food and a 'half crazy owner'.

The extract begins with Peters describing how during the course of the meal he visited the toilet and came across 'outrageous' letters of complaint posted on the walls with the restaurateur's very direct and unapologetic responses displayed alongside them (lines 1–10). Peters

[2] It should be noted here that this example embodies a structure that applies to many other cases of non-epiphanic stories. This is that the post-story summary is delivered in two parts. The initial part of the post-story is delivered as humorous comment (line 12). This is used to highlight the bizarreness of the events in the story rather than the point she subsequently makes. In the second part of the summary (lines 14–30), Moss Kanter then adopts a serious frame when suggesting that the ideas about creativity and innovation underlying what she had witnessed are more generally applicable.

[3] In considering the epiphanic or non-epihanic status of gurus' stories about change, it is important to bear in mind that gurus tell the same stories over and over and may frame the same story in different ways on different occasions. This is can be illustrated by reference to Daniel Goleman's story about his experience(s) when he caught a bus in New York, which he framed as an epiphanic experience in the example we considered in Chapter 3 (Extract 3.3). Greatbatch and Clark (2010) found that while on this occasion Goleman framed the story as depicting events that changed his life ('Now I am going to tell you the story that changed my life'), on another occasion he told the same story using very similar wording to illustrate the fifth element of Emotional Intelligence, which he defined in the story preface as 'handling emotions in relationships'.

reports that he was so affected by the quirkiness of these letters that when he returned to his table he and his wife seriously considered changing their careers and opening a restaurant (lines 30–34). Although the changes Peters and his wife discuss are potentially life changing, any change is momentary and confined to their conversation as they eat.

Extract 4.4 [Service with Soul: 0.05.50]

TP: Well the food was good. Very good in fact. And half way though the meal I had to go to the little boys room. And little boys rooms are located, like little boys rooms in restaurants all round the world you know, at the end of a long hall somewhere. And the long hall which has you know all the things posted on the wall, the Rotary Award, the Lion's Award all framed and stuff. And this had stuff on the wall too, but it was slightly different, because what was posted on the walls at Vilario's were the most OUTRAGEOUS LETTERS OF COMPLAINT that had ever been SENT.

Audience: LLLLLLLLLL LLLLLLLLLL LLLLLLLLLL LLLLLLLL

TP: Now if you had read the damn instructions you would have known what was coming because he said "look I love complaints but complain while your hear or your going to be sorry". Because next to the letter of complaints was his equally insulting response.

Audience: LLLLLLLLLL LLLLLLLLLL LLLLLLLLLL LLLLLLLLLL

TP: And the one that I most remember was a guy who was the Sales Director at the local Channel 3 television station OK. And this guy had written in and said your service wasn't any good and the white wine was really lousy. Vilario responds to him, he says "well I was disappointed to see that you didn't have time to complain while you were here during your three hour quote unquote business lunch,"

Aud: LLLLLLLLLL LLLLLLLLLL LLLLLLLLLL LLLLLLLLLL LL

TP: He said 'as for the white wine, this is an Italian restaurant we don't give a da::mn about white wine.'

Audience: LLLLLLLLLL LLLLLLLLLL LLLLLLLLLL LLLLLLLLLL LLLLLLLLLL LL[LL

TP: [When I got back (1.0) honest to gosh for the next I don't know thirty (0.2) forty-five minutes, something like that, (0.2) my wife and I sat at that table in that restaurant in Auckland (.) seriously discussing both of us giving up our professional careers and opening a restaurant

Audience: LL[LL

TP: [because it absolutely seemed like the most incredible way to sort of you know express yourself as a human being,

Audience: LLLL[LLLL

TP: [which is beautiful (.) you know and and you know I'm here and I didn't do it obviously.

Audience: [LLLLLLLLL

TP: [=But it was it was.=But but but let me let me now tie that back to what we are talking about here OK. Because words are important. (1.0) VILARIO'S DID NOT SATISFY THE CUSTOMER. Or to use that phenomenally stupid accountant engineering word 'IT DID NOT EXCEED EXPECTATIONS'.

Audience: LLLLLLLLL LLLLLLLLL LL

TP: What Vilario's does was an event, it was a transformation. (0.2) It is about a total redefinition about what is possible. (0.2) And I happen to think that it applies to the making of plastics, the making of software as well as the making of good tabbouleh. And so for the last several months we have been in pursuit of this idea of service with soul. We have found it in the damnedest places. In neighbourhood police work in the city of Chicago. In plumbing, heating and air conditioning in the San Wakeen Valley in California.

At lines 23–24, Peters feigns anger, smiles and bares his teeth as he relates how the owner rejected a customer's complaint about the quality of the white wine they ordered at the restaurant (line 20–23). Subsequently he remains silent, as audience members laugh, thereby confirming the relevance of this response. As the audience laughter fades away, he resumes speaking and adopts a quieter tone, drawing the audience attention into his intimate admission about him and his wife considering a possible change of career (lines 30–34). While he smiles throughout this section of his lecture, indicating his remarks can be understood as humorous, Peters speaks over and suppresses three brief episodes of audience laughter (lines, 35, 38 and 41). There is a sense of urgency in his talk. He gives the impression of wanting to get to the point in lines 42 to 46. In these lines he begins by announcing his intention of relating the story to the subject of his lecture, 'service with soul' (lines 42–43). He uses a loud and exaggerated tone of voice and contorts his face to demonstrate his utter disapproval of the phrase 'exceed expectations' (line 46). This evokes audience laughter, the relevance of which he confirms by ceding the floor as they laugh (line 47). Peters does not speak again until the laughter has completely died away. At this point he asserts that the lesson from this story has general applicability to very different types of work (lines 48–56).

As in the case of Rosabeth Moss Kanter's non-epiphanic story in Extract 4.3, the post-story summary is delivered in two parts. Peters configures it as a contrast, the first part of which is a negative assessment made in a hyperbolic tone of voice and with comic prosody (lines 42–46). This generates audience laughter (line 47). The second part of the contrast is delivered seriously, structured as a three-part list ('an event ... a transformation ... a total redefinition') and linked to his core theme of 'service with soul' (lines 48–56). This structure emphasises the generality of the point he is making in that he uses humour to disparage an alternative interpretation as vacuous management speak. The humour is used to underline the ridiculousness of this point of view. He therefore obtains laughter for a disparaging characterisation of a narrow alternative view of exceptional service before presenting his own broad idea of exceptional service on a serious footing. However, the idea is not delivered with the same certainty as it was in the previous cases, which includes his introduction of the notion of 'service with soul' earlier in the same lecture. Peters justifies broadening the applicability of his argument to a range of contexts by saying 'I happen to think that it applies' (lines 49–50). Thus, rather than stating the generic relevance of a point derived from a particular context with complete certainty, it is instead qualified by a conditional statement related to the core management idea.

Another example is Charles Handy's non-epiphanic story about an encounter he had with someone from whom he asked directions, which we considered in Chapter 3 (Extract 3.3).

Extract 4.5 – [Sigmoid curve: 0:11:56]

CH: I mean I was traveling in the Wicklow Hills behind the city where I was born Dublin (0.5) not so long ago. And I lost my way because the (.) hills in those days anyway didn't have any signposts. But then of course after a bit I saw an Irishman at the roadside so I stopped and I said 'can you tell me the way to Avoca'. And he said 'yes of course' he said.=He said 'it's very easy. You go on straight up this hill mm and then down the other side for about for for about a mile and a half (0.2) and you will see a bridge over the river a little bridge and Davy's Bar on the other side. (.) Its painted red you can't miss it. (.) Have you got that?' And I said 'well yes up the hill down the hill bridge Davy's Bar'. He he said 'well' he said 'half a mile before you get there turn right up the hill'.

Audience: LLLLLLLLLLLLLLLL

CH: And you see

Audience: L[LLLLL[LLLLL l-l-l-l-l-l-l

CH: [this [this is the problem. You only know where you should have turned r-h-h-ight up the hill (0.2) when you've passed it. (1.0) And I've met many many many firms many people at Davy's Bar downing their drinks saying that was good while its lasted but you know if only we'd listened, if only we'd (0.2) etcetera. (.) So it is very very difficult to know (0.2) and the only thing I can tell you is that when you're feeling pretty pleased with yourself with business or with life (.) that's the time to start thinking.

As in the previous example (Extract 4.4), the initial part of the post-story summary in Extract 4.5 is delivered as humorous (lines 12–13). Handy uses humour to underline a comment in relation to the specific context in the story. It therefore highlights the incongruous nature of the events in the story rather than the point he subsequently makes. Handy then assumes a serious footing when suggesting that what he saw in Davy's Bar is more generally applicable ('I've met many, many firms many people at Davy's Bar') (lines 19–24). The strength of this generic claim is presented conditionally in that he can only give a vague idea of when members of the audience should consider changing their lives ('when you're feeling pretty pleased with yourself') (lines 22–24).

In summary, whilst the generic applicability of the final messages following the non-epiphanic stories by Tom Peters and Charles Handy in Extracts 4.4 and 4.5 are clearly emphasised and expressed, the epistemological status of their claims is weaker than those made by Peters, Senge and Moss Kanter in Extracts 4.1–4.3. Rather than expressing their messages unequivocally 'with absolute certainty', they present them more equivocally and thereby perhaps leave more room for interpretation when their ideas are taken up by managerial audience members.

Conclusion

In this chapter we have shown how management gurus use stories about change to communicate the successful application and adaptability of their ideas. Regardless of whether these stories are framed as epiphanic or non-epiphanic, they exhibit three common practices. First, the stories exemplify the gurus' ideas by focusing on a particular case and on singular themes, making them more easily apprehensible and enabling the audience to collectively concentrate on a narrow set of events. Second, the stories are told in an engaging and entertaining manner, which heightens audience attentiveness and thereby makes the stories more memorable. Third, following the stories, gurus move from the particular to the general in order to demonstrate the applicability of the ideas exemplified by the stories to a wide range of contexts. This generally coincides with, and is marked by, a shift to a serious (or more serious) footing.

In both epiphanal and non-epiphanal stories about change the assertion of a general idea that the guru distils from the events described is initially delivered following a humorous conclusion to the story or a humorous remark by the guru relating to the specifics of the story. This emphasises the absurdness of an individual and actions in the story (Extracts 4.1, 4.2, 4.3 and 4.5) or an alternative interpretation of the point of the story (Extract 4.4). These humorous episodes provide an opportunity for the audience members to demonstrate a collective and positive response to the gurus' stories. Whether these episodes of collective audience laughter can be taken as demonstrating unequivocal agreement with the underlying values of the management practices that the events recounted in the stories are being used to convey is unclear (Greatbatch and Clark, 2003). Nevertheless, by producing displays of shared understanding of the humorous character of the gurus' remarks, the audience members who laugh do at the very least openly confirm themselves as members of an in-group that includes the guru (Greatbatch and Clark, 2003). These occurrences therefore provide an antecedent affiliative exchange between the gurus and audience members prior to the delivery of the gurus' core messages. The audience members and gurus are unified in a momentary display of mutual understanding which provides a positive environment in which the gurus can make their subsequent points. The residual positive dynamic from the laughter maximises the likelihood that the gurus' points will be received either neutrally or positively.

The gurus' assertions about the general applicability of their ideas are vague and high level and therefore allow for 'pragmatic ambiguity' (Giroux, 2006) in relation to how they are interpreted and taken up by management practitioners as audience members in different contexts. However, whilst the generic applicability of the final messages is clearly emphasised and expressed in all cases, the epistemological status of the claims varies. In some cases the message is expressed unequivocally with absolute certainty, whereas in others it is stated more equivocally. When gurus qualify definitions of their ideas, they increase their vagueness and thus effectively provide more space for interpretation by their audiences. It is possible, however, that the lack of specificity may weaken the impact and memorability of the ideas being promoted both during lectures and beyond. Regardless, our analysis underlines that pragmatic ambiguity is not only the result of the actions of management practitioners (including those in formal management roles and management consultants) during the diffusion and implementation process but is also constructed by gurus in ways that may enhance or inhibit possibilities for adaptability. Arguably, conveying the adaptability of ideas by management gurus can be considered a critical precondition for managerial agency in using management ideas in different contexts.

In Chapters 3 and 4 we have considered how management gurus generate a positive atmosphere in their lectures and exemplify and display the general applicability of their ideas. These two chapters shed light on the conditions that may increase the possibility of audience members leaving the auditorium with an enthusiasm for, and a willingness and intention to use, management ideas promoted by the gurus in their own organisations. We have noted that levels of affiliation with the guru's ideas may vary considerably among an audience, even in the context of displays of group cohesion through collective audience laughter. In Chapters 5 and 6, we shift our perspective to the audience members meaning making, and consider how and why individual audience members may vary in their interpretations of guru ideas. In so doing we consider how they may be 'variably active' and may potentially revise their orientations during the communication process. In the these chapters we thus examine the nature of these 'consumption orientations', as well as the main reasons for audience members to draw upon particular orientations in relation to specific gurus and their ideas.

5 Defining Audience Orientations

The previous two chapters explored core aspects of the immediate guru-audience interaction that is expected to enhance the impact of particular management ideas among a mass audience of managers. In particular, based on detailed analyses of real-time interaction during guru lectures, these chapters focused on processes that contribute to a positive atmosphere that enhances receptivity towards management ideas, and encourage application of the ideas following the events. The findings in these chapters provide important depth and nuance to our understanding of the rhetorical practices and persuasive strategies deployed by producers of management knowledge but also how audience activities are an inherent part of these processes. Overall, they have contributed to our general understanding of knowledge producers' ability not only to shape these ideas in ways that appeal to a managerial audience, but particularly how both the guru and audience activities may increase the likelihood that their ideas impact management and organisational practice via these audience members.

Together with Chapter 6, this chapter[1] zooms in on the individual management practitioners' meaning making in their role of audience members, and in particular we ask: *How and why do audience members vary in the way they are attracted to a guru and the management ideas they are promoting?* This issue is of particular importance not only to gain further insight into the potential agency of audience members in interpreting or 'decoding' the 'encoded' messages communicated by management gurus, but mainly because an audience's attractiveness towards particular management ideas can be considered as an essential precondition for intentions to adopt these ideas, and related actions to put them into practice (cf. Peters and Heusinkveld, 2010). Using analyses of interviews with management practitioners who have attended guru lectures, this chapter explores how audience members may display different orientations towards management ideas and the

[1] These two chapters draw in part on material published in Groß and colleagues (2015).

gurus that are promoting them and the role of audience members' background. Subsequently, in Chapter 6 we deepen our analysis by focusing on how and why consumption orientation may shift in relation to distinct audience activities.

Audience Members' Responses to Management Ideas

As outlined in Chapter 1, the extant literature has developed a number of explanations for the attraction of a guru and the ideas they are promoting, each drawing on a number of assumptions about the intended managerial audience. One stream of literature draws more or less implicitly upon psychoanalytical approaches to argue that guru-led ideas address several universal psychological needs associated with the managerial role (e.g. Gill and Whittle, 1993; Jackson, 1996; Watson, 1994). Audience members are attracted to the ideas that gurus promote because these enable them to obtain greater certainty, control and predictability over their responsibilities and working lives, particularly in their role as a management practitioner (Sturdy, 2004). Another area of research suggests that managerial audiences are collectively sensitive to a number of specific features in the design of management ideas by management gurus. It assumes that audience members hold a shared view of 'the' accepted key contemporary management problems (Abrahamson, 1996; Clark and Salaman, 1998), and are inherently attracted by the design of the best-selling books and guru lectures to make them easy to consume (e.g. Benders and van Veen, 2001; Clark and Greatbatch, 2004; Kieser, 1997).

Conceptually, the extant literature has provided important insights into these audiences' generic needs and collective responses but each strand of research draws on broad generalisations about the common factors that underpin audience members' receptivity to guru-led management ideas. Seen from a diffusion perspective, gurus' alleged impact on management remains largely explained in relation to their turnover of books and lectures, thereby portraying audience members as a homogeneous and relative passive group of knowledge consumers. As a result, one-dimensional images of audience members dominate present theorising which may contribute to a view of the meaning of management knowledge consumption as largely similar to each individual audience member. However, as we will argue in this chapter these understandings of the management practitioner as audience member and the potential impact of these ideas may be incomplete with regard to accounting for the complexities that stem from the specific nature of audiences.

The analyses in Chapters 3 and 4 have already recognised that both audience members' backgrounds and levels of affiliation to gurus and their ideas may vary considerably. Thus, it is recognised that mass communication events 'are not generally comprised of a homogeneous audience' (Greatbatch and Clark, 2005: 133) and that gurus present their messages in ways that are sensitive to this. However, because they involve video-based analysis of the rhetorical practices used by gurus during their live interactions with audiences, the chapters do not focus in detail on the ways in which an audience may be differentiated and how these differences have an impact on whether they find an idea attractive. In view of this, we now turn to consider what managerial audiences do, when and why they differ in what they do, and how this promotes and/or hampers the flow of ideas to organisational practice. The importance of developing a more advanced notion of audience differentiation stems not only from limitations in the extant literature on management gurus but also from more agentic and differentiated conceptualisations of management idea consumers in the growing literatures on organisational implementation indicating how organisational members may vary in their responses to management ideas (e.g. Ansari et al., 2010; Boiral, 2003; Kelemen, 2000; Kostova and Roth, 2002; Mueller and Whittle, 2011; van Grinsven et al., 2016).

To develop a detailed understanding of audience members' orientations towards management gurus and the ideas they promote, we draw in this chapter on a 'uses and gratification' perspective from the field of communication research (Biocca, 1988; Kim and Rubin, 1997; Levy and Windahl, 1984). As has already been discussed in Chapter 2, in this perspective, scholars have stressed the significance of studying individual members' experiences of audience activities in explaining how and why audience members may respond differently to media messages in mass communication settings (see Chapter 2 for a more detailed discussion). In other words, this strand of audience literature critically emphasises that to better understand the attraction of management ideas for an audience of management practitioners, it is essential to explore audience members' orientations towards the media and its contents related to different audience activities before, during and after management guru lectures in relation to the audience members' orientation. We will complement this perspective by drawing on the work of the critical media research tradition (cf. Hall, 1980; Morley, 2003) that stressed a view of audience responses to media messages as not being completely open-ended, but rather constrained by the way a message is encoded by its 'producer' and the socio-economic environment within which an individual audience member is embedded.

Our analysis in this chapter as well as in Chapters 6, 7 and 8 draws on the approach and findings of research on management practitioners' experiences as audience members in a range of different guru events (Groß et al., 2015). In particular, we use in-depth interviews with sixty-eight management practitioners some of these were interviewed twice who have participated in one or more guru events, but vary in their educational background, role, gender and organisation (see Table 5.1). Our sampling strategy was two-layered. The first stage involved interviewing a number of audience members at two different guru lectures, because we expected that this would enable us to collect a wide range of perceptions and activities from individual management practitioners during a single event (see Table 5.1, rows A and B). We selected these events because Guru A and Guru B are listed among the most popular and influential management thinkers in the context of the Netherlands (Haijtema, 2011). In addition, given that gurus may vary in style and message (Greatbatch and Clark, 2005; Huczynski, 1993), the selected events differed in terms of key characteristics such as duration, size, location and key topics. Keeping the national context constant ensures comparability of these characteristics. To understand better the specific contexts in which these audience members resided, we drew on additional sources such as interviews with the respective gurus, event organisor, and relevant written material from and about the lecture.

In a second stage we concentrated on selecting a number of informants who allowed us to learn more about their experiences across a number of different guru lectures. Therefore, we interviewed a number of management practitioners about their participation in a lecture series including four different US Gurus (see third row Table 5.1, labelled C), and a number of practitioners about their participation in a broad range of seminars by Dutch and/or international gurus (see last row Table 5.1, labelled D). By asking informants to explicitly compare their experiences of a range of guru events, we not only gained a better understanding of the differences reported by participants at lectures by Guru A and B, but also gained further insights into relevant audience activities and into the reasons for not attending certain seminars.

We adopted a semi-structured approach (Rubin and Rubin, 1995). In particular, questions focused on why informants selected a specific guru event, how they got involved in such an event, and whether and how they made use of the ideas after the respective event. Most of the interviews were held at the informants' offices and, on average, lasted around one hour. All interviews were transcribed and sent back to the informants for comments.

Using the perspectives discussed to analyse these in-depth interviews with management practitioners about their experiences as audience

Table 5.1 *Overview of interview data*

	Top manager	Middle manager	Staff	Self empl.	Total
No. of informants (some interviewed twice)	n=16 (♂=11; ♀=5)	n=30 (♂=21; ♀=9)	n=13 (♂=9; ♀=4)	n=9 (♂=6; ♀=3)	n=68 (♂=47; ♀=21)
1st stage of data sampling: exploring audience activities in relation to a single event					
NL Guru lecture A					
Informants	6	13	6	3	28
Additional sources	Director of event organisation (n=1); Management guru (n=1), event flyer, press reports, lecture slides, notes of observations				
Event characteristics	Duration: 8 hours, 995 euros (excl. VAT) Size: Large (>200 participants) Location: Large theatre Topic(s): Leadership, Management, Organisation, Performance, Strategy				
NL Guru lecture B					
Informants	9	5	3	2	19
Additional sources	Management guru (n=1), event flyers, press reports, lecture slides, respective guru book				
Event characteristics	Duration: 3–8 hours, costs up to 995 euros (excl. VAT) Size: Small 20–60 participants Location: Classroom setting Topic(s): Leadership				

Table 5.1 *(cont.)*

	Top manager	Middle manager	Staff	Self empl.	Total
No. of informants (some interviewed twice)	n=16 (♂=11; ♀=5)	n=30 (♂=21; ♀=9)	n=13 (♂=9; ♀=4)	n=9 (♂=6; ♀=3)	n=68 (♂=47; ♀=21)
2nd stage of data sampling: comparing audience activities across different events					
US Gurus lecture series C					
Informants	0	3	2	1	6
Additional sources	Event flyers				
Event series characteristics	Duration: 8 hours, 1,295 euros (excl. VAT) Sizes: ~160 participants Locations: Large theatre Topic(s): Change, Leadership, Strategy				
Diverse lectures D					
Informants	1	9	2	3	15
Event characteristics	Durations ranging from three hours up to several days, various sizes, settings and a broad range of topics, such as Innovation, Leadership, Management, Marketing, Organisation, Performance, Strategy				

members of guru lectures previous analyses of audience activities (Groß et al., 2015) we:

- identify four different key managerial audience members' consumption orientations (devoted, engaged, non-committal and critical) towards gurus and the management ideas they are promoting;
- show how audience members' orientations are constructed in relation to their perceptions of different key audience activities (selectivity, involvement and utility) at different stages of the consumption process;
- explain how, and to what extent the use of these orientations relates to the design of the guru lecture and the audience members' background characteristics.

As such, this study extends prior work on mass audiences in the dissemination of management ideas by providing a more advanced view of audience differentiation, elucidating how and why audience members relate to ideas as they are promoted in and beyond mass communication settings. This broader and more fine-grained understanding of consumption activity is essential in understanding when and how ideas disseminate and helps to better understand the success and impact of management ideas.

Orientations of Idea Consumption

In the analysis of the interview data, we concentrated on text fragments referring to audience members' understanding of *selectivity* (decision-making about media and media contents), *involvement* (emotionally engaging with media and media contents) and *utility* (putting media and media contents to use). These fragments can be seen as attributes of audience orientations and include reference to a broad range of activity types, such as physical, emotional and mental. Involvement of audience members in the context of guru lecture consumption, for example, can be associated with making notes during a lecture (physical activity), getting enthusiastic about an idea (emotional activity) or transferring an idea to one's own context (mental activity). In common with how 'activity' is understood in the audience literature, many of the activities reported by our informants were not physical ones, such as filling in a registration form for a lecture, but involve 'cognitive judgments' (Gunter, 1988: 113; see also Perse, 1990), such as evaluating the performance of a guru or thinking about the potential 'uses and gratifications' of attending a lecture.

In our analysis of the interviews, we searched for structures and core themes underlying the three audience activities (Corbin and Strauss, 1990; Miles and Huberman, 1994). By continuously comparing these emerging themes with the audience literature (Glaser and Strauss, 1967), we settled upon twelve different understandings of selectivity, involvement and utility activities as perceived by managerial audiences in a guru lecture context. After further rounds of reflection and refinement we grouped our core findings in terms of what we labelled 'consumption orientations' (an overview of each orientation is presented in Tables 5.2–5.5). In line with uses and gratification studies, 'consumption orientation' refers to the gratifications that individual audience members seek when engaged in media consumption activities (Levy and Windahl, 1984; Rubin and Perse, 1987).

In the sections that follow, we discuss four distinct consumption orientations (devoted, engaged, non-committal and critical), explicating the underlying gratifications that audience members seek in relation to guru lecture attendance. For each orientation we outline and illustrate the audience members' typical understandings of selectivity, involvement and utility, thereby indicating how and why the orientations of individual audience members' activities may vary.

Consumption Orientation 1: Devoted Consumption

The first consumption orientation that emerged from our data involved what we call 'devoted consumption' (see Table 5.2 for an overview). Here, audience activities are oriented primarily towards gaining knowledge to address work-related problems. We found various audience members emphasising that they seek guidance from gurus to improve the problems and situations they struggle with at their work – for example in their role as professionals, as managers, or as organisational members who need to design, manage, or undergo an organisational change programme. These audience members tended to consider themselves as newcomers in management and a central aspect of this orientation is a view of gurus as a source of superior knowledge who provide complete solutions to less knowledgeable apprentices.

Selectivity. Within this orientation, audience members framed selection activities in terms of learning specific solutions from the available stock of management knowledge. Informants' selection was triggered by specific issues at work, such as a reorganisation or the need to cope better with new positions or tasks. For instance, a manager responsible for a change-management project about new ways of smart working was searching the World Wide Web for information on this particular topic. Although he found a substantial amount of information and a relatively large variety of lecture suppliers, he was not convinced by the quality of most offers because: 'the content is the most important [reason to choose a lecture].

Table 5.2 *Devoted orientation: categories and exemplary evidence*

Devoted orientation of consumption	Selectivity	Involvement	Utility
Guru as charismatic expert *Audience members as followers* *Guru ideas as excellent/ unquestionable solutions for practitioners*	Select to learn '[Guru] gave a workshop of two hours [at our company] and I found it so interesting that I had a look whether he offers more things like that. I saw that he gave a [one day] lecture . . . and I signed up for it. . . . The topic was about leadership and I've got two groups to lead . . . and I wanted to learn his new perspective about how to . . . deal better with people as a leader.' (Informant B13)	Memorising ideas 'You're simply captivated from beginning to end. . . . I made notes about the things I wanted to remember.' (Informant A 18)	Taking over ideas 'He provided a very concrete solution [to my problem].' (Informant B7)
Typical audience activities	Active search Content-oriented search	Taking notes Listening carefully	(Seeking to) apply ideas directly Sharing ideas with colleagues, employees, underlings Recommending lecture to others
Background audience	From all functions, size of organisations, profit and non-profit, male and female; consultants are underrepresented		

There is such an unbelievable amount of trash about this in the market . . .' (Informant B11). The combination of watching several videos by Guru B on YouTube, complemented by reading several books by Guru B over the last few years, were considered critical in deciding whether to attend a one-day lecture. The key reasons for attending a lecture were twofold. First, the content of the lecture was convincing because: 'in my perception, new ways of working are mainly related to the question of how you can work more efficiently. And this fits with Guru B.' Second, this informant viewed lectures as providing more value than books and videos since they felt it is possible to interact with the author and allows for: 'deepening out an idea; because in a book, you impose your own ideas and they might differ from what the author intended; also YouTube videos are simply snapshots; . . . a lecture is deepening out ideas . . . my expectations were met' (Informant B11).

Involvement. The analysis revealed that, viewed from a devoted orientation, audience members' activities are primarily related to displaying a high degree of involvement. As informants actively look for new knowledge to resolve their problems, involvement is associated with activities such as actively listening, taking notes, exchanging thoughts with other participants about the messages and, if possible, in the respective lecture setting, asking questions of the guru about their own work-related problems. A director of a local school, for example, made notes throughout the evening and also observed that other participants 'wrote their fingers sore' (Informant B5). This audience member appreciated the guru message to such an extent that he attended this lecture twice. While listening the second time, he again experienced a relatively high level of emotional involvement with the ideas communicated by the guru, such as feeling relief when listening to a specific message: 'This was thus a real eye-opener. While [Guru B] was talking about this [concept], I thought that this, at one go, provides a way out of our misery' (Informant B5). Remarkably, reading this message earlier in the guru's book had not inspired our informant to apply it to his own organisation, a local school. In contrast, listening to the guru during the lecture, made him realise 'wow – that's what I can do with it!' By asking the guru during the lecture what his message would imply for the context of a school, he received a straightforward and helpful answer, which he readily accepted. Thus, typically in a devoted orientation the value of attending a guru lecture is strongly connected to a high degree of emotional involvement during a lecture. In addition, the way gurus tailor their messages in the interaction between speaker and audience, as already described in Chapters 3 and 4, are experienced as crucial in shaping this high-involvement level. As the school director explained: 'And that's the difference between reading a book and talking to the author and listening to him. This way, things come far more alive than by just reading a book' (Informant B5).

Utility. In a devoted orientation, utility activities are typically constructed as actively and purposefully making use of the knowledge gained, leading to direct implications for one's work. Our findings indicate that informants displaying this orientation related utility to reading back their notes, exchanging ideas with colleagues, recommending the lecture to others and making efforts to implement the solutions explained during a lecture. Informant A4, for example, a manager in the public sector, put the participation certificate on her office wall. This stimulated others to ask her about the lecture and allowed her to keep in the forefront of her mind the knowledge she had gained. Also, her extensive notes helped her to actually use the guru's ideas and to remember what he said.Informant C2, a benchmarking specialist from an industry association in the automobile sector, for instance, attended a lecture about the Balance Scorecard. During the break, he also received advice from the guru who asked him in person: 'Why don't you do it like that?'. He indicated that, based on this, he became actively involved in reformulating the Balance Scorecard used by his industry association, potentially affecting how member companies in the Dutch automotive sector use it: 'The effect is that, at present, we have unique operational Balanced Scorecards in the Netherlands [showing an example on his PC]' (Informant C2).

To summarise, in a devoted consumption orientation, the desire to learn is constructed as central in terms of need gratification. This becomes apparent in audience members' understanding of choosing a lecture, that is, with the intention to learn from a guru. Gurus are seen as outstanding experts, or even saviours, who are able to provide vital management knowledge to practitioners that consider themselves as relatively new in the 'world' of management. As audience members look for 'solutions' for their persistent problems by attending guru lectures, their level of involvement during these lectures is considered high as they seek to absorb gurus' wisdom by listening carefully, making notes and exchanging ideas with co-listeners. A devoted orientation also entails that the period after lectures is associated with actively reflecting on what they have learned by reading back notes, sharing their insights with colleagues and by seeking to actively apply guru ideas to transform their work practices.

While in our sample this consumption orientation primarily relates to those who experience (urgent) problems, we found it articulated by audience members with all kinds of personal and organisational backgrounds (lower, middle, high management; profit and non-profit organisations; male and female (see Appendix A). A devoted orientation seems not typically confined to audience members of a particular kind. However, also in comparison with other orientations, we found that for most informants that drew on a devoted orientation, attending a lecture was considered a single or irregular event, thereby offering few possibilities to make comparative judgements about these lectures in relation to lectures in general. In other words, guru lectures are only attended when specific knowledge is needed, not as a customary habit. In contrast, regularly visiting guru lectures was found as more common in audience members that used an 'engaged' consumption orientation, to which we now turn.

Consumption Orientation 2: Engaged Consumption

The second orientation that emerged from the data involved 'engaged consumption' (see Table 5.3 for an overview). This refers to the audience members' construction of audience activities as mainly oriented towards broadening one's own horizon as a management practitioner. People with this orientation typically attend guru lectures on a regular basis, sometimes several times a year, making the attendance of a specific lecture a less unique experience. In addition, compared to a devoted orientation, the relation between gurus and consumers is constructed much more in equal terms. In an engaged orientation, audience members do not seek guidance and enlightenment by a superior knowledge provider, but both gurus and audience members are viewed as knowledge experts albeit with different roles and related expectations. While the assumed role of gurus is to provide new insights, audience members regard themselves as co-producers of knowledge: they are the ones to select from gurus what is relevant for a specific situation. Adding their own practical knowledge and experience is thereby considered critical to making guru ideas relevant and useful in that context.

Selectivity. Viewed from an engaged orientation, activities of selection are primarily associated with a habitual consumption of guru products and services. In contrast to the first orientation of consumption, audience members tend to construct the scope of selectivity as more oriented towards following current developments in the management knowledge market in general rather than a commitment to specific ideas or an urgent need for a solution to specific work-related problems. A manager from a large financial company, for example, emphasised that regular attendance at guru lectures provided him with continuous and useful input for reflecting on his work. He explained how his selection activities implied following the developments of several gurus over a longer period of time: 'It makes sense to check their [gurus'] development and to see what they

Table 5.3 *Engaged orientation: categories and exemplary evidence*

Engaged orientation of consumption	Selectivity	Involvement	Utility
Guru as knowledge partner *Audience members as co-producers of knowledge* *Guru ideas as tools for practitioners to create own solutions in context*	Select to be stimulated 'The gurus [of a particular lecture series] are not [only] familiar with a single subject but they cover a very broad social-economic field of knowledge. This is why I'm interested in this lecture series as it fits with my long-time interest in broader insights.' (Informant C1)	Transforming ideas 'You are the one who has to add value [to guru knowledge]. While listening, you have to evaluate whether something is applicable or not . . . It is really hard work to make a good transfer [to your own situation].' (Informant A2)	Blending in ideas 'I have a broad interest [in management knowledge] . . . All [knowledge and insights] are put on a pile and based on that pile I do my work . . . I attend [lectures] for getting enriched and this may help [with my work] . . . in manifold ways but not straightforwardly.' (Informant D12)
Typical audience activities	Often regular attendance of lectures to broaden one's horizon	Direct selection of knowledge that fits own needs	Transforming knowledge into own knowledge by adapting it to own context
Background audience	From all functions, size of organisations, profit and non-profit, male and female; consultants are clearly overrepresented		

are busy with and what their current models are. I know various of these models from five or ten years ago' (Informant C6).

Involvement. Similar to the devoted orientation, audience members associated an engaged orientation with a high level of cognitive involvement. Our informants experienced that, in addition to physical activities such as making notes and talking with other participants about work-related topics, most activities were directed at becoming mentally involved with those ideas that are regarded as potentially useful for one's own work context. For instance, an owner of a small consulting company explained his active way of listening during a lecture in terms of sensitivity to ideas that could 'fit' his working context. He listened to Guru [A] in two different ways: 'First, thinking what can I use for my new job; and I paid particular attention to the examples he used. Second, thinking which ideas I currently apply. Mainly at the end of the [lecture], I was able to link what was said with the way I work' (Informant A3). While audience members using a devoted orientation tend to emphasise their absorption of certain ideas, for example by careful listening and making notes, involvement in the engaged consumption is viewed as primarily directed at continuously evaluating which ideas might serve one's own future needs. In addition, while listening, audience members see themselves as already mentally transferring particular ideas to a specific practice setting thereby assessing the potential value of an idea in context. This indicates that from an engaged perspective, audience members' own cognitive activities are considered as critical to make guru ideas ultimately relevant and of use. A senior manager of a bank explained why consumers' own reflection, experience and knowledge is needed to actually work with guru concepts and ideas:

> If you ask me, you get a kind of toolbox; you're provided with some things and then you have to choose what [fits for you]. ... when you talk about change projects, you cannot work with a 'best practice' because the number of factors is simply too high. (Informant B4)

Utility. From the viewpoint of engaged consumption, utility is linked with audience members' perception of knowledge producers as enriching practitioners' context-specific knowledge and experience, thereby offering material to enhance their toolbox. Activities after the lecture are considered as mainly directed at selecting ideas that could fit one's own contextual conditions, such as the size of the company, the industry, or the specific organisational culture. By doing so, audience members tend to present themselves as actors who co-create management knowledge and compared to the devoted orientation, gurus are considered of little relevance in contextualising the ideas they promote. As one informant explained:

> You take [concepts] to your daily practice. It's not that you give a presentation saying 'this guru said this and we've got the same problem, thus let's do it that way'. You acquire these things quite quickly in your own approach and it is as if you have come up with it yourself. (Informant A12)

In contrast to a devoted orientation, where gurus are seen as providing superior knowledge, an engaged orientation involves audience members viewing guru ideas as requiring contextual adaptation. Our informants stress that the ideas they have obtained during guru lectures are 'processed', transferred and accommodated by them. A central underpinning to these each of these utility activities is that the tools provided by gurus are not expected to deliver an immediate solution to a specific problem. An informant who had worked for the tax authorities for twenty-six years framed the utility of guru lectures in the following way:

> What I've found out more and more is to rely on myself. . . . Lectures or management gurus have a certain influence on me but it's not that I return from a lecture thinking: 'Yeah, tomorrow I really need to work like that!' Rather, I pick up things and these will probably be processed over time, but the most important is that after a lecture I better recognise the things that I do. (Informant D6)

In summary, from the perspective of an engaged orientation, management ideas do not need to satisfy an instant need for particular knowledge. We found that audience members using this orientation generally see themselves as an 'engaged multi-user' who selects potentially useful ideas and stores them for later (potential) use. Although, again, an engaged orientation is articulated by audience members holding different backgrounds, our sample indicates that it might be more common amongst consultants and higher-level managers from middle to large for-profit organisations (see Appendix A). These are the guru audience members who typically have the financial resources to attend lectures regularly in the first place. Managers from non-profit organisations, on the other hand, might need to use the whole annual educational budget of their management team to attend a single lecture, making attendance an exception rather than a rule. In addition, the need to have a general toolbox might fit better with the role expectations of consultants and higher-level managers not least given that an important part of their tasks entails impression management and in particular conveying the impression that they are at the forefront of management knowledge (see also Abrahamson, 1996). For consultants, attending lectures has an additional function in their daily work: as well as staying informed about the most important trends in management, they also invite clients to such lectures to strengthen their customer relationships. Whether to stay ahead or build relationships with clients, lectures are still selected for their content. However, the main motive is not built on an immediate need to find solutions to a particular problem.

The relation between guru and audiences suggests that audience members using an engaged orientation are typically less prone to be strongly impressed by a single guru lecture or a particular idea. Here, gurus and their audiences are framed as co-producers of knowledge: while gurus provide abstract ideas and define trends relevant to organisations, managers and consultants are the ones who, based on their practical wisdom, actually transform guru ideas into adequate solutions for real-world problems in organisations.

Consumption Orientation 3: Non-committal Consumption

The third orientation of consumption that we found in our analysis is what we termed 'non-committal' (see Table 5.4 for an overview). This refers to audience members' understanding of audience activities that are typically associated with a more pleasure-seeking orientation towards knowledge producers and the ideas they promote. In contrast to the first two consumption orientations, lectures are attended for a broad range of motives that are only loosely related to learning. Transferring knowledge is considered a secondary issue. Nevertheless, we found that gurus are often highly appreciated by audience members for their outstanding performance qualities, their entertaining presentations and the quality of their management anecdotes – elements that likely contribute to positive audience responses (see also Chapters 3 and 4). In other words, and in contrast to the first two orientations, a non-committal orientation entails audience members' highlighting general satisfaction of lecture attendance whilst framing the knowledge and ideas communicated in guru presentations as not relevant to them as consumers. From our data it emerges that audience members typically experience a fluctuation in their enthusiasm and receptivity to the ideas. During a lecture, they display appreciation towards the guru's performance. However, after a lecture they indicate very little motivation to apply the guru's messages in one way or another.

Selectivity. In contrast to a devoted or engaged orientation, a non-committal orientation is based on a view of selection activities as relatively unconnected to knowledge-related motives. Various audience members articulated that lectures are selected based on their desire to be entertained, to socialise with colleagues, to spend one's educational budget, or

Table 5.4 *Non-committal orientation: categories and exemplary evidence*

Non-committal orientation of consumption	Selectivity	Involvement	Utility
Guru as entertainer *Audience members as intangible/volatile* *Guru ideas as entertaining but irrelevant to practitioners*	Select to be diverted '[Attending the lecture] includes something like "let's sneak out of the everyday boredom and the daily craziness of a big company".' (Informant C1)	Being entertained 'Actually, I also talked quite some time about other things [unrelated to the lecture].' (Informant A14)	Letting ideas go '[T]here were some interesting eye-openers, which I have actually already forgotten . . . I can't remember them right now.' (Informant A14)
Typical audience activities	Selection based on coincidences, such as colleagues joining, need to spend educational budget, lecture part of educational guide	Relaxed listening, little note taking, enjoying network possibilities and low focus on content	Forgetting and ignoring knowledge Sharing lecture experience as refresher or fun activity
Background audience	From all functions, size of organisations, profit and non-profit, male and female; top managers are a little underrepresented; members of large for-profit organisations are overrepresented		

to experience a pleasant break from everyday work. For instance, one informant working for a large hospital described his selection activities related to a guru lecture as primarily motivated by the expected guru's performance rather than the usefulness of his ideas: 'My colleague had heard from a friend that the lecture is fantastic; so I thought: 'let's go, too, and make a nice day out of it'(Informant A1). As our informants reported, in these cases, the motives for attending these guru lectures are typically loosely coupled to the specific the contents, as in the case of a manager of a large telecommunication company:

> We received the lecture offer and the [name company] had negotiated a discount so that it precisely fitted with the educational budget; moreover, there were two colleagues of mine who were also interested in attending. That's when we said: 'Ok, let's do that.' (Informant A13)

Involvement. Our analysis revealed that, in relation to non-committal consumption, the level of involvement is primarily oriented towards pleasure-seeking activities such as enjoying the performance and setting of the venue, taking delight in the good food served and having pleasant conversations during the breaks. A manager from a large hospital quoted above, for example, described how he enjoyed being entertained instead of getting involved in content-related discussions: 'You're kept busy from the beginning till the end ... [by activities] such as making paper airplanes. The only boring moment was when [Guru A] went into depth ... [in] an academic discussion about things he had said beforehand' (Informant A1). In line with the low content-orientation, the entertainment qualities of the management guru are particularly relevant. This orientation does not exclude the possibility of learning, but it was framed as a low priority. As a senior manager at a large governmental institution explains: 'For me, it is 90 per cent relaxation. And 10 per cent is what sticks to you, what you take home. ... It's not that I just hang out during the lecture and don't listen; that isn't the case. I do listen but [learning] is something extra' (Informant B2).

Utility. A non-committal orientation is associated with an audience members' perception that includes an emphasis on a relatively low degree of utility after the event. Instead of an emphasis on actively transferring ideas from the lecture to their own work, informants reported how they had forgotten most of the things that had been communicated by the guru – and typically also did not actively enhance the possibility of remembering such as via taking notes – even though the ideas were experienced as inspiring during the event itself. The value of consuming guru lectures is primarily associated with the activities related to immediate pleasure-seeking rather than with more long-term activities aimed at putting these ideas into practice. Such a view is illustrated by the following statement from a manager in a large animal health company:

I like [Guru] a lot, great guy . . . a little cynical, giving things a humoristic twist . . . I didn't talk [with colleagues] about the lecture content, I only told others that it was really interesting, that they had missed something . . . Actually, I remember quite little [of the content]. (Informant B8)

In sum, a non-committal orientation is strongly connected to a low degree of utility after the lecture. In line with the subordinate role of learning attributed to guru lectures, audience members that draw on this orientation frame applying new ideas to improve one's own way of working as rather irrelevant. According to our data, and confirmed by the lecture organiser we interviewed, this orientation can be found amongst all types of audience members, but is particularly used by audience members in management roles employed at large for-profit companies (see Appendix A). The analysis suggests that it is more common that these companies make financial resources available to send a selected number of their employees to attend the same lecture or even offer an event as part of an employee's formal management training package. Compared to managers from large for-profit companies we found amongst the managers of non-profit organisations only isolated instances of a non-committal orientation as these audience members typically can be expected to have more limited financial possibilities to attend lectures for self-indulgent reasons.

The relationship between gurus and audiences in a non-committal orientation is expected to be of short duration: during events, audience members relate to gurus with high enthusiasm. This emotional involvement, however, is not perceived as affecting individual members' ways of working and is seen as offering limited opportunities to enhance entrenchment of the ideas promoted by the guru. As a result, gurus and audience members in this frame are considered to be part of separate worlds that only come together during the limited time of a lecture.

Consumption Orientation 4: Critical Consumption

The fourth orientation of consumption emerging from our data involved what we termed 'critical consumption' (see Table 5.5 for an overview). This orientation is primarily associated with activities that contribute to expressing audience members' dissatisfaction towards certain knowledge producers, their lectures and their ideas. The dissatisfaction we found in our data takes shape in two main ways: first, some audience members have a general critical stance towards management gurus. Although they

Table 5.5 *Critical orientation: categories and exemplary evidence*

Critical orientation of consumption	Selectivity	Involvement	Utility
Guru as overrated *Audience members as independent/thinkers* *Guru ideas as hot air*	Reject to distinguish oneself 'Maybe [Guru] has written a too [!] popular book. It's not taken seriously and some people laugh about it. . . . It has a semi-academic or maybe non-academic style; it's nice but nothing more. This was a reason for me to not attend a lecture by him. I've read the book and I've heard what others said and I thought I wouldn't go; for me it has nothing to add. (Informant D1)	Disengaging from ideas '[Guru] has a clear structure, like: these are the steps. But that's it, nothing else. . . . There is far better training than his one. . . . The level was quite superficial. . . . Look, I won't [join a game that includes] walking around with others, wearing a back-pack.' (Informant A10)	Rejecting ideas 'Their success [names 3 gurus] is to a large extent based on hot air. . . . This damages their messages . . . they become unappealing to me.' (Informant D12)
Typical audience activities	Attendants start with one of the other orientations	Getting annoyed, using smartphone, disconnecting from lecture and guru	Rejecting ideas and gurus Tell others not to join
Background audience	From all functions, size of organisations, profit and non-profit, male and female		

do attend guru lectures – on a sporadic or regular level – they also present themselves as critical observers of the management guru market. Second, audience members might select a guru lecture that ultimately does not fulfill their expectations. As a result, they take a critical stance towards the lecture, the guru and/or the ideas that have been communicated.

Selectivity. In relation to a critical consumption orientation, informants frame selection activities in terms of rejecting certain knowledge producers and the 'products' they offer. The above quoted director of a local school, who displayed a devoted orientation towards Guru B, articulated, at the same time, a critical orientation towards Guru A. He explained why he deliberately chose not to attend Guru A's lectures: 'If you claim that people can substitute [a whole study] with a one-week lecture, in my eyes you're a kind of charlatan .... I don't appreciate [Guru A] very much' (Informant B5). This case illustrates that audience members are not necessarily either in favour or against management gurus. Most informants using a critical orientation distinguish between 'good' and 'bad' or between 'relevant' and 'irrelevant' ones, thereby signalling their individual preferences in the context of the heterogeneity of the supply side (cf. Greatbatch and Clark, 2005). For example, a manager of a Public Higher School and consultant reported an ambiguous stance in relation to his experience of more than two decades of guru lecture consumption. His regular consumption, mostly being in line with an engaged orientation, was combined with an overall critical stance towards the evolving guru lecture market:

> Something has evolved in the market that it is prestigious to go to lectures from people who ask a lot of money for it. It is an expensive ambiance, it includes fine food, often several days with an overnight stay that is not needed at all. ... It creates an image of being up-to-date, modern, having the latest insights, and being someone who is willing to join a certain level of conversation. There is a lot of window-dressing. (Informant D1).

In addition to signaling serious doubts about the value of particular gurus or the market for guru lectures in general, we also found a second key motive for a critical consumption orientation. Specifically, our data indicated that a number of informants became disillusioned during an event arising from the fact that what they experienced during and/or after a lecture did not meet their a priori expectations. As discussed above, audience members can vary in the way they talk about their motivations when deciding to select a lecture: an urgent need for knowledge (devoted), a general interest, part of a habitual use, a need to stay up-to date (engaged), and non-committal activities such as entertainment, socialising with colleagues, or using one's educational budget. However, based on their experiences during and after attending a lecture, they become dissatisfied and display a critical orientation as described next.

Involvement. A critical orientation of consumption that is triggered by disappointment is linked to involvement activities that express audience members' frustration with the knowledge producer, the content of their ideas or the way these ideas are communicated. In particular, our informants linked involvement with not listening carefully, directing their attention to side activities such as checking their mobile or chatting with neighbours, getting annoyed and irritated during the lecture, and leaving the lecture before its official end. For example, an entrepreneur who appreciated the lecture of Guru B, described how he experienced a different guru, a famous Dutch sport and business coach, as patronising while attending one of his lectures. Involvement in his case meant that he experienced strong negative feelings that became apparent in the way he talked about it: 'Well, while this guy was giving his presentation, I really got an allergic reaction to the way he presented his ideas and the level of assertiveness he displayed. He's the kind of person who says: "That's how it is because I say it." Sorry, not for me!' (Informant B1).

Utility. In relation to a critical orientation that is triggered by disappointment, utility activities are oriented primarily towards rejecting the guru as well as the value of their ideas for management practitioners. Our informants linked utility to remembering the lecture as something that was not worth attending or advising colleagues and friends against attending a particular guru lecture. For example, an audience member who received a lecture as a birthday present from his father related the stage after the lecture had finished with talking to others about the low level of its utility value in relation to its price: 'I received it as a present but I think it is far too expensive. I also said the price should be at least halved. . . . I'd advise people to watch a summary of such a day on YouTube . . . . I'd never pay 1,000 euros for such a lecture myself' (Informant A7). Utility in the case of a critical orientation is not linked to seeking to apply guru ideas, but to rejecting them in relation to one's own situation, and eventually actively arguing against the ideas as well as the respective guru. A manager from a large for-profit company framed his activities after the lecture in terms of advising his colleagues in a management team to stop sending people to a certain guru lecture. 'I told the management team "Don't do that. . . . It doesn't have any added value. It's too general. He [the guru] touches upon topics, that's good, but I prefer more depth. . . . It's a waste of money"' (Informant A15). To summarise, audience members might reject certain guru lectures while enjoy consuming others, thereby signalling their individual taste and related cultural codes they identify with – managerial audiences tend to conspicuously appreciate a certain type of guru while disliking others. In our dataset, a critical consumption orientation was articulated by informants from a variety of individual and organisational backgrounds (see Appendix A). In this critical orientation, audience members typically frame some gurus as market criers, overrated puffers, or charlatans, and their ideas as hot air. Using this orientation, audience members show a distanced and critical relation with certain gurus and/or the management guru market in general, thereby emphasising their preferred tastes as well as their independence as consumers. From our data, the critical orientation not only indicates the need to conceptualise critical audience members as a heterogeneous group – the main motivation for drawing on this orientation varies significantly – but also suggests that orientations might change throughout the consumption process. This observation is developed in Chapter 6 where we will further explore audience dynamism.

Conclusion

Drawing on a 'uses and gratification' perspective, we have argued in this chapter that for a better understanding of the impact of particular management ideas among a mass audience of managers, we need to study individual members' construction of audience activities in mass communication settings. This follows from our findings in Chapters 3 and 4 which indicated that it cannot be assumed that gurus have a ready-made audience that is keen or receptive to hear what they have to say. Rather, the audience activities need to be considered as critical conditions that may either enhance or inhibit the likelihood that their ideas impact management and organisational practice via their audiences. Accordingly, in our analysis in the present chapter we explored *how* and *why* audience members may vary in the way they are attracted towards the guru and the management ideas they are promoting. We now consider a number of general findings and their implications for the conceptualisation of gurus and their audiences as well as the wider literature on the impact of management ideas.

First, our analysis of management practitioners attending guru lectures reveals that audience members can draw upon different consumption orientations: devoted, engaged, non-committal and critical, that is, the gratification that individual members seek which becomes apparent in the way they construct their activities related to the guru lecture (selectivity, involvement and utility). Thus, the results indicate that some audience members clearly affiliate with the guru and their ideas promoted at these events, albeit in different ways. In using a *devoted orientation*, individual members talk about their experiences of the guru event in line with what

Hall (1980) would call the 'preferred reading'. The management ideas presented by the guru are primarily seen as legitimate expert knowledge and, as such, these ideas are accepted as of particular value to management and organisational practice while alternatives are beyond belief. An *engaged orientation* would entail that audience members see management ideas presented by gurus as much more negotiated (Hall, 1980). That is, these members may typically frame management ideas as useful but reject the possibility that they are valuable to organisational practice per se as they fundamentally require adequate management practitioners' skills to adapt to context.

In a *non-committal orientation*, audience members also generally appreciate attending the guru event, albeit relate this particularly to the entertaining form in which ideas are presented. Concerning the content of idea this orientation signals that audience members do not perceive the need to use ideas for their own specific situation. In other words, whilst audience members may enjoy listening to the guru, and recognise the ideas they are promoting as of some interest, they do not see the value of putting energy into using these ideas further. Our findings also clearly indicate that a notable number of the audience show little positive involvement and/or explicitly and actively distance themselves from the guru event they have attended. This is remarkable given the assumption that managerial audiences may attend guru lectures on a voluntary basis, and despite the widely recognised efforts of the guru – and particularly those of high reputation – to create favourable conditions that enhance the receptivity to their ideas. The analysis also indicated that such a *critical orientation* is strongly connected to a specific guru or the market for management knowledge in general. In particular, we found that audience members may respond differently to various management gurus: while actively rejecting some gurus as 'hot air' and their ideas as of little value, practitioners may at the same time appreciate others.

Second, to shed further light on why there is differential attraction to management ideas among a mass audience, we explored the reasons for the likelihood of particular consumption orientations. In Chapter 3 we highlighted the complexities of the guru's task emanating from the differences in audience members' individual backgrounds, the organisations they are employed in as well as the audience expectations of the guru shaped prior to the event. Although the renowned studies of Morley (2003; 2005) strongly related audience members' interpretive position towards particular mass media messages to their socio-economic background (see also Kim, 2004), we found little evidence linking individual background characteristics of guru audience members directly and unambiguously to consumption orientations. In fact, the findings point out that all four main consumption orientations can be found amongst audience members of all kinds. Nevertheless, we found a number of notable patterns that could contribute to better understanding why some orientations may be more common among particular members than others. These concern reasons related to (1) the individual audience member's broader management knowledge consumption and (2) the organisation-level perks.

First, an important reason for the audience members' specific orientations relates to their broader *individual management knowledge consumption*. This entails the accumulated experiences generated from prior management media-related audience activities. The analysis suggests that management practitioners who consider themselves as frequent visitors to guru lectures may be more inclined to draw on an engaged orientation. These audience members typically experience a drive to remain up to date on the latest management insights, and develop a broad toolbox from which they could draw in different situations. Such a consumption pattern is more commonly found amongst audience members in consulting roles but also those who have occupied higher-level management positions for some time. In addition, regular attendance at guru lectures is more likely when audience members have access to financial resources and when these members may see this as an important pillar in signalling their occupational identity (see also Clark and Salaman, 1998). In terms of possible implications, frequently attending guru lectures thus likely coincides with more elaborate knowledge of the market for managerial solutions that allows these audience members to (1) more consciously select the lectures which are expected to be of value (thereby reducing the possibility of negative surprises or disappointments) and (2) develop a more detailed and well-substantiated critique on specific gurus or developments in the market that they do not experience as being in line with their occupational identity. In relative contrast, those audience members who see attending a guru lecture more as a single event may be more inclined to use a devoted orientation particularly given their limited possibilities to compare different gurus and lectures and develop a feeling for the market for management solutions. At the same time, limited experiences with guru lectures may also be related to a critical orientation as a lack of adequate expectations may increase the chances of disappointment and can be used to legitimise their distance towards the management knowledge industry.

When considering the nature of the event, experienced informants as well as the lecture organisers indicated that there is a large variety of guru lectures ranging from events that require relatively little prior management knowledge, to events that offer specific solution-focused knowledge and are mainly targeted at experienced practitioners. On the basis of our analysis it can be hypothesised that events that require relatively little prior knowledge may particularly attract relatively inexperienced practitioners and thereby increase the likelihood of possible orientations used by its audience members. This may also become apparent when comparing the variety of responses and motivations between audience members who have attended Guru A (variety of different management-related topics) with those who have participated in the lecture of Guru B (leadership of professionals). So, because of the broad contents and limited prior management knowledge that is required, Guru A may potentially appeal to more management practitioners, whilst at the same time this may increase the likelihood that audience members become dissatisfied for various reasons. The differences in variety between both lectures may provide additional evidence that the prior experiences of the target audience play a role in the potential variety of audience orientations, irrespective of their evaluation of the guru's actual performance during the lecture.

Second, another important reason for audience members' specific orientations relates to the potential role of *organisational characteristics*. We observed, for example, that managers from non-profit companies are mainly associated with learning-related motives to attend lectures, that is, the need to learn something specific, such as a particular management tool, or to 'update' their management knowledge. Non-committal motives, such as 'using one's educational budget', joining colleagues and 'enjoying the day', were absent amongst this group. Our data indicate that this might be explained by the more limited possibilities in a non-profit organisation to justify the allocation of financial means to these purposes, and the comparatively generous educational budgets for staff members in other sectors such as banking, finance and telecommunications. Thus, the occurrence of organisational perks may enhance the likelihood of a non-committal orientation amongst members of an audience.

Overall, our findings indicate that guru events produce people that display (among others) a devoted, engaged, non-committal or critical orientation which are related to their construction of activities prior to, during and after these mass events. Indeed, these people may not only act as carriers of ideas when they go back from an event to their organisation, but may also shape other members' attitudes to particular ideas being implemented in the organisation and may enhance or impede receptivity to ideas when these are 'sold' by consultants (e.g. Sturdy, 1997). However, such a potentially significant area of influence has received scant attention in the present literature on management ideas. Whether the guru performance has an impact primarily on those with a more engaged or devoted view or how the non-committal or critical group may contribute to 'spreading the word' will be further explored in Chapters 7 and 8. Indeed, a non-committal orientation may imply a positive consumption experience which may help preparing the ground for ideas in an organisation. Before turning to these important issues of organisational use of management ideas, we first need a more advanced understanding of the potential dynamics in the consumption orientations, which we address in Chapter 6.

6 Understanding Audience Dynamism

In Chapter 5 we explored how and why individual audience members may display different consumer orientations, that is, the variety in gratifications that managers seek when consuming management ideas such as via guru lectures. The identification of four key orientations (devoted, engaged, non-committal and critical) allowed us to develop a more advanced view on how exactly individual management practitioners may vary in the way they are attracted towards particular management ideas and the gurus who are promoting them. In seeking to explain why audience members may vary in their orientation, the chapter discussed how their orientations towards a guru event relate to their constructions of the activities prior to, during and after the event. Based on these analyses, we hypothesised that guru lectures that attract practitioners that have generated few experiences from prior management media-related audience activities can be expected to show a larger variety in orientations amongst its audience members. At the same time, the chapter also drew our attention to a number of complexities in how managerial audience members relate to these orientations. In particular, we noted that various audience members also could not be limited to one category as they displayed different orientations in relation to a single event and/or different gurus and that therefore audience orientations towards management ideas and the gurus that promote them should not be conceptualised as relatively static. As such, the findings from Chapter 5 not only shed important light on *how* and *why* audiences may be differentiated, but also generated an intricate issue – how to make sense of the potential multiple orientations amongst individual audience members.

In this chapter we explore shifts in audience orientations in more depth by asking: *How and why do audience members' consumption orientations shift throughout the communication process?* Addressing this question is of theoretical relevance, as theorists of consumption have emphasised the importance of accounting for the possible 'fragmentations and contradictions which characterize our actions as consumer' (Gabriel and Lang, 1995: 4). This may not only help in avoiding one-sided representations of management practitioners as audience members, but also contributes to a more fine-grained understanding of the inherent volatility and unpredictability that characterises the flow of ideas between different relevant contexts.

From Audience Differentiation to Audience Variability

As previously discussed, management gurus' success is primarily related to their ability to appeal to and deal with a more or less differentiated audience (see Chapters 3 and 4). As noted in Chapter 5, the importance of exploring audience differentiation in detail not only stems from advanced analyses of guru-audience interactions, but also from a growing stream of research on organisational implementation. The latter includes a large number of studies that sought to classify organisational members' responses to management ideas to relatively stable categories, including positive responses, responses unfavourable to a new idea and various partial forms of conformity (e.g. Ansari et al., 2014; Boiral, 2003; Kelemen, 2000).

A relatively small number of studies on management ideas in executive teaching such as MBA programmes also found 'intense ambivalence' towards management ideas to be the primary response of students (Sturdy and Gabriel, 2000: 986; see also Sturdy et al., 2006). Analysing Malaysian MBA students' response to Western management ideas, Sturdy and Gabriel (2000) showed that these students tend to downplay the importance of particular tools and techniques that were taught as a common part of the MBA programme, while at the same time stressing the significance of acquiring managerial language as part of their identity work. In addition, their findings indicate that on the one hand, students displayed a general attraction towards Western management ideas, and at the same time clearly displayed a critical attitude by considering many of them as 'irrelevant or wrong' (Sturdy and Gabriel, 2000: 992) mainly because these ideas did not fit the specific national and cultural context. Whilst these findings partly echo the variety of different responses towards these ideas as indicated in studies of organisational implementation, they also suggest that audience members cannot necessarily be related to one specific response category (see also Gabriel and Lang, 1995). As a result, given the tendency to classify audience members to single response categories and the relative contrast of this approach to studies that suggest that management practitioners may display multiple responses, there is a need to better account for the complexities and possible limitations in conceptualising managerial audiences.

This chapter builds further on the 'uses and gratification perspective' as employed in Chapter 5 where it helped in better understanding the way mass audiences may differ in their consumption orientation towards popular management ideas and the gurus who are promoting them. While both these chapters share an interest in analysing individual managerial audience members' experiences in mass events such as guru lectures to understand their attitudes towards management ideas, in the present chapter we undertake a more refined analysis of audience differentiation by mainly following a strand in the 'uses and gratification research' that developed a view of mass audiences not as passive or active per se, but as 'variably active' (Godlewski and Perse, 2010: 150; see also Blumler, 1979; Levy and Windahl, 1984; Rubin, 2009). This strand of uses and gratification research stresses that: (1) individual audience members may not necessarily be stable in how and why they consume particular media (cf. Blumler, 1979; Rubin, 2009; Ruggiero, 2000) and (2) there is therefore a need to account for the highly dynamic character of the consumption process, and in particular the potential volatile character of the individual audience members' perceived activities across phases of the communication and the gratifications associated with them. This suggests that to better understand the attraction of management ideas for an audience of management practitioners, it is essential to consider how individual orientations towards the audience activities around guru lectures in relation to needs gratification may vary during the communication process. In addressing this issue, we draw in particular on Palmgreen and Rayburn's (1982) view on expectancy-value (see Chapter 2) in order to develop a more fine-grained explanation of how gratification sought from attending guru lectures may relate to the gratifications obtained by different audience members. In line with this view, we explore how the broader design of guru events, the social context within which audience members are embedded, as well as their general consumption patterns may influence the possible shifts in orientation amongst individual audience members.

While Chapter 5 aimed to provide a better understanding of the way mass audiences may differ in their consumption of popular management ideas, this chapter focuses on the dynamic aspects of the consumption process. In particular, it seeks to explain *how* and *when* individual management practitioners as audience members may *shift* in consumption orientation throughout the communication process. Drawing on the interview data which we described in the previous chapter (see Table 5.1), and previous analyses of audience activities (Groß et al., 2015), we:

- identify three forms of shifts in managerial audience members' consumption orientation amongst individual audience members that may occur during the communication process;

- explain how these shifts are related to the design of the guru event, the social context of the audience members, and their individual consumption patterns.

In this chapter we add important nuance to our understanding of possible shifts in audience members' orientations towards management gurus and the ideas they are promoting, as well as the main factors that influence this variability. In other words, we stress the need for a more dynamic understanding of audience responses that can account for the individual-level variability in consumption orientations.

Audience Variability and Idea Consumption

Our interview data indicated that, in line with the uses and gratification literature, individual audience members' orientations display significant changes in relation to a particular idea and the guru who promotes it. We found such shifts in about half of the informants who attended guru lecture A and about one-third of the informants who attended lecture B (see Appendix A). Obviously, these data should be considered with some caution given that the audience members we investigated were not part of a random sample (see also Zbaracki, 1998). Nevertheless, given the size of the analytical sample and the variety in the characteristics of the informants, they indicate that shifts cannot be seen as a trivial or insignificant phenomenon in understanding audience orientations.

We found three typical shifts in consumption, referring to how individual audience members may change in orientations during their consumption process (the final categories are presented in Tables 6.1–6.3). Thus, in addition to the possibility of (a) consistency ('no shifts') in orientation, the analysis revealed three alternative forms of shift throughout consumption activities: (b) 'involvement-induced', (c) 'utility-induced' and (d) 'alternating'. These shifts illustrate and add support to the significance of developing a conceptualisation of audiences as 'variably active' to better understand audience members' possible attraction towards management ideas. In the sections that follow, we discuss how the underlying orientations of individual audience members' consumption activities *may or may not shift* throughout the consumption process and explain when these shifts are more likely to occur by showing the audience members' main motivations for each shift.

No Shift: Consistency in Consumption Orientation

In our study, we found relative consistency in orientations towards a guru and the ideas that have been promoted amongst a majority of our informants. These audience members displayed no shift in their consumption orientation in relation to a specific lecture as they basically received what they had expected. This implies that their view of selectivity, involvement and utility was experienced as relatively stable throughout a particular event and beyond: the main motives for choosing a particular guru lecture (selectivity) were constructed as in line with the way audience members engaged in the lecture (involvement) and made use of what they received (utility).

Informants who displayed a *devoted* orientation invariably framed their experiences of a guru lecture in terms of seeking and receiving valuable knowledge from a legitimate expert that constitutes a solution to relevant practical problems. This entails that, typically, audience members not only expected a concrete solution to a pressing problem but also report that they obtained some form of ready-made concept that actually helped them in their daily work. Our informants relate a 'no shift' primarily to general consistency between the form and contents of the lecture, with multiple and positive experiences with the guru prior to the lecture (for instance in the form of attending previous performances, reading articles, books, columns, or advertisements), in combination with favourable opinions expressed in an audience member's personal network. In addition, our informants perceive a relatively concrete view on how and where the insights from the lecture can be applied as of significance in maintaining a primarily devoted orientation.

For instance, one school director explained his consistency in orientation towards guru lecture B not only by referring to the actual lecture and the guru's performance. Rather he also accounted for the fact that he had met Guru B several times, experienced these meetings as very positive, had prior discussion with colleagues about Guru B, found consistency in the guru's main message, and experienced this message as directly applicable and in line with his work-related issues and objectives, that is, enhancing leadership in professional organisations:

> In terms of contents, I find [Guru B] very strong and, in addition to that, he also has a lot of humour. By the way, I had heard his story twice; we invited him to speak for our alliance some time ago. I suggested that the P&O staff of our central office invite this person [Guru B] to give a talk to the group of leaders within the alliance. I give talks about my own ideas of organising to our department managers in our school on a regular basis. However, I do not speak about this to the school leaders in our alliance. Of course, it is difficult to invite Prahalad or Hamel to a school, but he [Guru B] lives close by and equally has something to say. The talk that he gave for the school managers was not entirely the same; at least 50 per cent corresponded to the lecture that I recently attended as it was particularly adapted to the specific [lecture organiser] audience. (Informant B5)

In explaining consistency in the use of an *engaged* orientation throughout the consumption process, informants also referred to correspondence in what they had expected and obtained as a management practitioner. In particular, audience members typically framed all the different activities they employed in terms of the possibilities sought and received to add new ideas to their toolbox and generate necessary energy for potential later application and refinement to practice. In addition, the informants attribute this consistency to the limited expectations of specialness of the general lecture experience (especially compared to the typical US gurus), as well as their inherent reservations concerning direct practical applicability of the guru's proposed solutions to their own context. Generally, expectations of lectures are 'stripped of' any mythical qualities due to audience members being well informed about the guru and their message, possibly in combination with regular attendance at similar events. Thus, in an engaged orientation, gratifications sought are typically and consistently met when the guru shows expertise on a specific topic and provides some fresh ideas that audience members may use after significant adaptation. As such, compared to a no shift in a devoted orientation, particularly the scope and nature of gratification sought concerning utility can be seen as more limited. The head of HRM in a large healthcare organisation talked about the different motivations for her consistency in orientation as follows:

> Last year, I participated in the [event organiser] evenings for the first time. I found this particularly interesting because I work in a town close by and it is a good way to become up-to-date again. Following a large MBA is simply not possible right now, and perhaps I also don't want to. As such, doing these lectures, including the one from Guru B, is then a very attractive alternative. I had heard about Guru B before, also that he did something together with an HR manager in healthcare. So Guru B was known to me and his book on the topic is something that fits well. So although his ideas are well known, I found it attractive to revisit them. I did not read his book before the lecture but had a general idea of his specific view on the topic. (Informant B3)

Consistency in an audience member's *non-committal* orientation is mainly related to their perception of whether the guru and the broader event actually delivers on the more or less explicit expectation of providing a generally entertaining experience. In particular, various informants indicated that they had attended lectures for primarily hedonistic reasons and mentioned their general satisfaction with the specific guru's performance, the ambiance, or for example the networking possibilities during lecture. Informants explain that their expectations stem from a generic association of management gurus with fun and the specific guru as having the capabilities to deliver this. It is suggested that consistency is more likely when audience members are well informed about the performance qualities and specific style of the guru, preferably by drawing on their personal network. In contrast to the previous two types of orientations (devoted and engaged), the scope of expectations related to consistency in non-committal orientation typically does not go beyond issues of involvement, not least given that informants perceive immediate pleasure-seeking as relatively unrelated to applying ideas. With regard to consistency in non-committal orientation, utility is considered a peripheral or irrelevant issue.

For example, a product manager in a large telecommunication company attended a lecture by Guru A. He persistently expressed a non-committal orientation throughout the interview and attributed this explicitly to several instances in relation to selectivity where he sought to become relatively well informed about the qualities of Guru A, also in comparison with other gurus on the market:

> Well, I think that I had heard about him [Guru A] somewhere, I can't remember in which context. In our company each of us has an employability budget of 1,000 euros, and by coincidence the lecture organised by [conference organisation] was 995 euros. So, just like a lot of my colleagues, I found it just nice to experience such a lecture. My expectations were quite in line what just happened, so a thrilling show within which ideas from different gurus were discussed. In fact, I experienced it as even a little bit more thrilling than I had understood from others. Some compared Guru A with [another well-known guru on the market], but that simply does not make sense; it is really different. Guru A relates much more to research and has a different approach. He considers matters more from a scientific perspective; I found that quite refreshing and it was generally in line with what I expected. (Informant A14)

In contrast to the first three orientations, consistency in a *critical* orientation typically implies an a priori and persistent incompatibility between gratifications sought from media consumption and what is provided by the guru lecture. The informants' views indicate that some lectures are simply never able to meet particular audience members' expectations, irrespective of the actual performance of the guru. In other words, in relation to a consistent critical orientation it can be assumed that the scope of expectations lies beyond the lecture concerned. In explaining the likelihood that audience members display such a consistent critical orientation, informants generally refer to the possibility that they may not appreciate the guru phenomenon in general, or do not like the specific topic(s) discussed in the lecture per se. In various instances audience members also motivate their consistent dislike to their extensive knowledge and experience in relation to the guru market, and refer to their perceived capabilities of producing some form of solutions to management, thereby putting their own work on a relatively equal footing to that of the gurus.

One telling example comes from a manager working for a large international bank. In talking about the main motivations for his primarily critical orientation towards the guru lecture series provided by a well-known lecture organiser he refers to a number of earlier occasions in which he met the gurus concerned. For instance, he stated that: 'I knew Prahalad very well. I went to the University of Michigan to do an MBA and he was one of the lecturers', and later he signalled his familiarity with Covey because in the bank: 'I was involved in the development of a coaching programme for our managers to promote their skills in advancing team performance. We have asked Covey or his son to do a short lecture and pushed all our senior managers through our programme' (Informant C6). By reference to his familiarity with different gurus, his ability to compare them, and his involvement in producing management solutions he states that: 'it makes me very critical, and generally speaking I don't get much out of a lecture' (Informant C6). Whereas a lot of audience members may suggest consistency in their consumer orientation, underlying there may be important variations, particularly in the scope of expectations. In the following sections we will focus on the audience dynamism by discussing three typical shifts in audience orientations and explore when these are more likely to occur by explaining the main motivations of audience members.

Shift 1: Involvement-Induced

The first type of consumption shift that emerged from our data refers to the possibility that audience members' experiences of involvement and utility activities are not consistent with expectations that emanate from activities primarily associated with selectivity (see Table 6.1). The main trigger for this shift is typically that the fulfilment sought by audience members differs from that they have obtained from a knowledge producer primarily during a guru lecture. Our analysis indicates that the latter may exceed expectations but can also easily be experienced as much less than expected.

First, an involvement-induced shift can be triggered when the 'gratifications obtained' are considered higher than audience members' expectations. For instance, while a lecture may have been chosen for fun or to stay up-to-date, the actual knowledge presented might have inspired audience members to get more involved than they had foreseen, learn more than they imagined beforehand, and perceive many more possibilities to productively apply insights to their daily work. Table 6.1 provides

Table 6.1 *Involvement-induced shift: patterns and exemplary evidence*

	Selectivity	Involvement	Utility
Devoted	A13		
Engaged	C5	A17	A17
Non-com	A22, A17, A15	A13	A13
Critical		A22, C5, A15	A22, C5, A15
Main motivations	Expectations are not met or surpassed by/during lecture; expectations can be related to content, personality guru, performance of guru, entertainment quality, relevance for audience member/daily work		
Informant A17	Non-committal 'I know [Guru]. I've got to know him during a get-together . . . and I had this personal educational budget at [company]. I still had that money, so I thought: "Let's go to [Guru]".'	Engaged 'He knows how to motivate people . . . . It was a refresher, a moment of rest to look back. To bring back the various training and lectures you've obtained [until then]. . . . It stimulates you in certain ways; it triggers you to notice certain aspects of yourself and to get into action.'	Engaged 'Yeah, I've got several things out of it. For example: "Are you a leader or follower?" This was an important one for me . . . I really changed my way of working . . . I needed that trigger to get into action. . . . [Among other things], I said goodbye to two people. That's something where I really thought: "Let's tackle things now!"'
Informant A22	Non-committal 'I didn't have any expectations, I remember that. Normally, you've got expectations and you read a little upfront, you have a learning objective. . . . This wasn't the case here. For [this lecture] it was more like: "For once in a while, let's attend such a lecture and let's see what's going to happen." . . . Honestly speaking, it was a day off.'	Critical 'All three of us thought that [Guru] is an awful person. An awful guy. We had the idea that he was drugged up to his eyeballs to get through the day. . . . [H]e doesn't affect you emotionally. I think that's the essence . . . he doesn't reach your heart at all.'	Critical '[D]oes anything remain? No! Nothing remains. . . . It's a waste of money.'

an exemplary overview of this shift, which we found in a number of informants (A13, A17, A22, C5). Informant A17, for example, who works for a large company in the telecommunication sector already knew Guru A in person from a business event. As he had not spent his educational budget, he thought 'let's simply go for a day to [Guru A]', thereby displaying a non-committal orientation with respect to how he selected the lecture. During the lecture, however, he indicated that he surprisingly became positively inspired, which was perceived as the main motivation for turning to an engaged orientation as the lecture brought various concrete and valuable, albeit unforeseen, insights during the processes of involvement.

Second, we also found a number of instances in which audience members report they had expected to receive a concrete solution for an urgent problem at work, but felt they did not obtain any managerial insights that they regard as valuable. This generally means that audience members acknowledge that they had received some form of management knowledge, but at the same time considered this as being too much on an abstract level so that it could not be applied instantly without significant resources and efforts to mould, adapt and supplement it to actually make it useful in practice. Also audience members that have attended lectures mainly for more non-committal reasons, such as developing shared experiences with a colleague or simply spending the educational budget, can get frustrated when the style of presentation or any other aspect of the lecture such as the personality of the guru or the setting does not contribute to a primarily entertaining experience.

The account of Informant A15 exemplifies such a shift. Remarkably, this manager has attended the same guru lecture and works at the same Dutch telecommunication company as A17, but, in contrast to A17, his gratifications obtained from the guru lecture generally failed to meet his expectations. His consumption orientation changed in relation to the three core dimensions of audience activity, that is, selectivity, involvement and utility.

Selectivity. Informant A15's selectivity orientation, his main motives to attend the lecture of Guru A, can primarily be characterised as non-committal. During the interview he explained how he wanted to join a younger colleague from his team, for whom the topic of the lecture was new. He phrased this as follows:

> [My colleague asked] '[Name informant] are you going? I think it'll be interesting.' And he didn't know all these management concepts and it's someone from my group. Thus, I thought it's nice to join . . . maybe I will get something out of it, a kind of refresher. Actually, I was also curious how someone would set up such a day. (Informant A15)

Our informant indicated that Guru A's lecture was mentioned in the company's educational catalogue, and he had a 'standard' educational budget, which he could use without the need to obtain any further approval, which facilitated his selection and subscription to the event. Similar to other informants who displayed a non-committal orientation, he reported that the 'fit' of the organisational educational budget (1.000 euros) with the costs of the lecture (995 euros) did not obstruct his attendance. He recounted that without the pre-fixed educational budget: 'I would not have attended . . . and I think that 350 of the 400 other people [of the company] would not have attended without the budget' (Informant A15). We found that the primary non-committal orientation that informant A15 displayed in relation to selectivity shifted when he expressed his view about actually attending the lecture. While the gratifications he sought by attending the lecture were not particularly high in relation to knowledge, what he obtained during the lecture was even less, as becomes clear when analysing how he constructed the activities associated with involvement. In particular, he experienced the set-up of the lecture as being far too superficial to actually learn anything. Triggered by his dissatisfaction about the lecture and the way Guru A presented various management ideas, his consumption orientation shifted from mainly non-committal to critical: 'I didn't expect to learn a lot of new things, but I had expected some more depth. For me . . . it was just like a seagull flying in, shitting all over everything, and then flying out again. . . . It was simply too much; too much in a short time' (Informant A15).

While he gives credit to the guru's ability to present management ideas in an attractive way to a large managerial audience, and 'keep up their attention', he also experienced the content of the ideas presented during the lecture as far too thin: 'it is delivered in a playful way and some things do stick but [I doubt] that it actually adds any value' (Informant A15). This was considered an important trigger for getting involved in a critical way during the lecture. For example, this manager regarded it as 'useless to ask a question' or to make notes; the main involvement was networking during the day, but 'to do that, you have other opportunities'.

Informant A15 also regards the *utility* of the lecture as relatively low, thereby signalling a shift – compared with his construction of selectivity – to a critical orientation. In particular, during the interview he denied that he transferred or used any of the ideas presented at the lecture to his work. The 'event-bag' with hand-outs of the presentation and CDs to listen again to the presented management ideas: 'rests unused in the corner; I haven't looked inside.' Rather, he reported that the main activities after the lecture involved telling others about the low value of the lecture in relation to its cost. He remembered how he advised management colleagues in his department not to attend the lecture:

> I discussed [the lecture] in the management team. And I told them: 'We shouldn't do that [again]. . . . . It has no added value.' . . . It is too general; . . . I prefer to have something more specific. Also as [company], I would say: never do it again. In particular as about 400 people from [company] go there. (Informant A15)

To summarise, an involvement-induced shift can be seen as a change in orientation of individual audience members that is primarily characterised by a lack of consistency between the way selectivity is constructed compared to other key activities. This inconsistency is mainly triggered by a perceived discrepancy in the gratifications sought from involvement-related activities and those obtained. The informants emphasised that the reason for this discrepancy lies generally in becoming dissatisfied with the content and the style of the lecture, and thereby realising that they did not receive what they expected. While the data showed several instances of a shift to a critical orientation, we also found a few instances of audience members being positively surprised by what they received. This indicates that gurus might exceed as well as fail to meet their audience members' expectations in relation to involvement.

In our sample, we found an involvement-induced shift amongst a variety of different informants, thereby suggesting that it cannot be directly linked to personal or organisational backgrounds. Rather, the informants connected the inconsistency in the orientations that they displayed to the expectations that emanated from selectivity, often concerning audience activities prior to the actual lecture. These management practitioners may have selected a lecture, but the basis for the gratifications sought are seen as relatively absent. Specifically, our informants acknowledge that, apart from being aware to some degree of the general reputation of the guru in the field of management, they typically had limited experiences of attending lectures and relatively little prior knowledge about the specific expertise and style of the guru. As a result, the knowledge obtained may more easily be experienced as too abstract or the style and values as incongruent with personal preferences. In addition, the audience members we interviewed related an involvement-induced shift to a lack of strong connection of the lecture to their personal interests; elements such as organisational perks or joining colleagues seem to have dominated processes of selectivity. Overall, the expectations raised in relation to selectivity (or the lack thereof) may not be directly related to the actual guru performance (although shaped by prior performances and general reputation), but may have significant implications for an audience member's experience of other consumption activities.

Shift 2: Utility-Induced

A second typical way in which individual audience members' view of their consumption activities may lack consistency is what we have called 'utility-induced' shift. The informants indicated that the main triggers that are typically associated with utility-induced shift in consumption orientation relate to their perceived discrepancy between the experienced applicability of ideas in management and organisational practice, and their expectations emanating from attending the guru lecture. In other words, such a shift in consumption orientation may occur when an audience member constructs activities related to utility as different from the primary orientation that characterises their perception of selectivity and involvement. Our analysis of the data revealed several instances in which audience members displayed this specific type of shift in orientation (see Table 6.2 for examples). Similar to the involvement-induced type of shift, we found that the experienced need gratification may have exceeded or failed to meet the gratifications sought from using management ideas that were obtained during attending a guru lecture. We will further elaborate on and illustrate both possibilities.

First, a utility-induced shift in consumption orientation may imply that audience members construct the practical value of the ideas obtained during a guru lecture in management and organisational practice as much higher than expected. For instance, Informant C3, a senior manager in a medium-sized petrochemical company, reported a utility-induced shift from an engaged to a devoted consumption orientation. By regularly reading management books and by attending several lectures per year, he seeks to address his need to keep his knowledge on new management ideas up to date and aims to obtain general input to reflect on and enhance his own work. In particular, he framed his *selectivity* of a lecture series in terms of his general interest in management knowledge, and his persistent desire to better understand how he and his company work:

> In my normal work as a manager, I'm [continuously] searching for ways to structure things. I've always been someone who structures things. ... I have [for example] always used the balance scorecard to check: what is relevant in life? ... I have always really liked the [various] perspectives and I use the concept a lot in my organisation. (Informant C3)

In line with a form of engaged consumption, he systematically associated his *involvement* during the lecture series with activities such as holding a particular notebook to make notes and actively selecting ideas that he considered relevant for his work. As a regular consumer of management ideas, his main gratification sought from attending guru lectures is not

Table 6.2 *Utility-induced shift: patterns and exemplary evidence*

	Selectivity	Involvement	Utility
Devoted	A12	A12	C3
Engaged	C3, D1, D3	C3, D1; D3	A12
Non-com			D1
Critical			D3
Main motivations	Expectations are not met or surpassed after lecture; expectations can be related to content, personality guru, performance of guru, entertainment quality, relevance for audience member/daily work		
Informant D1	Engaged '[I went there because Guru] has the reputation of being very flamboyant and inspiring and of having a really good story. I'd been told that several times by colleagues who had been there.'	Engaged '[Guru] asked provoking questions . . . and by his very inspiring way of asking questions you got detached from your daily routine. . . . This was the most important thing to me.'	Non-committal 'In terms of content not much has remained. Actually, I can't even remember the title of the lecture.'
Informant A12	Devoted '[I selected the lecture] because I'm really interested in business administration . . . and to see what I may use in my daily work.'	Devoted '[The lecture] was a feast of recognising things! . . . There were really practical things . . . that help you to be sharp in your daily work. Something like: "Wait, if I do it like that, then I'll become more effective or efficient".'	Engaged 'One shouldn't exaggerate things, you pick some things and you use them. . . . But it's not that you do things in a completely different way. It's not that you, based on such a one-day event, introduce a new way of working.'

gaining new knowledge, but being motivated to take ownership of ideas and make them valuable for one's own practice. He phrased this in the following way:

> often not that I learn something new, but rather that you get inspired to apply a new piece [of an already known idea]; ... you forget these things in your daily life. The very moment [you attend a lecture], you think: gosh, this is something I need to pay attention to. (Informant C3)

During one of the lectures, he also took the opportunity to contact one of the co-presenters, a Dutch top manager who became famous for successfully managing a major turnaround in one of the biggest companies in the country. This resulted in a one-hour conversation during the lunch break about the top manager's own experiences during this turnaround. Although Informant C3 did not select the lecture as a means to find a concrete solution to an organisational problem, nor was his lunch talk with a co-presenter about his own work, the input received during this lecture triggered him to address a long-standing problem at his own company in an alternative and more promising way. Concerning *utility*, informant C3 described the value and effect of his lunch talk: 'I talked for an hour with [co-presenter] about his experiences and how he felt about [the re-organisation of a large Dutch-based multi-national]. So that was an added value [of the lecture]' (Informant C3). While the talk was unrelated to Informant C3's own company, the experience of the co-presenter inspired him to take a clear stance towards those who he regarded as the source of an ongoing problem at his own company. Thus for C3, the utility-induced shift was particularly triggered when he experienced that the lecture had a different, albeit much more valuable, type of utility than expected. In the case of Informant C3, the lecture exceeded his expectations and ultimately was associated with a change in the strategy of his department:

> One of the topics we talked about was 'how do you find the courage to change [company]?' So, this was mainly about the mental background of daring to do something like that ... During that time we had a lot of problems with [a] contractor ... and oddly enough the talk with [co-presenter] inspired me to change everything ... I made a whole strategy then to go to the top of the [contractor] company ... and to tell them: 'I'm not happy with your performance; it's either up or out.' It was absolutely the talk with [co-presenter] ... This was very valuable for me ... We're still busy with this new strategy. (Informant C3)

Second, our data also included a number of cases of utility-induced shifts in orientation (see Table 6.2), in which the lecture did not fulfil the specific audience member's expectations, particularly with regard to the practical value of the ideas that have been presented during the lecture.

Informant A12, for example, a product manager at a large telecommunication company with extensive work experience in the IT field and an education at the Maritime Academy, mainly attended the lecture of Guru A to get more knowledge about new and effective management ideas. In his construction of processes of selectivity, he mainly reflected a devoted orientation with his focus on searching for concrete input to better solve management problems and on becoming a better manager in general.

While he experienced the lecture as generally providing the input he sought, back at his workplace, he realised that the interesting management ideas might not be directly or as easily applicable in his work as he expected. Instead of a continued emphasis on directly using ideas as presented, the informant showed a shift towards a more engaged orientation, thereby emphasising the wider value of the ideas transmitted during the lecture, while at the same time showing lower expectations towards their local implications: 'do you actually work in a different way? – No, that's of course not the case. It is not that such a one-day event makes you introduce a new working process' (Informant A12). This indicates that he came to realise that some ideas promoted by the guru seemed valuable during the lecture, but did not turn out to be applicable to his company at all, for instance because they were perceived as lacking fit with the company's culture, as 'we never work that way [here]'. As a result, this audience member was triggered to distance himself further from the ideas that were transmitted during the lecture in terms of their practical value, whilst laying much more emphasis on activities such as making a 'free translation of a useful model' to better fit them to his own situation. Informant A12 even emphasised that, after discussing the guru advice with several colleagues, he decided not to apply these interesting ideas. While pointing at the reference book he received from the guru lecture, informant A12 explained:

> Absolutely, those management ideas [provided during the lecture] are very recognisable in our own situation. For instance, a very nice model presented at the lecture is the one from Eli Goldratt. However, in contrast to his idea we just add a lot to our work; we introduce new products, a new process – it just has to be bigger and more. In fact we almost never say goodbye to anything – and that was one of the things that I discussed with a colleague – we just never do that. We always add things to the work process, but we never cut out anything. So did we translate this idea into practice . . . actually no. (Informant A12)

A number of informants in our sample displayed a *utility-induced shift* in consumption orientation. Such a shift is more likely to occur when audience members realise after the lecture that the gratification they sought concerning the practical value of ideas was either not met or exceeded expectations. In our analysis of the data, we could not relate this type of shift to specific audience members' background characteristics or function (managers and staff). Rather, our informants emphasised that utility-induced shift are to be connected to (1) an audience member's perception of an idea's applicability in their own situation, compared to (2) what is generally suggested in the lecture.

One key element, an idea's perceived applicability, not only stems from the audience member's assessment of the 'fit' of an idea with their working context, but also to the experienced possibilities for agency in taking up an idea in this specific context. In various instances, our informants emphasised that, despite their favourable intentions, they were not yet able to translate some useful ideas obtained during a lecture into practice. Intuitively, possibilities for agency may, directly or indirectly, be related to hierarchical position in an organisation given that it is often connected to power and related access to time and resources. However, the lack of a clear connection of utility-induced shifts to function suggests that, independent of hierarchical position, audience members may or may not see possibilities to translate ideas into practice. We seek to further explore how resources related to power plays a role in audience member's intra-organisational use of management ideas in Chapter 7.

Another important element, and one that may easily be overlooked, that shapes a utility-induced shift concerns the expectations raised by the management guru prior to and during the lecture. In line with our analysis of guru lectures in Chapter 4, the informants confirm that demonstrating the potential applicability of the ideas in a variety of different contexts generally enhances the likelihood that audience members may be inspired by attending the lecture and obtain energy and confidence to put it into practice. However, our exemplary data also indicates that illustrating the successful use of ideas by management gurus may not necessarily encourage application by individual audience members. Rather, the informants explain that, for instance, the use of success stories may be experienced as motivation to apply an idea promoted by a guru, whilst at the same time it can be discouraging when these are accompanied by large promises and related expectations. Also, utility-induced shifts can occur when gurus may assume substantial managerial agency, but individual audience members do not see possibilities in their organisation (time and resources) or capacities to enact this idea. Thus, overall, while the guru and the ideas they are promoting during a lecture may be considered as inspiring, their perceived value is connected to audience members' view on realising their expectations in relation to a specific context of application.

Shift 3: Alternating

The third type of shift that emerged from our data is 'alternating', referring to a continuous shift in consumers' orientations in relation to a particular lecture and single consumption activity (see Table 6.3). We found examples of this type of shift in various instances (e.g. A5, A11, A20, A26, B1 and D10). Whereas involvement-induced and utility-induced shifts can be relatively clearly connected to inconsistencies between the audience member orientation of different consumer activities, 'alternating' is characterised by inconsistencies in relation to a single consumption activity. Such an alternating type of shift implies that audience members switch back and forth in expressing what they like and dislike of a single lecture, guru, and/or lecture content both during and after the lecture; ambivalence seems to be the key feature in each of the relevant stages (see Sturdy et al., 2006).

One telling example of alternating shifts in the consumption of a guru lecture came from Informant A5. Based on her work as a talent programme manager for a large Dutch bank, she can be considered a very experienced, well-informed and intensive consumer of international management ideas providers. It is part of her work to regularly attend international conferences and meet well-known speakers. In line with her professional need to attend lectures, conferences and business schools, her critical view on the multitude offers on the management market, and her personal preference for not staying out of the office for a whole working day, we found multiple instances of engaged, non-committal and critical orientation towards the lecture of Guru A in relation to selectivity, involvement and utility.

In relation to *selectivity*, Informant A5 signalled an engaged as well as a non-committal orientation. Her engaged orientation was linked to the wish to find out 'what does he actually do during the [lecture] day', and whether the guru 'actually is someone to potentially hire' for their in-house talent programme. In this role, international business schools regularly invite her to meetings, lectures and conferences as a form of:

> 'relationship management'. We do that, for example, regularly, for business schools abroad; that way you see what faculty they have ... [In addition,] I'm a member of a client advisory boards of INSEAD. You go there twice a year and get, among other things, insight in the new professors they have. (Informant A5)

During the interview, her non-committal stance became visible in her account of how her registration had been triggered by an email invitation from the lecture organiser that included a present for personal use. Additionally, the lecture took place in walking distance from her

Table 6.3 *Alternating: patterns and exemplary evidence*

	Selectivity	Involvement	Utility
Devoted	A20	A20, D10	A20, D10
Engaged	A5, A11, A26, B1, D10*	A5, A11, A26, B1, D10	A5, A26, B1, D10
Non-com	A5, A11, A20, A26	A5, A11, A20, A26	A5
Critical		A5, A11, B1	A11
Main motivations	Ambivalence of consumption; sources are multiple, parallel expectations of audience members which might be partially conflicting and/or are only partially met		
Informant A26	Engaged and non-committal Engaged: 'I had expected to get some distance during the lecture from the daily . . . "rat race" so that I would have the chance to reflect on various philosophies and approaches without getting distracted.' Non-committal: 'I went [to the lecture] like: "I'll wait and see". I didn't prepare myself.'	Engaged and non-committal Engaged: '[Guru A] is enthralling . . . and he can easily play with the crowd. . . . I have learned a lot [from the lecture].' Non-committal: 'In some respects it felt like an entertainment show. '	Engaged Engaged: 'I have talked a lot to colleagues about it and I still do so. . . . The lecture made me think. . . . I became inspired and I picked up some topics. . . . I've read several books about [these topics]. . . . These [two topics] are the two most important things I've learned and we still use them.'
Informant A11	Engaged and non-committal Engaged: '[I selected the lecture] 'to gain general insights from [Guru] about management; how he puts ideas about management together.'	Engaged, non-committal and critical Engaged and critical: 'It was very fast and at a certain moment you think "that's interesting" and you start reflecting about it but then he's already gone on.'	Critical Critical: 'I listened to some of his summaries on CD [after the lecture] but I've found them completely void of meaning. . . . If you ask whether [the lecture] was useful . . . he touched upon

	Non-committal: 'Each employee has an educational budget of 1,000 euros. Yeah, well, colleagues went there as well.'	Non-committal: 'My perception of the day is very positive, but if you ask whether I attended any training? No, actually not. . . . because for training you expect self-reflection and that you get really involved. . . . you're more consuming than actually being active yourself. . . . it was simply entertainment.'	some aspects but I don't think that you get more effective from that. If I wasn't there, was I less effective? For sure I can say that this is not the case.'

* Informant D10 has attended a broad variety of guru lectures, leading to a devoted, engaged and critical consumption orientation as illustrated in Appendix A. The pattern of 'alternating', included in this table, refers to a lecture where she displayed a devoted and an engaged orientation only.

office – it was 'just around the corner' – making attendance easy and resonating with her personal dislike of being out of the office for long.

> I had heard all the advertisement before and I had doubts about whether to register or not. [The personal email invitation included] a nice offer with a discount coupon [from an internet store], which I found really attractive. That was the trigger to subscribe. (Informant A5)

Concerning *involvement* activities, we found that Informant A5 alternated between three orientations with regard to the specific guru lecture: engaged, non-committal and critical. She showed signs of an engaged orientation by explaining how she felt strongly involved with the content, thereby more or less implicitly referring to her role as the bank's talent programme manager: 'I was really impressed by his way of presenting; you're really sitting there and making notes, thinking "wow, I recognise these [ideas]"' (Informant A5). At the same time, however, she reported a non-committal stance towards the ideas that were communicated by the guru during the lecture. This can be seen in the light of her extensive experience in visiting guru lectures and the related possibilities to compare a management guru's expertise and capabilities to what is offered on the market for management knowledge. For example, she perceived the content of guru lecture A as: 'pretty superficial. I mean, it is a kind of party, it's nice, but it's not like: "wow, now I go home purified" . . . I haven't heard anything new, let's put it that way' (Informant A5).

Finally, in relation to involvement, she also displayed a *critical* orientation. While the lecture was experienced 'as a refresher of ideas' and the presentation style as competent, she considered some parts of the lecture as 'too dazzling', and the dance show at the end as 'completely dull' and 'absolutely terrible'. In contrast to what was written about the lecture in the Dutch media, she regarded Guru A not as a leading thinker on his own, but simply a clever salesperson:

> Simply someone who has a smart commercial offer. And who does an outstanding presentation, he does that stunningly well. For me, a guru is someone who has an own theory, who writes a book on an academic level . . . He's absolutely no management guru, . . . but his lecture set-up is really interesting. (Informant A5)

In the analysis of the interview, we discovered that Informant A5 also alternated between different (engaged and non-committal) orientations with regard to utility. When asked about the impact of the lecture on her work, she displayed an engaged orientation only with regard to a single aspect that she suggested to her manager be incorporated into their own in-house training workshops: '[Guru] makes a very nice link between various books and times during which books have been written; and this is something we can really do better in our own programme. ... That's how I used the content of the lecture' (Informant A5). Her non-committal orientation was particularly associated with an absence of any follow-up activities: not subsequently listening to the summaries of the lecture on CD, not reading back her notes and also not talking with others about the one-liners that seemed inspiring to her during the lecture itself. In explaining her post-lecture activities, she even stated that she would avoid being associated with the lecture to signal some kind of knowledge or expertise: 'I would never put attendance on my CV as it is no lecture, it is pure entertainment – I really see it that way.' But, at the same time, when asked about the costs of the lecture (995 euros), she did not regard them too high. Asked whether the lecture is worth the money, she explained:

> Of course you always prefer to pay less. I don't see it as wasted money, however, as you also receive the CDs. Even if I had to pay it myself, I would have seen it as worthwhile as it is something special; it takes place only twice a year. Then you also have the feeling of 'I take part in something special'.

As a whole, the example of Informant A5 illustrates how and when audience members may alternate between different consumption orientations. This type of shift highlights the possibility that one audience member may be inconsistent in their consumption orientation in relation to a particular lecture *and* single consumption activity. In contrast to other types of shifts which are primarily triggered by perceived differences in gratifications sought and obtained (e.g. expectations that are not met), the key motivation for displaying an alternating consumption orientation is more related to audience members' multiple reference points against which they may assess the value of a lecture, or particular consumption activities. As exemplified by Informant A5, informants talked in terms of alternating orientations in relation to different roles, backgrounds and the variety of interests and needs that emanate from them, thereby introducing a general ambiguity into the consumption process. In other words, a central issue in understanding alternating consumption orientations amongst individual audience members involves the question: in relation to *what* or *whom*?

Seen from this view, the occurrence of alternating orientations may be more likely when audience members are knowledgeable about the management guru market *and* have the possibility to relate a lecture to different situations in which management practitioners (including themselves in other roles) may reside. In line with this, we found these instances mainly involved experienced multi-users who regularly consume management guru ideas for their work; as described above, regular consumption of ideas is most prominent for members of large for-profit organisations as these organisations can afford to allocate the financial means to pay for lectures.

Conclusion

Building on the uses and gratification perspective which informed Chapter 5, this chapter sought to address the need to further develop our conceptualisation of audience dynamism to better understand audience members' experiences of mass events and the implications for the flow of management ideas. Whilst the main focus of Chapter 5 lay in identifying key differences in audience members' orientations towards management ideas and the gurus that promote them, this analysis also revealed that during the communication process, a substantial number of informants showed important variation in their consumption orientation, thereby suggesting considerable volatility in terms of the attachment they had to the gurus and their ideas. Drawing from studies that have conceptualised mass audiences as primarily 'variable active' (e.g. Blumler, 1979; Rubin, 2009; Ruggiero, 2000) we focused in this chapter on possible shifts that can occur in the orientations that audience members may draw upon. In line with this, the present chapter explored how and when individual audience members may shift in consumption orientation throughout the communication process. Our findings on these two issues have a number of important implications for future research.

First, by showing how individual audience members' orientations are not necessarily limited to a single category (devoted, engaged, non-committal or critical) and cannot be considered a permanent state, our findings seek to move beyond conceptions of managers' attitudes towards management gurus and their ideas as relatively static. Rather, our findings stress the need for a more dynamic understanding of audience responses that can account for the individual-level variability in consumption orientations. Specifically, the analysis revealed that while some informants consistently drew on a single consumption orientation in relation to a single idea or management guru, others displayed important shifts between multiple orientations.

Concerning the former, a large proportion of our informants displayed a single ('no shifts') consumption orientation towards a particular guru lecture that they have attended. As indicated in our findings, consistency in orientation implies that the audience member's view of selectivity, involvement and utility with regard to a specific guru lecture is considered as relatively invariable. However, despite the fact that in terms of shifts, consistency in consumer orientation is presented as one specific type (the

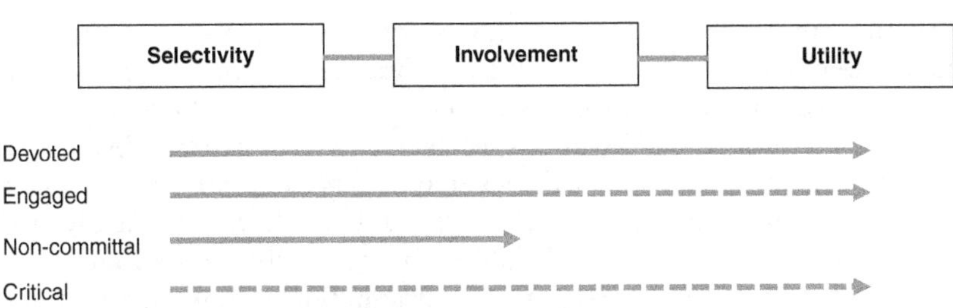

Figure 6.1 Perceived scope of audience expectations

absence of major inconsistencies), we found important variation in the audience members' perceived understanding of consistency in terms of the scope of expectations across the distinct orientations (see Figure 6.1). In particular, whereas a consistency in a devoted orientation entails that the expectations are relatively high across different activities, audience members typically proposed much lower expectations with regard to utility in relation to an engaged orientation. In contrast, using a non-committal orientation suggests that the scope of expectations particularly applies to selectivity and involvement and is generally absent when they talk about utility. In a critical orientation, expectations are considered beyond the guru event.

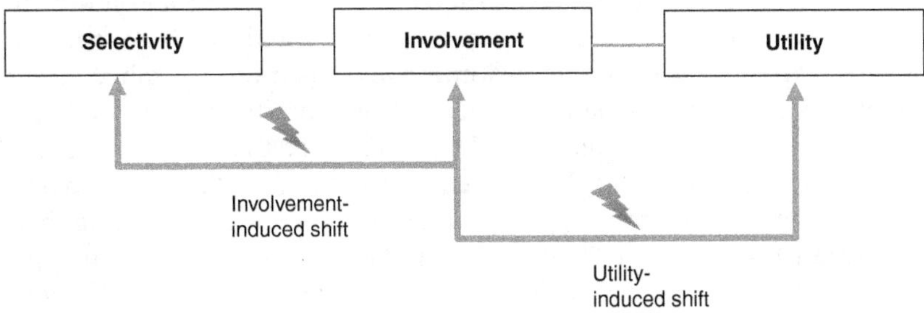

Figure 6.2 Perceived shifts in audience orientations

With regard to the informants who displayed shifts between multiple orientations, our research reveals three types of movements between the main orientations, 'involvement-induced', 'utility-induced' and 'alternating'. These movements are confined primarily to those whose selectivity is devoted, engaged or non-committal (see Figure 6.2 for an overview). An involvement-induced shift refers to the inconsistency between the orientation that underlies an audience member's framing of selectivity and the way they talk about involvement and utility. The findings show that this inconsistency can be experienced as favourable or unfavourable to the guru lecture. In addition, various informants also showed what we have called utility-induced shift which is seen as a lack of consistency in the way audience members construct activities of utility compared to the main orientation that characterises selectivity and involvement. Finally, we defined the alternating type of shift as the possibility that an audience member may lack consistency in their orientation towards a particular lecture and a single consumption activity.

Second, even though some theorists have provided important insights into how management practitioners may display multiple responses towards management ideas at the same time (e.g. Sturdy, 1998; Watson, 1994), prior work has provided little detail about *when* these practitioners may show different and even conflicting orientations. In exploring the conditions under which these shifts are more likely to occur, we analysed the audience members' main motivations for each type of shift and we found a number of key reasons related to the individual audience members' (1) expectations and related (2) broader management knowledge-consumption pattern.

First, an important reason for the occurrence of shifts in consumer orientations is related to the question whether *expectations of a specific audience member are not met or are exceeded.* The informants' motivations suggest that consistency, that is a lack of shifts, is based on lectures fulfiling their expectations – whether these are gaining a solution to a pressing problem (devoted orientation), expanding one's toolbox (engaged orientation) or rather hedonistic motives (non-committal orientation). In line with this view, involvement- and utility-induced shifts are more likely when gratifications sought are perceived to be at odds with the gratifications obtained (cf. Palmgreen and Rayburn, 1982). Obviously, this connects directly to what the guru has done specifically during their performance directly in front of the audience. As such, the findings confirm that inconsistency in orientation may not only be about a guru's perceived inability to create an atmosphere favourable to the reception of ideas (Chapter 3) but may also concern a perceived failure in conveying the practical applicability of these ideas (see Chapter 4). Notably, we also found instances in which the gurus *exceeded* the expectations of the individual audience members.

At the same time, the audience members' views also indicate that, in addition to the actual guru performance, the expectations raised prior to the event play a crucial role in possible shifts in orientation. Indeed, informants refer to their experiences with communications by the event organisation as mainly stemming from information-collecting activities such as watching YouTube videos of the guru or reading advertisements and e-mailings in the run-up to the guru event. However, the findings also reveal that at least as important in shaping the expectation, is the perceived reputation of the guru in terms of contents and style. Compared to the communications of the event organiser, activities such as reading books written by the guru, their media appearances and shared experiences by audience members from prior performances (including those in videos) are generally seen as essential in shaping expectations, and thus the possibility of (in)consistencies. In particular, the likelihood of involvement-induced shifts is primarily related to the way the guru event is designed in line with the audience members perception of – as a result of information-collecting activities prior to the event – what the guru has done in the recent past. To enhance consistency, creating a positive atmosphere involves not only the promotion of attractive ideas but also maintaining a link with the guru's prior work. In a similar way, utility-induced shifts are less likely to occur when the expectations raised during a lecture are in line with what audience members would expect is possible in a work situation. Thus, a guru may promote an idea's practical applicability, but needs also to keep expectations low to prevent audience members' perception of inconsistency with activities they are expected to perform in daily work. Overall, our findings direct our attention to a broader understanding of the audience activities that are performed prior to, or are expected after, the guru event that shape audience orientations though are beyond the immediate performance of the guru.

Second, our analysis also suggested that individual level management knowledge-consumption patterns need to be seen as important in understanding possible shifts in orientation. Again, we found little evidence linking function or socio-economic background to possible shifts. Rather, particularly interesting for understanding shifts in consumer orientation is the group of what may be considered as relatively heavy users of management knowledge commodities. These audience members are typically very experienced in attending lectures and discuss their experiences with peers on a regular basis. Under these conditions, they have a better overview of the field and thus have a stronger basis for making adequate comparisons between different gurus. Because of this overview, audience members are better able to choose the lecture they appreciate, and develop a more realistic view on what a guru lecture might entail and its potential value for their daily work, thereby making shifts in orientations less likely. In contrast, an audience member's lack of prior knowledge of the guru market and a relative absence of a strong prior connection to their personal interests makes shifts in orientation more likely to occur. At the same time, as people become more and more experienced, they might also become more ambivalent towards the guru phenomenon: they have typically obtained a variety of different experiences and can draw on different reference points to assess what they can expect from a guru lecture and what they can get out of such an event. In some respects, this type of audience member is too experienced to talk about a guru lecture in terms of one single category. Thus, alternating may also be inherent to a particular group of audience members, whatever gurus do.

The identification of various shifts in individual consumption orientation is of theoretical significance because it indicates the need for a more fluid and variable understanding of management practitioners' responses towards management ideas. Some audience members clearly affiliate with the guru and their ideas during the communication process, but not all, and not necessarily on a continuous basis. Whilst obviously important caution is needed given that we do not base our conclusion on a randomised sample, it nevertheless can be concluded that audience members displaying a consistent devoted orientation is just one of the many possible categories, and most likely not the largest one. At the same time, however, we cannot assume that such management audience variability is likely or even possible in every context. Also, the possible focus on pleasure-seeking orientations in the context of guru lectures and identity processes in the setting of an MBA programme (Sturdy et al., 2006) suggests that different dynamics and logics may operate in contexts prior to idea implementation. Compared with the assumed setting of management idea implementation, the specific context of guru events is typically outside the constraints and pressures of an organisation. Indeed, as discussed in Chapter 3, these events are designed to loosen attendees' organisational attachments and create an 'in-group' (Greatbatch and Clark, 2003) with the consequence that they may change their views more easily. Therefore, in Chapter 7 we will shift our focus to explore managerial audiences in the context of organisations as the assumed main social setting concerning the use of management ideas.

7 Managerial Audiences in Organisational Contexts

As explained in our analysis of guru lectures in Chapters 3 and 4, the creation of a positive atmosphere around particular management ideas and the promotion of their applicability are considered crucial conditions for the widespread appreciation of these ideas and their potential use amongst a large managerial audience. Yet, whilst recognising that these factors may enhance receptivity towards particular management ideas and encourage application, it does not preclude a number of different orientations amongst individual audience members towards both these ideas and the gurus who are promoting them. As such, in Chapters 5 and 6 we not only shed more light on the differential attraction of ideas and gurus amongst managerial audiences that participate in guru lectures, but also showed how and why individual audience members' orientations towards a guru and their ideas are not necessarily limited to a single category (devoted, engaged, non-committal or critical), and cannot be considered as a permanent state per se. Overall, these findings allowed us to better account for the role of audience members' activities in understanding management practitioners' orientations towards management ideas that are promoted in mass communication settings.

Yet, the general consumption orientations we discussed in the previous two chapters are still largely disconnected from the specific social settings and relational interaction in which ideas usage generally tends to take place. In particular, guru-audience interactions typically occur outside the conventions and power relations of an organisational context (Greatbatch and Clark, 2005) which is widely assumed to be the 'natural setting' of management idea implementation (e.g. Mueller and Whittle, 2011; Outilla et al., 2020; Reay et al., 2013). As discussed in Chapter 1, the primary focus in studies of idea implementation is limited to the settings of 'adopting organizations' (Ansari et al., 2014). Remarkably, these implementation studies have paid scant attention to the critical question of the origin of these ideas, beyond the assumption that various external pressures may have enhanced their organisational adoption. The widespread attraction and adoption of these ideas at the organisational level is treated as a given and starting point for exploring how these are translated into practice.

We still know little about how management practitioners, who have been exposed to particular ideas in different media, come to use these ideas in different relevant contexts and assimilate them into their work context. This chapter therefore aims to further our understanding of managerial audiences by moving the analysis from a focus on management practitioners' more general need gratification to the specific organisation as the assumed main social context for the actual use of management ideas (e.g. Clark, 2004a). Thus, beyond the recognition that audience members may vary in their orientations towards management ideas we ask the question: *How is the social use of management ideas in organisational contexts related to the relative power positions of individual audience members?*

This is an important question because extant literature suggests not only that the widespread promotion of these management ideas produces predominantly positive management practitioners, but also that, as consumers of management ideas, these practitioners play an important role in the intra-organisational processes aimed at translating ideas into practice (e.g. Mueller and Whittle, 2011; Reay et al., 2013). In the light of this, the present chapter explores audience members' intra-organisational use of management ideas in relation to three forms of resource-related power, and explains how these forms are deployed and reconstituted in the relative power positions individual audience members hold towards different targets of influence.

The Organisational Use of Guru-Led Ideas

Management gurus are generally assumed to have a high level of influence on the business community in different ways. This assumption is not only based on the sales figures of their books, the numbers of managers that have attended their lectures, or the attention they receive in the managerial media and managerial discourse (Furusten, 1999; Greatbatch and Clark, 2005; Pagel and Westerfelhaus, 2005). The numerous organisational changes programmes that have been associated with the ideas legitimated by management gurus over the years (cf. David and Strang, 2006; Knights and McCabe, 1998; Suddaby and Greenwood, 2001) also suggest a direct influence on the organisational practices and work of many individuals. Despite this, as we discussed in Chapter 1, prior research offers little detail on the organisational use of particular management ideas promoted in mass communication settings, beyond the assumption that different media channels play an important role in their widespread appreciation amongst management practitioners. Whilst recognising that a large number of these practitioners may find particular management ideas highly attractive, and may display predominantly positive orientations towards them, for instance in relation to attending mass events such as guru lectures, this research has been unable to develop a deeper understanding of the meanings attributed to these ideas as well as of their construction in management and organisational practice by these practitioners as audience members.

Developing a better understanding of how audience members might bring these ideas into organisations and construct their deployment and social use, is of particular significance given the growing literature on the their organisational implementation (Sturdy et al., 2019). Studies of organisational implementation have shed important light on role of managerial agency in shaping the translation of ideas into practice (e.g. McCabe, 2011; McCabe and Russell, 2017; McCann et al., 2015; Reay et al., 2013; van Grinsven et al., 2016). As detailed in Chapter 1, a growing stream of literature on management idea implementation has focused on managers' micro-level practices aimed at promoting an idea and facilitating its widespread organisational use, thereby 'mobilizing change at the level of the firm' (Morris and Lancaster, 2006: 215). This suggests that once accepted by top management as a critical 'entry point', an idea trickles downward to other organisational members (e.g. DeCock and Hipkin, 1997; Kelemen, 2000; Outila et al., 2020). In other words, studies of organisational implementation suggest (1) the initiatives of a generally positive (top) management, and (2) a *primarily top-down organisation-wide* change programme as key to understanding the social use of ideas. However, a critical issue relates to how audience members with different backgrounds and, to various degrees, shifting orientations may actively employ ideas from guru lectures in a specific organisational context.

This chapter seeks to address this issue by drawing from seminal studies on the social use of mass media as a conceptual lens (e.g. Lull, 1980; Morley, 2005). Here, as seen in Chapter 2, media and its contents are primarily conceptualised as important resources to individual audience members for 'establishing, sustaining and improving social relations' (Lull, 1980: 332). In other words, these studies focus attention on understanding different media uses in relation to the audience members' social position in a specific context, and their interpersonal objectives to maintain or enhance power and influence. This is in line with broader understandings of power as primarily tied to relational interaction around asymmetrical distributed structural resources (e.g. Lawrence et al., 2001). Indeed, institutional analyses relate the success of 'institutional entrepreneurs' to their access to the right resources and their skills in leveraging those resources (Fligstein, 1997). More specifically, following Scott's (2001) conceptualisation of power, Lawrence and colleagues (2001, 2005; see also Kipnis, Schmidt, and Wilkinson, 1980; Yukl and Falbe, 1990) found that forms of power vary in relation to the way they seek to affect social action with (1) 'influence' as emanating from the use of culturally appropriate social skills such as involving 'moral suasion, negotiation, persuasion, ingratiation, and exchange' (Lawrence et al., 2005: 184; see also Fligstein, 1997), (2) 'force' as tied to authority to restrict specific actions of others, and (3) 'domination' as having the ability to shape entire systems of power within which others are 'imprisoned'. Drawing on this perspective to analyse the in-depth interviews with sixty-eight audience members as described in Chapter 5, we:

- reveal how the interpersonal use of management ideas involves three different forms of resource-related power (influence, force and domination);
- explain how these forms are reproduced through their recursive deployment and reconstitution;
- elaborate how different directions of agency may relate to the relative power positions individual audience members may hold towards their assumed targets as they address subordinates (downward), peers (lateral) and superiors (upward).

Our analysis not only indicates that once within an organisation, audience members' use of management ideas is inextricably connected to the use of power, but also that this is systematically associated with the relative power position towards their assumed target (e.g. at a lower, similar or higher hierarchical level). Overall, the findings suggest that relative position plays an important role in the possibilities for putting ideas into practice as well as in enhancing the legitimacy of the power-related resources employed in this process. These findings are of particular significance as they shed essential light on how and why different audience members may actively use management ideas in an organisational context as the 'natural setting' of idea consumption, and allow for the development of a much broader and more nuanced conceptualisation of the recursive and multidirectional ways in which ideas promoted in mass communication settings may potentially shape and maintain management and organisational practice.

Media Use and Social Resources

As indicated, in the sections that follow we discuss and illustrate how the social use of management ideas in an organisational context relates to three distinct forms of power and we show how these forms are simultaneously deployed and reconstituted in the relative power positions individual audience members hold towards different targets of influence. In analysing our data from the in-depth interviews described earlier in the book (see Table 5.1), we were directed to the reproduction of resource-related power as individual audience members both draw upon and reinforce their positions when using management ideas. The analysis revealed how audience members' relative power positions in an organisation shape the use of management ideas, which, simultaneously, provides a basis to reconstitute these same power positions.

In particular, three forms of resource-related power emerged as being crucial in understanding the audience members' intended use of management ideas in an organisational context: (1) influence, (2) force and (3) domination. In addition, the data also showed that these forms were not only associated with realising interpersonal objectives in a hierarchical downward direction, that is, top managers in relation to their subordinates. Rather, the audience members exercised interaction patterns involving (a) downward, (b) lateral and (c) upward relations (see Tables 7.1, 7.2 and 7.3 for an overview and illustrative examples). The next sections provide further details on these forms of resource-related power as well as the background and main orientations of the audience members that are involved in the organisational use of management ideas.

Deploying and Reconstituting Influence

A first form of power through which individual audience members constructed the use of management ideas in an organisational context is influence. We found in our analysis that influence is considered relatively untied to audience members' formal organisational positions but revolves primarily around the individual's social skills to get things done in line with one's interpersonal objectives, for example via persuading others to appreciate a particular viewpoint by referring to gurus and their ideas. The data showed that after attending a lecture some audience members drew on their social skills as an essential resource in introducing specific management ideas in their organisation.

Our analysis also revealed that audience members not only sought to exercise influence in relational interaction as a way to affect the broader perception and interpretation of the idea and shape the understanding of organisational issues in line with their personal views and interests, but also to maintain or enhance influence as a resource in their relative power position. In addition, the data exhibited that, in seeking to influence others, audience members not only targeted their

Table 7.1 *Deploying and reconstituting 'influence': overview and exemplary evidence*

Primary direction	Deploying and reconstituting influence: illustrative examples	Formal role	Main orientation
Downward	*Deploy* That really depends on how you can convey that yourself. I talked about it really . . . see, that adventure from last week that could not have worked if I had not been able to make them enthusiastic about the idea.	*Informant A26* MM in large organisation	Engaged Non-committal
	Reconstitute Sometimes it is just very convenient to put such an authority next to it. So, in that sense, it has the consequence that conversations proceed more easily. Some people are in that sense very impressed by authority.	*Informant A28* TM in medium-size organisation	Engaged
Lateral	*Deploy* Yes, I've been to the lecture together with a colleague, so we also talked a lot about it, and particularly how we could use ideas in our change trajectory. We have also advised several other colleagues to attend that specific [Guru B] lecture.	*Informant B11* MM in medium-size organisation	Devoted Engaged
	Reconstitute This sheet, I literally used this sheet to start up the project. So, it is very simple and only just one thing and it might be only a fiftieth of what has been told, but that was something that to me was immediately applicable. (Informant A20)	*Informant A20* EMP in large organisation	Devoted Non-committal
Upward	*Deploy* I don't think that in this company you can simply go to the CEO and say we just need to change this structure because I went to	*Informant B3* STAFF in large organisation	Engaged

Table 7.1 *(cont.)*

Primary direction	Deploying and reconstituting influence: illustrative examples	Formal role	Main orientation
	a particular Masterclass and that's totally it. But I can of course explain in the bilateral meeting with my senior management how I would like to be managed myself.		
	Reconstitute	*Informant A16*	
	To incorporate that in the message you have to give to others in a couple of weeks. For example, the management team. And then it is a good story if those things contribute to . . .	STAFF in large organisation	Devoted

subordinates, but also appealed to peers and superiors in a lateral and upward direction respectively (see Table 7.1 for an overview). For each direction we now outline and illustrate how audience members sought to deploy and reconstitute influence in the organisational use of management ideas against the background of their role and main orientation.

Direction 1: Downward Influence. Our findings revealed that the audience members' deployment of influence in a downward direction is important in understanding the use of management ideas. In particular, we found accounts of relational interaction in which audience members drew on their personal skills to promote the use of management ideas in an organisational context in line with their views and interests, thereby seeking to shape organisational interpretations of managing and organising in a downward direction. For instance, a commercial director of a regional bank (TM) who signalled a primarily devoted orientation towards Guru B, explained how he habitually engages in low-profile talks with his four deputy directors and their sixty employees. These day-to-day talks were taken as an occasion to 'discuss' his experiences of the lecture by Guru B and the management ideas that were communicated during this event. These talks were used to influence how people lower in the hierarchy do their work:

> That is also a little bit part of my own character. What I always do is directly apply what I have learned. I take notes and I share them continuously. Look, these four managers, I talk to them on a weekly basis; also to the people in the department individually. That is very low profile. (Informant B14)

Ideas he introduced after attending a lecture by Guru B concern, for example, how to stimulate people to improve their work and which mindset is needed for actually managing professionals who enjoy – according to Guru B – working autonomously without rigid control. This involved him drawing on his personal skills, such as via enthusiastically, albeit in a concealed manner 'spreading the word' every now and then, thereby seeking to influence other practitioners through the use of management ideas. He also gave the guru's book to one of his subordinates, a person who 'seeks to keep tight control' on how work is done, suggesting to him:

> 'Read that book at some point and, when you've finished it, I'd like to know what you think about it.' So, that's how I seed these things at the bank. It might take some time but I'm really positive about such gurus; they bring one-liners to us and we, as directors, use them. That's what I do with [guru books and lectures]. (Informant B14)

In addition, audience members also drew on management ideas to reconstitute the legitimacy of these personal resources. In the words of Informant B14, they 'translate them into what I myself regard as useful' and from which he expects '100 per cent positive results'. In this way, management ideas not only provide useful language to shape the understanding of organisational issues, but also offer a vocabulary through which audience members can maintain or enhance their relative power position in an organisational context. For instance, in a downward direction, one top manager in a large public sector organisation – who displayed a mainly non-committal orientation towards Guru B – described how he used the notes that he made during the guru lecture to convincingly clarify the official management view on particular matters to one of his subordinates in a performance interview:

> This morning, for example, I had a performance interview with an employee. And I needed arguments to be more convincing and that was what this is about. Because [the subordinate] is not guided by the interests of the organisation but he is a real professional [lawyer] who is unable to switch . . . from his professional perspective to what the organisation regards as important . . . This [concept from the lecture] I can use very well, so then I select that . . . so that this person understands how I think about it at that moment. (Informant B2)

Direction 2: Lateral Influence. The analysis also indicated that audience members construct the use of management ideas through the deployment of influence in a lateral mode. This entails drawing on their social skills as a critical resource in convincing organisational members in similar hierarchical positions of the value of particular management ideas, thereby promoting their own understanding of organisational issues. One of the informants, an internal advisor providing audit, tax and advisory services within an international company, whilst displaying a both an engaged and a critical consumption orientation, indicated that by sharing what she had learned during the lecture by Guru A, she promoted the personal and organisational benefits of Guru A's ideas among her direct colleagues:

> So, I really learned something new from [Guru A], an effective method that I could actually use the day after the lecture without much additional study and reading; for me it entailed a substantial change in my own habitual way of working. Yes, and afterwards I shared the ways of working and the methods that I learned. I disseminated them throughout the department because I thought others would be able to benefit from it. It also made others follow his lecture. (Informant D3)

However, we also found that audience members drew on the management ideas conveyed during a guru lecture, or specific elements of them, in reconstituting influence as a form of power in (lateral) interaction with peers. This involves the construction of management ideas as a means to enhance an audience member's personal (expert) status amongst organisational members in relatively similar hierarchical positions. For instance, a leading economist employed at a large bank who demonstrated a non-committal and critical orientation towards Guru A indicated that she sought to demonstrate competence towards peers by signaling her access to certain prestigious items obtained during Guru A's lecture. In this case these items were then used as 'bridges' (Corrigan, 1995: 46) towards particular authoritative visions in the area of management and organisation:

> [Guru A] had a fair number of aphorisms about organisational change and the role of the manager, and they were all printed on these 'wisdom tiles'. So I took a couple of them home and, for a while, I used to put them in my colleagues' mailboxes. That was great fun and a good reason to talk about them. I also told them that I have the CD box [from the lecture] at my office and that everyone can come and borrow literature from me. (Informant A10)

She mentioned that one wisdom tile specifically helped her to improve the communication with her colleague about how to conduct an increasing number of dismissal interviews. As the bank was going through a reorganisation, the economist had noticed that doing these interviews was problematic for her colleague as they did not correspond with his self-image of 'Mr Nice Guy'. One tile about leadership served as a tool to have a discussion on how to take the lead in these 'rather unpleasant talks' and, in particular, how to finish them well. According to her colleague, she gave him this tile 'at just the right moment' providing him an extra 'boost' to change his perception and approach.

Direction 3: Upward Influence. A final form of influence-driven use of management ideas that emerged from the data is considered as part of upward interaction. We found that audience members in lower-ranked positions or staff functions, in particular, constructed the use of management ideas primarily through the deployment of personal social resources to shape the views of powerful others in line with their specific interests. An internal senior consultant of a large bank (Informant C1), who was a member of a team of five consultants, specified the significance of using his social skills to convince higher-level managers of the added value of a particular management idea. As he has no managerial authority, he generally seeks to employ 'a ruse' to enhance the possibility of putting a specific issue on the corporate agenda. Whilst displaying both engaged and non-committal orientations, the input this management practitioner received by regularly attending guru lectures was constructed as a means to convince those in higher-ranked positions:

> Then I am talking about coming up with ruses with which I can [convince] our management to first discuss this just within [our internal consultant team] and then indicate how this can help them progress. And then at a certain point in time, the subject can be prioritised collectively . . . I really have to come up with a ruse, because taking that kind of strategy development to a higher level, that absolutely exceeds my circle of influence. (Informant C1)

Also, in an upward motion, the data revealed various accounts of relational interaction in which management practitioners as audience members drew upon a management idea in strengthening their position with respect to influence as a form of personal power. As such, this influence becomes apparent when management ideas provide audience members in lower hierarchical levels or staff functions with an opportunity to become recognised as experts on issues that people in higher levels consider valuable to the organisation. In this way, signalling expertise in management ideas, for instance by attending guru lectures, allows audience members to gain better access to conversations with organisational members in more powerful positions, and to have more resources to convince them. Informant B12, working in a middle management function at a municipality, in the following quotation, described this form of upward influence related to civil servants changing their way of working. Although he displayed a predominantly non-committal orientation towards the lecture of Guru B on how to lead professionals, he 'got convinced that this is the [timely] way of working' and that they cannot 'carry on' like they did.

> I used [Guru B's] general account to elaborate what we are working on right now. Because in our sector we are working on an organisational development, and in

two weeks I am going to take it to the management team, to sound it out, to discuss it: is this the new direction? Can we agree on the way we need to manage? And, if so, are we going to record these agreements in the annual plan? So [Guru B] taught me to just present these things in the management team. We just need to keep up with the times and reposition ourselves. (Informant B12)

Deploying and Reconstituting Force

A second form of power intimately connected to the way audience members constructed the organisational use of management ideas involves the recursive deployment and reconstitution of force. Whereas influence is associated with personal sources of power and the use of informal networks, our findings indicated that force is tied to the legitimacy of formal positions that may grant management practitioners the authority to restrict particular actions of others (see also Lawrence et al., 2001; 2005). However, similar to influence, we could discern interactions in different directions associated with this form of management idea use, although we found few accounts of upward interactions. See Table 7.2 for an overview and exemplary evidence. Again, for each relevant direction (downward and lateral) we outline and illustrate how audience members may deploy and reconstitute force in the organisational use of management ideas against the background of their role and main orientation.

Direction 1: Downward Force. Deploying force emerged from our data as an important form of power through which individual audience members constructed the use of management ideas in a downward interaction with other organisational members. In particular, audience members' accounts revealed that they drew on their formal position in the organisation as a resource in their accounts of the uptake of a particular management idea conveyed during a guru lecture. The informants indicated that constructing particular ideas via the deployment of a downward force is primarily associated with promoting their own specific understanding of organisational issues and at the same time limiting the interpretations and discretionary actions of members in lower hierarchical positions. For example, Informant B1, previously a manager of a large bank who started his own consulting business, was hired by his former employer as an interim manager for realising a particular strategic project. As the project was evolving, it became clear that he had to deal with the tension between the need to finish the project on time because it would end soon, and to give these people some space in order to 'to get the best out of them' (Informant B1). In relation to the ideas presented by Guru B (to which he showed both an engaged *and* critical orientation), he

Table 7.2 *Deploying and reconstituting 'force': overview and exemplary evidence*

Primary direction	Deploying and reconstituting force: Illustrative examples	Formal role	Main orientation
Downward	*Deploy* Well, I put that idea to a manager of our office. I told him 'I heard this account yesterday or the day before, let's see what you can do with it'.	*Informant B14* TM in large organisation	Devoted
	Reconstitute What I did, and it did work here, is indicate to that group of professionals that they should realise what I'm doing. Realise that I am your shield and that we, me, but they too should carry that responsibility towards higher management.	*Informant B1* SE in small organisation	Engaged Critical
Lateral	*Deploy* My business partner is an ex-sportsman, and those people are not necessarily good managers. He is very operational, so that was very difficult. So what I did was put some of the statements of that day on paper and send them to him with the remark that we have to talk about it together. At first he was a little sceptical, but in the end he realised that it was only a good thing.	*Informant A7* SE in small organisation	Non-committal Critical
	Reconstitute Yes, it does bestow some status towards colleagues and principals. People are able to say that they attended a lecture by [guru]. It heightens your prestige that you attended a couple of these lectures. And then people don't even have to remember the content, but the name will speak for itself.	*Informant D1* MM in large organisation	Engaged Non-committal Critical

described how he used his legitimate organisational position to arrange different sessions in which he directed his subordinates in their thinking about how the project should take shape:

And what I did then was schedule a couple of sessions with a group of about fifteen professionals in which I did emphasise the 'beginning with the end in mind', which is one of those things of [the guru] that works. I asked 'guys, where do we want to go together?' And that is how I used that, just scheduling these two sessions and giving direction together, not more than that. ... giving direction to each professional and to what is his [sic] contribution for the next two months. (Informant B1)

In addition, accounts showed that, in using management ideas, individual audience members not only deployed force as a form of power in pursuing their interpersonal objectives, but also drew upon management ideas in reconstituting this specific form of power. This refers to accounts of relational interaction through which audience members sought to shape other practitioners' views of the appropriateness of using force in relation to particular organisational roles and the audience members' alignment with these role expectations. The head of the HR department of a Dutch university, who displayed a primary engaged orientation towards a lecture by Guru B that she had attended, described how she used a management idea obtained from the lecture to enforce what she viewed as her legitimate position in relation to her subordinates:

Simply knowing the way their senior management wants to go, provides them with a sense of direction. ... also the idea that the vision that I have in mind implicitly, to put that on paper. And now I have the time for that. So that I should not take over things from them, but that I just have to ... I have to frame it for them. They just need someone who explains the frameworks within which they may operate ... So yes, this allowed me to limit my anxiety and enhanced my trust, also in my staff. (Informant B16)

Direction 2: Lateral Force. The findings also revealed how, in an organisational context, using management ideas entails the deployment of force in relational interaction of a lateral kind. This involves audience members drawing upon their extant hierarchical position in the organisation to stimulate direct colleagues to use particular ideas primarily to impose specific interpretations and promulgate the appropriateness of particular actions and downplay 'alternative' views that may be put forward by others. For example, one of the directors of a language training institution (Informant B9), and a regular lecture attendee, described how she sought to push particular ideas forward amongst the other members of the management team that she had obtained from attending a lecture by

Guru B. After the lecture, in relation to which she primarily displayed an engaged orientation, she found it useful to talk about it with her peers, in this case a colleague who is also a management team member: 'I outlined the general message [of Guru B] and indicated that I find it important, and would like to do something with it' (Informant B9). Specifically, this informant's account indicates that, by using management ideas communicated during the guru lecture in this way, she sought to enhance her leverage over others and thereby shape the organisation in line with her view:

> So, I discussed the lecture with him in general terms and stressed the significance of actually using some of the ideas. Also I proposed a number of changes that I find important to make amongst our young and older staff members, such as related to the e-learning trajectory; I told him that this is one area in which I would use the ideas . . . (Informant B9)

The analyses revealed that, also in a lateral direction, individual audience members used management ideas promoted during guru lectures in reconstituting force as a power-related resource amongst their peers in an organisational context. Informants' accounts showed that guru lecture attendance and 'knowledge' about the presented management ideas were exercised to contribute to their 'esteemed position' (Lull, 1980: 206), or form of expert power within the organisation. Informant A4, for example, a manager in the government of a small city, explained how she used insights obtained during the lecture of Guru A (to which she showed a mainly devoted orientation) as a way to back-up and push a long-held desire to introduce her view – towards her direct colleagues – on how the various departments are to be designed:

> I never got the co-operation [from other organisational members] to do things differently, more flexibly. But now I can say 'guys, these are insights that have been researched and are backed up with literature. They show that diversity offers a range of possibilities.' . . . I'm looking for more flexibility and that is why I do that. (Informant A4)

Deploying and Reconstituting Domination

A third form of power through which audience members constructed the use of management ideas in an organisational context involves domination. In contrast to other forms of power discussed above, domination is not so much about shaping an idea's perceived relative advantage nor the appropriateness of specific actions, but rather about shaping encompassing systems aimed at enhancing control over others (cf. Lawrence et al.,

Table 7.3 *Deploying and reconstituting domination: overview and exemplary evidence*

Primary direction	Deploying and reconstituting domination: Illustrative examples	Formal role	Main orientation
Downward	*Deploy* As a result of that lecture I changed my department. And I appointed a top-ranking official so that all of that could be centralised, all the administrative tasks.	*Informant B18* TM in large organisation	Engaged
	Reconstitute So now I am working on it to see how we can use and abuse these quotes for an argumentation of functions and functionalities within the software. To advance the management conscience of these lawyers.	*Informant A6* TM in small organisation	Engaged

2001, 2005). Even though domination is generally conceptualised as a systemic form of power, we found that its deployment and reconstitution in the social use of management ideas is associated with audience members' initiatives and their access to critical resources. Our analysis indicated that, in an organisational context, these resources particularly relate to audience members' ability to shape organisation-wide control systems, and their possibilities in steering decision-making on the initiation of formal change programmes designed to institutionalise these systems. Perhaps unsurprisingly we only found this form of power in relation to *downward* interactions. See Table 7.3 for an overview and exemplary evidence. We now outline and illustrate how audience members may deploy and reconstitute dominance in the organisational use of management ideas against the background of their role and main orientation.

With regard to deploying domination as a relevant form of audience members' use of management ideas, the informants indicated that an organisation-wide uptake of ideas conveyed at a guru lecture is unlikely without individuals holding the ability to control organisational members in less dominant positions. In this way, audience members may further regulate others' behaviour in relation to their access to valued material and immaterial resources. For example, a high-level manager at a large bank specified how the deployment of dominance had been key in ensuring the take-up of ideas from guru lectures in his organisation. In particular, he had decided to dispense with the current administrative system of registering working hours for his direct subordinates. While this created confusion amongst his subordinates, his aim was to shape the organisation in line with his view of Guru B's idea that professionals work best if granted a high level of autonomy:

> The first thing I got rid of was registering working hours. Well, people got confused. But it is a burden to me, because what should I do with all these reports? It is very time consuming to make these reports, so we dispensed with them. I only want to see the results. So, we are going to look at the output. But how can we measure that? I say 'if you want to be professionals, then you have to look at your own results and I am not going to measure you all the time'. (Informant B4)

Similar to the other two sources of power (influence and force), we noted that managerial audience members also used management ideas derived from lectures to reconstitute domination as a power base in their organisational contexts. The informants experienced that in downward interactions, dominant actors sought to shape others' perceptions of role expectations concerning their own specific positions (for example by framing them in terms of professionals, such as in the exemplary quote from Informant B4), and the power attributed to these positions in organisations. The use of management ideas may then confirm the audience members' central role in decision-making about control systems in the organisation and in initiating programmes aimed at changing these systems. A director of a local school, for example, used the ideas obtained from the lecture and the status of the specific guru to make clear that experienced, long-term teachers also might need to obtain new knowledge, such as how to use IT in the classroom. Telling experienced teachers that they did not have sufficient knowledge, 'would directly lead to a conflict' (Informant B5). Instead, he referred to the lecture of Guru B in relation to which he displayed a both devoted and critical orientation. During the interview he pictured how managerial audiences simultaneously draw upon their own resources to implement an idea in an organisation, whereas the concept itself is used to legitimise the proposed changes and their own roles as the initiators.

> And we are going to have young colleagues educate older colleagues ... and the fact that ... last week I gave a presentation in which I used that graph of [Guru B], with which you can show them that scientific research indicates [the decline of knowledge]. Well, and if you can indicate properly what research there is then that

saves you a lot of fighting to get things done. So, there is a need for a legitimation to say to people 'your knowledge is no longer at the level it should be'. (Informant B5)

Conclusion

This chapter sought to shed more light on managerial audience members' use of management ideas in an organisational context. After exploring in our previous chapters how management ideas are presented to encourage application, as well as how and why audience members' consumption orientations towards these ideas may vary, we moved our main focus to the organisational context as the assumed 'natural setting' of idea use. In particular Chapter 5 and Chapter 6 have provided important insight into the audience members' consumption orientation towards particular gurus and their ideas, but these analyses offered limited detail about how and why these particular individuals may use these ideas in an organisational context beyond the assumption that large numbers of organisations have formally adopted some of these ideas and have invested significant resources into change programmes aimed at implementing them. Drawing on studies of the social uses of mass media as an analytical lens, we explored different forms of power through which audience members, within the context of an organisation, construct the use of management ideas, and we set out to explain how these forms of power are deployed and reconstituted in the relative power positions these individuals hold towards different assumed targets of influence. The findings have a number of key implications for research on the flow of management ideas and studies on the impact of management gurus in particular.

First, by providing a broader view on the *nature of agency* that plays a role shaping the organisational use and ultimate impact of management ideas (see also van Grinsven et al., 2016), the findings presented in this chapter demonstrate that future analyses of the impact of these ideas need to move beyond the assumption that management idea use is primarily connected to dominance as a systemic form of power. As indicated above, prior studies of implementation consider the organisational use of management ideas mainly in relation to large-scale programmes aimed at achieving some form of system-wide changes at firm level (e.g. Ansari et al., 2014; Mueller and Whittle, 2011; Radaelli and Sitton-Kent, 2016; Reay et al., 2013). Yet, our data suggest a much larger range of forms of power through which individual audience members construct the use of management ideas in their respective organisational contexts (see Tables 7.1, 7.2 and 7.3). Specifically, the informants' accounts revealed how not only dominance, but also influence, and force are equally considered as relevant forms of power which are inextricably related to the organisational use of management ideas. The individual audience member's social use of management ideas in an organisational context is thus simultaneously related to the deployment of three different forms of power as it is a reconstitution of these same forms of power. This chapter stresses the significance of viewing audience members' agency in shaping the organisational impact of ideas not as a given, but in relation to available resources.

Second, by adopting a social use of media perspective we highlighted the *direction* of agency in the intra-organisational use of management ideas. The primary focus in the literature on organisational implementation is on how managerial agency influences the way ideas are adapted when they move from higher to lower hierarchical levels (e.g. Ansari et al., 2014; Reay et al., 2013), thereby easily viewing responses from people in subordinate positions in terms of their potential deviance from a managerial interpretation. Yet, rather than considering agency in the organisational use of management ideas mainly in terms of such a top-down direction, our analysis suggests the importance of accounting for multiple directions as audience members' accounts reveal how the forms of power are deployed and reconstituted in relational interactions of a downward, lateral or upward fashion. In other words, an individual audience member's social use of management ideas in an organisational setting not only varies in terms of how it becomes apparent in the deployment and reconstitution of resource-related power, but also depends on the relative power position towards their assumed targets, as they may be subordinates, peers or superiors.

Third, our analysis also contributes to the development of a more *differentiated view of the background and attitudes of the key agents* that play a role in the organisational use of management ideas. Prior work focusing on the organisational implementation of management ideas mainly depicts those in (top) management roles as particularly enthusiastic towards these ideas and considers them as vital carriers and an essential starting point for the organisational use of ideas. Yet, our findings indicate that management ideas do not only arrive in an organisation via those in management positions. Our focus on a wider variety of management practitioners participating in guru lectures allowed us to stress the role of audience members of different hierarchical levels as relevant in understanding the use of management ideas in an organisational setting. Organisations need to be considered as much more permeable to management ideas than is often suggested. In other words, although individuals in high-rank management positions are easily considered as some form of 'obligatory passage point' (cf. Bloomfield and Danieli, 1995) for management ideas to enter organisations, our findings clearly indicate that a much broader range of actors may be actively carrying ideas into organisations and contribute to and even promote their use. This suggests that management ideas may be seen as important resources for audience members in different organisational positions in a variety of interactions. Overall management ideas may thus 'enter' an organisation via a variety of different actors, and initiatives to use these ideas need to be seen as much more dispersed.

Finally, our findings indicate that management ideas enter an organisation not only via those who are unambiguously positive towards a particular guru or guru-led ideas. Given the main focus on managers' micro-level actions including those aimed at promoting a management idea amongst other organisational members (Gondo and Amis, 2013; Reay et al., 2013), prior studies of organisational implementation tend to suggest that audience members who display a primarily devoted orientation after media exposure are the ones who typically act as champions of ideas when they return to their respective organisations, thereby considering others only as recipients of their initiatives. Instead, we found accounts of the deployment of forms of power in relation to the use of management ideas amongst informants holding devoted, engaged, non-committal and critical consumption orientations as well as combinations of these. The informants' accounts clearly show that intra-organisational use is not restricted to audience members who display a primarily devoted orientation, but also involve actors with other or mixed orientations towards the gurus and management ideas promoted by them. As such, future analyses should be more sensitive towards organisational members' orientation towards particular management ideas and their orientation towards the specific managerial interpretation of these ideas.

We show that a broad range of actors with different orientations may be involved in carrying ideas into organisations and that their agency in shaping the organisational impact of these ideas is related to the resources available to them in the relative power position towards their assumed targets. This stresses the need to develop a more differentiated understanding of the consumer of management ideas in an organisational context, as well as the way ideas are handled (cf. van Grinsven et al., 2020). Yet, although the present chapter has advanced our understanding of the audience members' use of management ideas in organisational contexts, it provided little detail about how these ideas may be used beyond this specific setting. To gain further insight into this relatively unexplored area, Chapter 8 examines how audience members may extend their involvement with guru events, and the ideas that are promoted there, beyond immediate and organisation-related use. This is of particular significance because it enables researchers to shed light on the potential impact of management ideas in important but relatively neglected contexts.

8 Managerial Audiences and Fan Involvement

Throughout the book, and in the light of the broader flow of ideas, we have gradually shifted our focus from considering managerial audience members in relation to the mass communication setting within which management ideas are typically conveyed, to important social and situational contexts of idea use. The previous chapters revealed how, before management ideas are introduced into organisations, they are filtered and critically appraised via a primarily differentiated and volatile audience, as well as showing how audience members may subsequently construct the use of ideas in their particular organisational settings. With regard to the latter, our analysis in Chapter 7 showed how, within the context of organisations, audience members may construct the use of an idea through different forms of power and how these forms are deployed and reconstituted in the relative power positions the individuals hold towards different assumed targets of influence. These findings provide a broader and much more nuanced understanding of the background and orientation of those involved in the use of management ideas in organisations, as well as of the nature and direction of their agency.

Our analysis in Chapter 7 emphasised the need to study the social use of management ideas beyond a habitual focus on the organisational implementation of management-induced, organisation-wide change programmes, but has still paid scant attention to the possibility that using these ideas may also, and to a significant degree, occur beyond organisational settings. Therefore, in this chapter we focus on developing a broader understanding of the audience members' use of management ideas by asking: *How and why do audience members become involved in using management ideas in their wider social contexts?* Addressing this question is of particular significance since the prevailing view of management idea consumption remains limited to 'managers acting as active users of popular management concepts within their organizations' (Wilhelm and Bort, 2013: 428), thereby neglecting other, equally important, areas of potential impact. Indeed, assuming that managerial audiences adopt ideas via management gurus with a sole purpose of using them in organisational settings would be at variance not only with a view of consumption as central to everyday life (DuGay, 1996; Hancock and Tyler, 2019), but also with contemporary views of audience members as both spectators *and* performers, which is seen as particularly relevant in the context of new business media (e.g. Abercrombie and Longhurst, 1998; see also Hill, 2018). Viewing audience members in these different roles may shed essential light on a critical, but relatively neglected issue of how using ideas 'coincides with or even (re-)starts production' (Heusinkveld et al., 2011: 141). Analysing the in-depth interviews with the range of different audience members described earlier in the book (see Table 5.1), this chapter explores different forms of audience members' protracted involvement with ideas beyond their direct use in an organisational setting. We show how these forms vary significantly in their main drivers which are rooted in audience members' differential skills sets and relevant communities – outside the setting of an organisation – they relate to. In addition, we show how these skills are made productive via different identification and commodification practices, and explain how these have specific implications for how the production and consumption of ideas may relate.

Management Idea Use beyond Organisational Settings

Although much theorising tends to consider organisations as the primary social setting concerning the use of management ideas, a few studies also suggest the significance of processes across and beyond organisational boundaries. Overall, little is known about (1) how exactly management ideas may enter an organisation and (2) how organisations, and management practitioners in particular, may play a role in the further dissemination of these ideas.

First, whereas most studies suggest some form of external (mimetic) pressures as a main cue for internal processes of use (e.g. McCann et al., 2015; Morris and Lancaster, 2006; Reay et al., 2013), some have provided a few hints about how ideas may enter an organisation. For instance, in his detailed analyses, Zbaracki (1998) concluded that reports of TQM uses and successes in other organisations were considered important motivations for organisational members to initiate processes of implementation in their own organisation. More recently, a number of theorists took issue with the limited systematic research attention in the literature on management ideas to the way ideas may enter organisations. For instance, Radaelli and Sitton Kent (2016) identified 'idea acquisition' as one of the important micro-level practices aimed at the organisational implementation of ideas. However, whilst they found indications that management practitioners will access ideas via a variety of different channels, they also concluded, particularly with regard to middle managers (MM) that 'there is no available theory to explain how MMs assimilate and organize these inputs' (Radaelli and Sitton-Kent, 2016: 317). In line with this, Huising emphasised the need to gain more insight into the role of *extra-local communities* in relation to processes of idea implementation. She revealed how managers, acting as change agents in their organisations, had 'participated in BPR seminars, practice consortia, and bench visits, settings in which they could interact with others interested in BPR' (2016: 399). This analysis also indicated important changes in how these change agents view and may relate to this extra-local community, that is, from a source of information initially to a 'source of inspiration and a space of belonging' in later stages (Huising, 2016: 387).

Second, a number of the accounts signalled that extra-local communities may not only influence the use of ideas within organisations, but may, in turn, be shaped by organisational members and their specific experiences with using an idea. More generally, theorists have indicated that implementation experiences may have important implications for an idea's broader reputation and its related possibilities to become entrenched (Benders et al., 2019; Giroux, 2006; Scarbrough et al., 2015). More specifically, Zbaracki found different ways in which organisational members, and most notably those in management functions, sought to display what the organisation has done to various external (TQM) audiences such as TQM propagators in the field or other organisations interested in adopting TQM. In this way, managers sought to address an organisational need to 'display a positive image' (Zbaracki, 1998: 626) and personally 'take credit for successes' (Zbaracki, 1998: 627). These findings suggest that the organisational use – or highly stylised views of it – may thus also invigorate processes of diffusion: 'The seemingly innocuous managerial claims of success might ultimately fuel the fads and fashions that continually sweep through organisational practice' (Zbaracki, 1998: 632–3).

A small number of studies go even further by arguing that those directly involved in the organisational use of management ideas can simultaneously play a central role in processes of diffusion, thereby suggesting a further blurring of boundaries between 'producers' and 'consumers' of these ideas. As Sahlin-Andersson and Engwall write 'it is impossible to make a clear distinction between those creating, those mediating and those using ideas' (2002: 17). Similarly, Røvik (2011) suggested that, viewed from a virus perspective, management practitioners cannot be considered as 'pure' consumers of ideas as they are generally part of processes of co-production and co-consumption. In one of the few empirical studies on this issue, van Veen and colleagues (2011) provide a detailed account of how various management practitioners, after attending guru seminars and a series of company visits, not only used particular management ideas on Quality Management in their own organisations, but also actively promoted these ideas themselves. This demonstrates that in parallel to their role in implementing the ideas in their own organisation, management practitioners can translate their experiences into a more portable form, actively promote these ideas and facilitate other organisations in putting them into practice, or as van Veen and colleagues phrased it: "managers' involvement in the fashion process does not stop after the translation of a concept to their specific context. Simultaneously, they can become active carriers of this concept and are potentially diffusing it to other contexts' (van Veen et al., 2011: 160).

Thus, although in the current literature increased attention has been given to the actual use of management ideas in organisational contexts, little is known about how these ideas are used beyond this specific setting. To gain further insight into this relatively unexplored area, this chapter will draw on a spectacle/performance perspective (cf. Abercrombie and Longhurst, 1998), and studies of fans and fandom in particular. This growing literature has found that although fan(atic)s are easily viewed in pejorative terms, their omnipresence and wide acceptance marks the need to view them as a natural phenomenon in contemporary societies (Sandvoss et al., 2017). As Abercrombie and Longhurst have put it: 'ordinary audience members are more like fans and enthusiasts than might initially be thought' (1998: 122). In line with Sandvoss who considers fandom as 'the regular, emotionally involved consumption of a given popular narrative or text' (2005: 8), this chapter explores how audience members may extend their involvement with guru events and the ideas that are promoted there beyond immediate and organisation-related use. Based on our analysis of the interviews with sixty-eight audience members discussed previously (see also Table 5.1), we:

- identify three main forms of fan involvement associated with the use of management ideas which primarily occur outside an organisation (exaltation, socialisation and marketisation);
- explain how these forms relate to analytically distinct drivers and audience members' perceptions of differential identification and commodification practices.

Whereas the consumption of management ideas is typically associated with translating these ideas to audience members' own (organisational) context, the analysis shows that they may extend their (media) involvement beyond immediate and organisation-related use. The findings presented in this chapter shed important light on significant but relatively unexplored areas of potential impact related to the social use of these ideas. In addition, the chapter not only allows further exploration of why and how audience members may continue their involvement with a particular guru event, but also contributes to specifying whether and how they become productive (Jenkins, 2013) in relation to such an event and how this may impact the (re)construction of identities and the ideas related to the event. Finally, our analysis provides an important basis for rethinking the role of management practitioners and the nature of their work.

Fan Involvement and Management Ideas

Whilst the social use of management ideas is habitually connected to the intra-organisational translation of these ideas into practice, the informants' accounts include many references to uses of ideas unrelated to immediate organisational application. When we explored these references in more detail, we found that the consumption of management ideas needs to be considered as comprising a much broader variety of use, generally 'located' beyond organisational settings. In particular, in line with the spectacle/performance perspective as developed by Abercrombie and Longhurst (1998) the audience members stressed that the knowledge and skills that have been acquired via past experiences of media exposure, such as regularly attending guru lectures or reading management books, are made 'productive' through the way they construct and reconstruct themselves in relation to particular management ideas or management gurus (*identification practices*), as well as their protracted (re)construction of the language and related material artefacts that are obtained from, and associated with a guru event (*commodification practices*).

The analysis also indicated that these audience members have become productive beyond the Guru event in various analytically distinct ways, each associated with specific points of reference and related motivations, and having a specific bearing on the use of management ideas beyond the scope of a particular organisation. Indeed, whereas in some instances reference is made to an *imaginary relationship* between the audience member and the guru as driving the use of ideas, the informants also related 'use' to their embeddedness and status in an *imaginary management community* or their market value to *imagined consumers*. The audience members' accounts suggest varying degrees of fan involvement and association with more than one form of involvement (see Appendix A for an overview).

In the following sections we discuss three key forms of fan involvement that emerged from our analysis of the interview data discussed previously: (1) exaltation, (2) socialisation and (3) marketisation, and we explain how these forms relate to informants' perceptions of the main drivers and their typical (identification and commodification) practices (see Table 8.1).

Exaltation

One important form of managerial fan involvement that we found in our data we have termed 'exaltation'. This refers to a form of management idea use associated with addressing a need to establish and maintain an imagined relationship with a specific guru, idea or management genre, and is strongly related to heavy media exposure. Our informants indicated that they did not necessarily use guru lectures and the ideas promoted in these lectures for direct organisational application, but mainly to signal and explain their own specific taste concerning preferred approaches to management. In other words, rather than the question of how to put an idea into organisational practice, the central concern in exaltation involves: *How do I enable and justify a strong emotional attachment to a specific management idea, guru or management genre in general?*

Key Driver We found that exaltation as form of fan involvement was particularly motivated by a perceived individual need to establish and maintain a strong personal and often emotional attachment to a particular idea and/or guru, mainly as an end in itself. One experienced audience member – working at a large consultancy as a specialist in guiding consulting teams in processes of tendering and a heavy user of management training events – even perceived a clear analogy with the desire to bring about feelings associated with fan involvement in popular music: 'I think that it is partly a similar kind of feeling that you experience when you are fan of a popstar. It is always great to see such people in person and actually hear them telling their story' (Informant D3).

When talking about the guru lectures, a range of audience members recognised some form of individual passion for these ideas and experienced this as the main driver for their interest. For instance, informant C4 – a self-employed interim manager and certified Covey leadership trainer – framed attending guru lectures as 'a great present to myself'. He indicated that whilst guru events offer ample opportunities for networking, his primary aim is to establish some form of attachment to the ideas and the guru:

> The genuine goal is to advance my own knowledge development to consider whether the combination of guru book and theme really fits me and my

Table 8.1 *Forms of fan involvement, key drivers and main practices*

Form of fan involvement	Key driver	Main practices
Exaltation – *addressing and shaping (imagined) relationship demands with, or affective link to, specific guru, idea or management genre*	Establishment and maintenance of strong personal attachment to ideas and/or gurus as primary end in itself	• *Identification* – constructing elements of a guru or management idea in relation to or as part of themselves (e.g. via resembling or copying) • *Commodification* – displacing and reinvigorating language and representative artefacts of a guru event as part of ongoing matters in daily life
Socialisation – *addressing and shaping demands and expectations of imagined management community*	Establishment and maintenance of social position as member of imagined management community to enhance status and embeddedness	• *Identification* – using elements of a guru or management idea in constructing themselves in relation to a management community (e.g. via pretending, authenticating and transcending) • *Commodification* – using elements of a guru or management idea in creating and circulating specialised texts and materials as part of the habitual interactions in a loosely defined managerial (cult) community
Marketisation – *addressing and shaping demands and expectations of imagined consumer and general market*	Establishment and maintenance of position as innovative knowledge entrepreneur in an imagined market to enhance business	• *Identification* – using elements of a guru or management idea in constructing themselves as leading actor in a management knowledge market (e.g. via appraising and intermediating) • *Commodification* – using elements of a guru or management idea as part of addressing perceived market needs

passion – then I also delve into their books much more. This was clearly the case with Covey and Kotter. (Informant C4)

In line with this, another informant, holding a middle management level position in a regional governmental tax agency, also signalled an intrinsic drive to immerse himself in particular ideas and management thinkers who are promoting them.

The main reason for me is that I just really like to hear people talk about their ideas and motivations and what their main basis is of their theories as well as how they have developed them. [...] In that light I also tend to read guru books. [...] Often, I then would like to know more about the person, so I proceed collecting information. (Informant D6)

Various informants even explicitly referred to the role-related expectations typically associated with fans, thereby framing their seemingly unconditional attachment to ideas or gurus as a more or less natural condition. For instance, a manager employed at a large non-profit organisation who considered himself a regular visitor of guru events, linked his continued interest in reading and re-reading a specific management book with a view of himself as a fan: 'Yes, I'm a great fan of management books, particularly *Good to Great* by Collins. This is one of my favourite books, I really like this one. I read it twice – left it for two years and then read it again' (Informant D2). Indeed, referring to a fan role is considered an important way for audience members to signal and explain an ongoing desire to gain experiences connected to an idea or a person and related heavy media exposure. A manager from a petrochemical company reported that his colleagues recognised his intrinsic drive for developing strong attachments towards particular management ideas or gurus and, as a consequence, more or less automatically assumed interest in other guru related artefacts or events:

If my boss receives a management book then I often get it from him – he knows that I enjoy reading these books. I guess that most people in our company are not able to mention the big names. Perhaps they might have heard about Covey, but definitely not from Prahalad or Kotter. Most of them know that I like this kind of management literature and that I'm really interested in it [...] So in this case, attending a lecture by Covey is for my colleagues only a confirmation of what they already thought about my passion. (Informant C3)

Identification Practices With regard to exaltation, audience members are involved in constructing and reconstructing elements of a guru or their ideas in relation to themselves in various ways. First, in talking about these events, the use of guru ideas and lectures was being viewed as instrumental to define oneself via *resembling*. In particular, we found various instances in which informants expressed a desire to be similar to the star or the identity they were promoting. In wanting to be like particular promotors of management ideas, audience members constructed particular management thinkers as some kind of aspirational identity for themselves in their role as manager as well as citizen. In this way, they positioned themselves as eager followers of particular ideas and related thought leaders. One of our informants, a commercial director of a bank, emphasised his wish to bear a resemblance to Guru B and/or his ideas on leadership. In doing so, he constructed a view of himself in aspirational terms:

> Yes, I particularly experience no-nonsense and authenticity when he [Guru B] talks about his ideas. Also, humour is what characterises him; he also looks untouchable, independent and represents a powerful personality. These are things that I also would like to have a little bit more of. I'm impressed how he uses humour to address serious matters and right from the start he captures the attention of the group – that is really difficult and something I would like to master. These are the things I have great respect for. (Informant B14)

Second, in constructing themself as a person and/or management practitioner, audience members also identified with particular management ideas or gurus as expressed via accounts of *copying*. This is shown by audience members articulating a view of 'self' as being formed by emulating elements that are typically associated with particular gurus and their ideas. In other words, to enhance personal attachment, audience members thus sought to model themselves on a star or the ideology they are promoting. One example comes from a primarily devoted organisational member employed at a large bank tasked with IT security issues in relation to sales, who explicitly recognised that he sought to mimic Guru A's presentation style:

> He discussed a lot of different topics and was able to maintain the audience's attention to his story. And if you're able to keep people involved during your lecture, then you're simply a very good speaker. It also signals his own involvement in the subject which I find very appealing. Personally, I also like to be highly involved in my work and like to talk about it. As such, I try to copy that from him or other people to use that in the message that I would like to convey to my colleagues in a few weeks, for instance to the management team. (Informant A16)

Commodification Practices In relation to exaltation our analysis revealed that matters concerning the knowledge commodity – the guru event – were being made 'productive' by audience members – they displaced and reinvigorated language and representative artefacts as part of their ongoing matters in daily life. By bringing the guru language or representative artefacts into their working life, audience members aimed at enhancing experiences of proximity, and signalling their attachment to their 'star' guru.

First, our informants explained that they sought to establish a strong attachment to a particular management guru via re-using the language this star typically draws upon in phrasing their management ideas. In this way, the audience members became textually productive through constructing everyday life in a particular guru's terminology. For instance, one staff member of a large bank tasked with strategy development in a role as internal consultant and highly experienced in attending guru events, explicitly used the language of one of the US Gurus as the main measure to consider a large change process in his organisation.

> Within our bank, a large change programme has been initiated with the inspiring term ... comprising the development and implementation of a new style of working. ... This involves a massive change trajectory. I really dug into this, and, in my view, it closely relates to [US Guru B's] way of thinking. In fact, [US Guru B] has inspired me to a large extent in the way I consider this trajectory as representative of the company's Works Council. Thus, I'm not directly responsible for this trajectory, but the Works Council follows that change trajectory closely and thoroughly and comments on it. It is also one of my main areas of attention. As such, I talk to programme managers of that trajectory on a regular basis, and the way I talk to them, view them and assess them is directly inspired by the ideas of [US Guru B]. (Informant C1)

Second, our analysis revealed that audience members not only seek to obtain management ideas and artefacts related to the knowledge commodity – the guru event – but also make them productive in some way. The interviews contain ample examples of audience members talking about getting hold of the obvious souvenirs, such as books authored by the guru and their lecture slides. In addition, our informants indicated that they may also collect artefacts that are connected to a specific guru event such as 'wisdom tiles' (Informant A10) displaying a telling aphorism from a management guru, and even more personal artefacts from a guru such as an autograph: 'During the lecture there was much interaction and at the end you could get his autograph ... and I did' (Informant D9). However, in relation to exaltation, these artefacts not only remain connected to the context of production, such as a guru lecture, they are also used by audience members to signal personal and emotional attachment thereby extending the relation between guru and audience member beyond a lecture setting. These guru-related artefacts are constructed and reconstructed in the context of everyday life as form of fan involvement. One informant, a manager in a local municipality, explained how she sought to maintain her personal association with Guru A and his ideas via the certificate that she obtained after attending the lecture:

Yes, I have put the certificate on my bulletin board. Initially, I did this just for myself to remember the lecture that I attended and to keep thinking about it. You have to continuously invite yourself to rethink this mainly because it is tempting to just keep on doing things the way you did them the day before. And such a certificate provides a good occasion. (Informant A4)

Overall, collecting material objects – gadgets – from the guru event is experienced as enhancing one's perceived proximity to the guru's realm, as well as an opportunity to construct life in terms of particular stars and the ideas that they represent. Here, audience members were not so much engaged in translating guru ideas into their own management and organisational practice. Rather, audience members primarily used key elements from these events to signal some form of attachment with particular management ideas or those that promote them.

Socialisation

Another notable form of fan involvement that emerged from our analysis we describe as 'socialisation'. In their accounts of the guru event, the audience members referred to a use of ideas that is not related to specific organisational contexts, but one that is primarily associated with their engagement in a broader management community. This form of use is thus not concerned with translating particular ideas into practice, but mainly with the question: *How do I establish and maintain a legitimate position in a management community, and contribute to the further development of this community?*

Key Driver Our informants related 'socialisation' as form of fan involvement to the perceived individual audience members' needs to address the assumed demands and expectations of an imagined management community, primarily to enhance their status and social embeddedness in this community. Particularly, audience members present a view in which they stress a general need to engage with the subculture that has developed around management as an occupation. For instance, one top manager from a large bank, showing a mainly engaged orientation in his role as audience member of Guru B's lecture, emphasised the significance of the role-related expectations for management practitioners that are associated with what he referred to as a 'management cult'. Although he signals some discomfort with the assumed pressures that emanate from these expectations, he also appreciates the genre: 'Well, a number of these gurus are really good and their ideas very useful. However, there is also some kind of guru event attendance cult thereby assuming that if you attend these guru lectures then you're automatically up to date' (Informant B4).

Overall, the informants indicate that a perceived need to relate to an imagined management community is not only associated with a desire for some kind of belonging or social embeddedness in a community of people that share a particular occupation, but is particularly connected to a longing for social status in this community. Specifically, being actively engaged in a broader management community may signal the availability of time and monetary resources which, in turn, are considered necessary conditions for addressing a wish to access this community, such as via regular guru lecture attendance. One experienced management practitioner and heavy media 'user' formulated this as follows:

> There is an emerging belief in the market that it's very prestigious to go to the lecture of those who ask a lot of money. It's an expensive environment, including good food, comprising multiple days and overnight accommodation which I think is not really necessary. In that case gurus are only used to enhance people's status. If you did not attend the latest event, it gives the impression that you're lagging. Guru lectures may contribute to creating an image of someone who wants to be up to date and modern, absorbs the latest insights and spends a lot on the opportunity to participate in discussions on a certain level. (Informant D1)

Identification Practices With regard to socialisation, we found that audience members used gurus and their ideas in constructing themselves as members of a broader management community. As such, whilst management ideas and management gurus are seen as an important component of this community, our informants explain that they tend to express identification not with these ideas or star persons per se, but primarily with the subculture that has developed around it. Thus, using management ideas serves mainly as a function to position a person in an imaginary network of like-minded people who share particular specialised management-related interests. In this context, audience members contribute to a view of themselves as someone being part of that cult albeit in a way that hints at some form of social hierarchy.

First, the analysis of the audience members' accounts revealed that, in talking about guru lectures and management ideas, they constructed themselves via *pretending* to be part of an imagined community. It involved signalling the aspiration of being a recognised member of a management community in response to role-related expectations. These audience members typically embraced the need and the willingness to learn the cultural repertoire and develop as a manager as a critical part of themselves. For instance, one of the audience members embraced being part of a management community as an aspirational identity and considered attending a guru lecture as an important means to address a perceived lack of experience.

We attended the lecture with four relatively new managers, all trying to find their place in this job, and exploring how one would deal with things. We are also part of a department mainly consisting of technicians remotely so we had the feeling that we could use some guidelines given this particular group. … I found the lecture very useful particularly given the fact that I just started in a management role and still need to learn everything. Someone who has been in such a job for twenty years might view things differently, but for me it is all new. … I would definitely recommend this to people who just started in a management job because you hear many things that you can use in your work. Particularly in the first few years you need to learn a lot and this lecture offers a large number of tips and tricks. (Informant A16)

Second, we found that some audience members talked about themselves in relation to guru lectures through *authenticating* their membership of an imagined community. This involved presenting a view of 'self' as being an experienced and genuine member of the managerial community. In constructing themselves in this way, reference was generally made to their extensive experiences in attending guru lectures which, at the same time, allowed them to distinguish themselves from relative novices in the field of management. Indeed, informants explained that a lack of substantial managerial knowledge not only hampers effectively generating value from attending guru lectures, but also undermines the possibility to genuinely construct oneself as being an established member of the management community. A top manager from a telecommunication company who had attended Guru A's lecture identified the possession of background knowledge as important in becoming engaged in a managerial subculture, thereby simultaneously presenting a view of himself as experienced and knowledgeable:

I think that it requires some background to attend these lectures. If you are still a rookie in management then you really have to work very hard to absorb all this and translate it to your own situation. … Of course, it is good when young managers who have never heard Covey or Kolter attend these lectures, but it would be better if you knew some of the basics. Concerning Covey, his book on the seven habits represents a number of things that I find important and recognisable when they are being discussed during the lecture, but if a novice is just being thrown in at the deep end, I think that they will leave the place less enthusiastically. (Informant A17)

Third, our analysis also indicated that some audience members' accounts of the guru lectures comprised views of themselves as frontrunners in the management community by ways of what can be phrased as *transcending* the general level of knowledge and involvement in the imagined community. This means that in their talk, they presented a view of 'self' as a member of the management community that, to a certain degree, leads the way on issues of management and actively enthuses others to follow suit. Particularly, by constructing themselves as engaging in circles of management thinkers, these audience members sought to develop a perception of themselves as relative insiders thereby enhancing their social position. As Informant C5 – a senior consultant from a large consultancy – noted: 'yes, it certainly enhances your status when you can say "I had lunch with Covey last week".' Thus, having a brief conversation with a guru shortly after their lecture was not necessarily considered as a way to amplify or intensify their experience, but primarily to support the construction of their social status by signalling audience members' connection to a producers' network as well as the ability to converse with them at seemingly the same level. Managerial audience members sought to derive their social status via constructing themselves in proximity to gurus as well as creating the impression that they can have conversations on relatively equal terms and may even contribute to the further development of the gurus' ideas albeit in more individual-level interactions (cf. Chapters 3 and 4). A top manager in a healthcare organisation expressed this viewpoint:

> I found it rather remarkable because a few days after Guru B's lecture I had a meeting with a number of HR advisors. I told them that I attended that lecture and they were very impressed that I had read Guru B's books and had actually seen him in person. So, for them he genuinely has a guru status. For us it is way to learn and prevent any stagnation in the organisation. In the disabled care sector, we are a big player, and thus others look at us to take the lead in addressing issues in this sector. So, we feel a great responsibility to keep things in motion. (Informant B3)

Commodification Practices From our analysis, a number of audience practices related to the guru event – as management knowledge commodity – emerged as critical in defining the shape of socialisation as a form of fan involvement. In particular, we found that audience members provided detailed accounts of the various ways in which they have engaged in creating and circulating specialised talk and texts as part of the habitual interactions in a loosely defined managerial (cult) community.

First, the data showed that audience members became textually productive via constructing and reconstructing the management ideas and related artefacts derived from guru events in such a way that it helped *entering* networking activities. In other words, audience members adapted the guru's lecture in such a way that it could be used as some form of 'entry ticket' to be able to participate in what are generally considered as regular managerial community-related activities. Our informants indicated that this may occur particularly via making detailed comparisons between ideas and the gurus that are promoting them. Through the practice of comparing, audience members not only displayed their prior experiences in engaging with well-known management gurus but also developed an important base for 'valuation' (cf. O'Mahoney et al., 2013), that is, showing their ability to their peers to distinguish good from bad taste in management ideas. This can, for instance, be seen in the following account from a bank manager who – interestingly in the light of Chapters 3 and 4 – in his comparisons referred to the speaking styles of different US gurus:

> [US Guru A] is always interesting and dynamic. I found [US Guru B] also great, and particularly recently better than in his first years. [US Guru C] was much more interesting than I expected. I now better understand the Balanced Scorecard – you could very well compare it to Six Sigma. [US Guru B] is just good particularly because of his story about the iceberg – I also liked his style. [US Guru A] also has a great style, but is a bit more, you have to like it – I can understand that some people don't. (Informant C6)

In this way, management practitioners not only aimed at reconstituting their status in the managerial community, but also contributed to reinforcing a view of some ideas and experiences as a 'normal' part of the body of management knowledge. A self-employed consultant explained how she would refrain from talking about her participation in guru events in more formal communication, but emphasised their importance in other, more informal occasions:

> I would not put it on my CV that I have attended particular guru lectures, but I would definitely refer to it if I wanted to join a particular conversation. In this way you can signal that you have experienced things and therefore have something to say. Partly it is a status thing. You are expected to come up with something new and if you can mention that you've attended these events, then it likely increases your value and perceived status – although it is obviously not the same as a large car or such. (Informant D8)

Second, another important way in which audience members become textually productive in relation to guru lectures involves *enthusing* others in their network about particular management knowledge commodities. This set of commodification practices contributed to socialisation as a form of fan involvement through translating guru ideas and related artefacts into textual recommendations to other management practitioners. This was expected to contribute to the further dissemination of the ideas presented in the guru lecture as well as to the further development of the managerial community and subculture that is generally associated with these ideas. We found various instances in which audience members sought to re-invigorate interest for particular lectures, books and articles amongst their peers in their network situated outside their organisation. For example, a director of a service company described this as follows:

> I'm part of a network of about fifteen entrepreneurs in [city X] which comes together once a month. It appeared that one of them – I did not know that – had also attended the guru event, so it became a 'hook' for a conversation about the contents. In such a case, everybody has their own typical question about it – one of them asked about facilities and how many security people were working at the event – but overall, I tend to speak enthusiastically about my experiences and how I look back on that day my own way. From these fifteen entrepreneurs, I think that four indicated that they would have joined me if I had asked them. But there are also others who say: nice to hear this, but that would do nothing for me. (Informant D15)

In addition, the informants' accounts indicated that the creation and circulation of texts may also occur via virtual communities. This shows that knowledge commodities were used by audience members to involve other people in sharing their interests, in particular management ideologies via various channels such as LinkedIn:

> I posted a message on LinkedIn particularly to share my enthusiasm about that guru event. Just to show that it was really interesting and something that could be recommended for people who are looking for things in this area. In response to that, I received a number of personal messages from people who asked why I decided to attend the event, how it was, and whether it could be of interest to their organisation ... In general, I really enjoy thinking about how it could apply to others and in particular when others then respond to that. In that case you have a really nice conversation which may also be beneficial to you. It becomes a sort of productive interplay. (Informant D14)

Third, some informants also referred to socialisation in relation to translating the gurus' ideas and related artefacts into texts comprising their own specific storyline. We found various occasions where audience members talked about producing 'new' articles based on the gurus' ideas as well as the possibilities to shape their texts in such a way that it appeals to their peers, as one consultant explained: 'What is currently on my to-do list, following from the guru lecture, is to internally and externally publish an article on Porter. The lecture encouraged me to further disseminate the ideas' (Informant C1). In this way, a knowledge commodity such as a guru event was used by audience members to produce text that effectively promotes their own specific management style and view on management in a management community. This form of textual production was thus not only aimed at amplifying the attention to particular gurus and their ideas, but also at potentially shaping a managerial community by encouraging others to follow a particular interpretation of it. For example, a leading accountant, responsible for professional quality and related education efforts for 160 accountants working at a large number of different offices, talked about Guru B in terms of using him for disseminating a particular ideology amongst leading professionals. In addition, this informant also stressed the significance of having some self-confidence as being essential to engage in the textual reproduction of gurus' ideas:

> Because of my study in business administration I got the opportunity to deepen my initial specialisation, that is, accounting, and I even wrote a number of articles. I think that without my business administration study I couldn't have written these articles, at least, I wouldn't have had the courage to write them. But now I think I can do it mainly because I have got the tools to write via that study which particularly enhanced your self-confidence about how an article should be written. At the same time, I recognise that I'm not yet an advanced storyteller. (Informant B7)

Marketisation

A final important form of fan involvement associated with management ideas that could be discerned from the data analysis is what we term 'marketisation'. Similar to the first two forms – exaltation and socialisation – discussed above, the informants' views indicated that marketisation constitutes a way of using management ideas that is unrelated to their more or less direct translation into organisational practice. Rather, in relation to the guru lectures they have attended, various audience members talked about the use of these ideas as primarily aimed at addressing and shaping expectations of imagined consumers or the general market, thereby enhancing their own business. Exemplifying this form of involvement was an account of Informant C5, a consultant and heavy 'user' of guru events, as he explicitly indicates that management ideas are not primarily used in the context of his or his clients' organisation, but in the context of developing a market relation:

> Indeed, I did not translate this lecture into action, nor did my clients. Rather, it has been good to spend a day together and have the chance to talk and share thoughts – in fact it did not change anything, it is primarily aimed at networking. (Informant C5)

Unsurprisingly we found accounts about this type of involvement mainly amongst audience members with a consulting background, as well as amongst those audience members that are considered to be potential clients of consulting services. Whatever their background, overall the audience members engaged in marketisation are mainly concerned with the question: *How do I establish and maintain a position as an innovative knowledge entrepreneur in the management knowledge market?*

Key Driver With regard to marketisation as form of fan involvement, audience members explained that they are not driven by the expectations of a specific management community per se, but mainly by what they experience as 'the market'. Here reference is typically made to the assumed 'needs' in the universe of an imagined consumer in the context of a general management knowledge market, particularly those needs that are still in a latent and relatively undefined stage. In addressing these consumer needs, audience members indicated that they sought to capitalise on the opportunities offered by the fact that some management ideas have become widely accepted – as they are promoted by recognised authorities in the field.

I have my own company and made a deal with myself that every year I need to attend at least one lecture including one or two speakers. In this way, I take care of my own 'research and development'. ... I'm not sure whether visiting particular lectures directly enhances my status or my market reputation, but there are occasions where I would mention that these are part of my own development and I think that a client always wants to see that: those who are helping me are dedicated to developing themselves. (Informant C4)

In their accounts, the informants stressed that adequately addressing these assumed consumer needs is not an end in itself, but of critical importance in generating paid assignments. As such, management ideas and guru lectures were intimately connected to creating possibilities for audience members to maintain or enhance their own business. An inability to adequately address the demands and expectations of the imagined consumers is generally viewed as undermining one's reputation and hampering potential commercial successes. This became apparent in the account of one of the audience members who works for a large and established consultancy:

Yes, if clients ask questions that most likely stem from reading particular management books, then we also have to know these books. We always have to be able to make connections between the client and their specific world on the one hand and on the other hand the ideas and theories that are available in this world. If a client says that they have read something and your answer is 'please give me two weeks to also read it', then you're not doing a very good job. (Informant C5)

Identification Practices In our analysis of the data we found that audience members actively constructed a sense of self in terms of some form of aspirational elite identity (Visscher et al., 2018) in relation to a management knowledge market in various ways.

First, audience members were involved in *appraising* themselves as possessing valuable management knowledge. In this context, the use of powerful management ideas and management thinkers was seen as instrumental to presenting a view of themselves as leading management progress, thereby contributing to a favourable reputation within the market. Indeed, our informants emphasised the significance of the ability to capitalise on their reputation – such as emanating from guru lecture attendance – in addressing the assumed needs of imagined consumers. One experienced management practitioner explained this as follows:

> Yes, it enhances your status towards colleagues and clients if you could say that you have attended a lecture by Mintzberg. Attending a number of these events has a bearing on your prestige, irrespective of the contents and the specific names. Consultants can then say they are aware of the most recent developments because they go to particular gurus and are involved in developing these ideas. Clients really like to hear this until it is factored in the price. (Informant D1)

Second, in the accounts of the informants we also found that they constructed themselves through *intermediating* – portraying themselves in terms of helping consumers make sense of management ideas on the one hand, and their own specific situation on the other. Our analysis indicated that the ability of audience members to connect gurus and their ideas to potential client problems, and adequately presenting themselves as the one possessing the appropriate reputation and repertoire to adequately use these ideas to solve the specific client issues, is seen as critical in maintaining their business. As one consultant explained:

> [Consultancy X] is one of the oldest consulting firms in the Netherlands. It has a good name that is associated with being a little headstrong, and we like that image. As such, we generally don't follow management hypes but tend to get the knowledge directly from the source. That is the main reason why we invite these gurus and bring them here ... Those four names generally appeal to all our clients – they are famous people who have been around for a long time in the world of management. So, it is not only what we think is important but also what our clients expect from [consultancy X] and identify us with. (Informant C5)

Commodification Practices The main commodification practices related to marketisation that we found in the accounts of the audience members involved adapting guru-related language and their ideas as part of client concerns such as via (1) legitimating particular products and services, (2) explicating and steering potential client concerns and (3) developing a broader repertoire that can be drawn upon immediately when opportunities may occur.

A first set of commodification practices that were experienced by audience members as relevant as part of marketisation focused primarily on using guru ideas from guru lectures in further enhancing their reputation as well as that of their products and services. In this way, audience members did not seek to translate these ideas into organisational practice, but sought to textually process the ideas in such a way that it fits their commercial offerings. For instance, one director of a company who had attended an event by Guru A considered reconstructing this guru's texts as part of the marketing of his software packages aimed at law firms.

I did not specifically use it to consider my own situation, but I'm planning to use relevant quotes from management gurus on our website as a commercial hook to promote our software. So, I'm seriously exploring how we can use these quotes to support the functionalities within that software, and at the same time enhance the management awareness of the lawyers and make them just better entrepreneurs. (Informant A6)

In addition, this director also emphasised that his efforts related to incorporating the guru's ideas and language into his software packages. In this way, management ideas are not rewritten to support the legitimation of particular products, but essentially become materialised in some form as a part of a commercial product that is offered on the market.

Well, I try to remember the lecture in the sense that, in the light of the computerisation of law firms we seek to include management ideas in our software. In this way we feel we can better understand the clients' working processes and provide better support. For instance, we have considered how our software could indicate the 'bottlenecks' in client organisations and similar things. (Informant A6)

A second set of commodification practices was considered as contributing to processes of market-related agenda setting. Various informants emphasised their involvement in reconstructing the ideas presented at guru lectures as part of convincing potential clients that particular managerial issues should be seen as relevant to them. Their accounts suggested that they drew on guru events and ideas to explicate and shape opportunities amongst key individuals in client organisations and generate fee-paying assignments. For instance, in line with the image that informant C5 sought to convey to his potential clientele, he saw co-organising and attending guru events as an important occasion not only to identify himself with star management thinkers, but also to build relationships with potential clients and influence their agenda.

I had good conversations with my clients, mainly because at these occasions you are not directly working on an assignment. Rather, it allows you to consider their organisation from a higher level of abstraction and ask: 'What do we see if we use this perspective to analyse your organisation?' This not only produces great conversations, but generally enhances the likelihood that, at a later stage, this client may think that they need to address particular issues in their organisation and then they will certainly come back and give us a call. So, it may give the clients an extra push in the right direction. Clients may ask me questions which I can then translate to the specific guru and indicate that we have an 'answer' that can be useful. (Informant C5)

One HR manager from a large healthcare institution also noted that in relation to guru events, she received invitations from various management knowledge entrepreneurs on a regular basis. She recognised that these invitations have to be seen in the light of marketisation – using guru lectures and guru ideas as part of relationship-building practices by firms with an interest in exploring possibilities for generating assignments. In relation to these occasions, informants recognised that people are not so much engaged in translating management ideas into organisational practice, but are mainly constructing such ideas as some kind of common ground to enhance the likelihood of establishing market relationships.

Yes, I do get these invitations, but that is generally relationship management – a particular firm that seeks to contact me mainly because of my function as HR manager. By inviting you to these events they try to get into a conversation. Afterwards, there is generally a network meeting in which people talk to each other on a relatively informal basis and try to do business. (Informant D10)

A third set of commodification practices that emerged from our analysis of the audience members accounts concerned (re-)constructing ideas and models promoted by gurus in their lectures into concrete guidelines, thereby making the ideas more operational and accessible. As such, the use of ideas from guru lectures is intimately connected to the development of an audience member's repertoire of legitimate language and tools. This repertoire is then assumed to enhance the likelihood of being able to offer an immediate and practical 'answer' to specific client questions (cf. Heusinkveld and Benders, 2005), or in the words of Informant C2: 'It's not about knowing everything from the book in general. Rather, and that is my main motivation, developing tools that an entrepreneur can use immediately to their advantage.' In line with this, Informant B6 explained his efforts in using elements that he obtained from attending Guru B's lecture in order to develop a repertoire to support the performance of his commercial projects:

I obtained the slides from [Guru B's] lecture and found them very useful. Incorporating these in our knowledge base is still an item on my to-do list. In these instances, we generally ask what elements from these lectures we can use for own knowledge base, and where we could refer to them at a later stage. As business consultants, we have a sort of repository within which we thematically seek to collect things. It is not really a formal knowledge system, but simply a collection of interesting things. If we do client projects, we do specific things in a start-up phase, a phase of analysis and an evaluation phase and each phase includes particular subjects and models. (Informant B6)

So overall, what we found in the interview data is that, in addition to the possibility of organisational use, audience members emphasise the significance of using gurus and their management ideas to commercial ends thereby indicating how they can be considered both as members of the audience and 'petty producers' (Abercrombie and Longhurst, 1998: 140).

Conclusion

This chapter sought to shed more light on a relatively unexplored area in the literature on the flow of management ideas, that is, the use of these ideas beyond organisational settings. After exploring in Chapter 7 how, within the context of organisations, audience members construct the use of idea through different forms of power, our analysis emphasised the need to study the social use of management ideas not directly related to organisational implementation. In particular, drawing on a spectacle/performance perspective, we explored in the present chapter how audience members may engage in different forms of fan involvement (i.e. exaltation, socialisation and marketisation), each having a specific bearing on the way they construct and reconstruct themselves and the management ideas and artefacts associated with a guru event. We furthered our insight into the way audience members can become 'textually productive' in various analytically distinct ways, and how these are associated with specific imaginary communities that act as points of reference beyond the scope of a specific organisation. In the following paragraphs, we discuss the main implications of these findings for our understanding of the main drivers for using management ideas, their role in relation to managerial identity and our understanding of how the production and consumption of ideas may relate.

First, the findings advance our view on the potential scope and primary aims of management idea use beyond implementation in an organisational context. In the prior literature, the use of ideas is considered to be primarily driven by the desire to translate abstract ideas into management and organisational practice. This is largely based on the assumption that translating ideas into practice contributes to the interest of organisations or their organisational members in relation to their work such as related to efficiency, legitimacy or power (cf. Morris and Lancaster, 2006; Reay et al., 2013; van Grinsven et al., 2016). At the same time, Watson noted that management ideas cannot only be seen as relevant in relation to organisations by referring to what he calls the management practitioner's 'double control' problem, that is: 'dealing simultaneously with issues of the shaping of their personal life and interests and issues of the shaping of the work of the organization' (1994: 898).

Building on this, our findings indicate that the desire to use management ideas is not necessarily dictated by work and organisation-related considerations, but is rooted in different points of reference. In particular, the analysis revealed that audience members derive their main motivation for idea use also from their *imagined relationship* with a guru as an end in itself, from their embeddedness and status in an *imaginary management community* or from their market value in relation to *imagined consumers*. As the overview in Appendix A indicates, individual audience members signal various forms of fan involvement. Indeed, whereas some display little fan involvement, others' accounts show multiple forms. The audience members relate these forms to various conditions such as their experience in attending guru lectures and in performing different managerial roles such as director, line manager, or consultant. Whilst displaying exaltation may not be specifically related to particular preconditions, the findings show that socialisation at least requires awareness of, and connectivity to some (imagined) community or network. The informants' accounts indicate that particularly directors tend to emphasise the significance of these networks in the valuation of particular guru events and ideas. Others refer to imagined management communities to show their knowledge and experience in relation to a management cult or signal the aspiration to become more knowledgeable about this subculture. The latter is often apparent in accounts of audience members who have relatively little experience in management roles and/or attending guru lectures. Finally, and perhaps unsurprisingly, marketisation as form of fan involvement is particularly apparent in the accounts of those in consulting roles. These audience members typically associate themselves with international 'star' gurus and tend to consider themselves as heavy users and active translators of abstract guru ideas to their own audiences.

In relative contrast to organisational contexts, these relations and communities are much less defined by the constraints of space and time, whilst at the same time they all share some form of social hierarchy within which audience members can distinguish themselves from others in the context of a specific form of fan involvement. For instance, audience members experience differences in social status in relation to a management community, but in a similar way may also perceive substantial variety in personal attachments to what they may perceive as star gurus or market value to consumers. Irrespective of their social position the findings show that guru events provide important resources for audience members' 'complex imaginative worlds' (Abercrombie and Longhurst, 1998: 106), thereby indicating the substantial scope of potential influence beyond organisational settings, as well as potentially reinforcing each other.

Second, our analysis contributes to further specifying our understanding of the role of identity in relation to management ideas and management gurus. Extant work has emphasised how the construction of managerial identity is of particular significance in enhancing the appeal for particular management ideas amongst a managerial audience: 'gurus not only represent and define core management skills and attitudes (and values); they also define senior managers' roles and identities' (Clark and Salaman, 1998: 153). More recently, research has shown how identity relates to how management practitioners shape processes of organisational implementation (van Grinsven et al., 2020), thereby stressing the significance of different forms of identity work as crucial in understanding the use of management ideas in organisational contexts. Building on this, the present chapter further specifies how management ideas are central to the construction of audience members' identity in various ways. Specifically, the accounts of our informants show that audience members may construct elements of an idea as part of their own identity, or they may construct themselves as part of a management community or create a view of themselves as leading management progress. In other words, through talking about management ideas, audience members define themselves not only in terms of someone involved in organisational implementation (cf. van Grinsven et al., 2020), but also as management fan, management cultist or management knowledge entrepreneur. Overall, this indicates the importance of not only considering what audience members do with management ideas in the context of organisational implementation, but also of considering who they are beyond organisational settings (cf. Abercrombie and Longhurst, 1998).

Moreover, prior work tends to consider explicit identification with a management idea or management guru as having a pejorative bearing on management practitioners for various reasons. For instance, Sturdy noted that management practitioners who show a strong explicit attachment to particular ideas, enhance the possibility of being considered by their colleagues as 'guru groupies' or 'whores', and explains this can be viewed as mainly stemming from 'the threat that consultants/ideas may pose to managers' identities as competent and "in control" and, relatedly, to their careers and job security' (1997: 403). In contrast, our findings signal the importance of considering such strong identifications with an idea or star as a normal aspect of idea use, and even as status-enhancing such as can be found in many accounts of identification practices which often include reference to management ideas to signal some form of aspirational (elite) identity. Rather than presenting explicit attachment to management ideas as a potential issue, many of our informants saw some form of fan involvement as a common element of managerial audience members and generally were not inclined to conceal this involvement.

Third, the findings presented in this chapter contribute to developing a more informed critique and nuance of habitually used distinctions between production/consumption and supply/demand that prevail in much of our conceptualisation of management ideas (Sturdy and Fleming, 2003). Indeed, the broad literature on management ideas generally attributes the 'production' of management ideas as well as the related rhetoric and artefacts to different knowledge entrepreneurs. In a similar way the 'consumption' of ideas is typically associated with management practitioners' activities aimed at promoting intra-organisational acceptance and inducing processes of implementation (Gondo and Amis, 2013; Kelemen, 2000; Radaelli and Sitton-Kent, 2016; Zbaracki, 1998). This chapter indicates that audience members not only become textually productive in processes of organisational implementation. Rather, the results indicate how audience members' skills acquired via past experiences of media exposure, such as regularly attending guru lectures or reading management books, are being made 'productive' in a variety of different ways beyond organisational settings which may entail important implications for the general attention to these ideas amongst (management) practitioners. In other words, audience members not only 'implement' ideas obtained from guru lectures in the context of their organisation, but they also use these ideas as a critical resource to 'perform' in relation to different imaginary communities.

The way audience members perform in relation to these imaginary communities – textually construct and reconstruct themselves, as well as the ideas, language and material artefacts that are obtained from, and associated with a guru event – may not only directly contribute to the attention particular ideas (and audience members themselves) receive in these communities. Indeed, results show that the potential influence of audience members' performances goes far beyond coincidental infectious effects (cf. Røvik, 2011) of some fan-related enthusiasm, but include wide-scale and systematic efforts aimed at promoting a management cult in which some management ideas are seen as common 'knowledge' (see Figure 8.1).

The informants' accounts suggest that, together with (A) regular media exposure to 'new' ideas, the (B) audience members performances

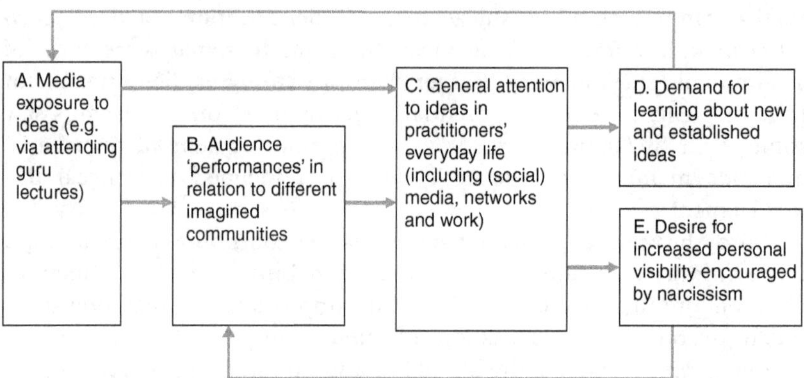

Figure 8.1 Managerial audiences and media performance

targeted at different imaginary communities may (C) contribute to the perceived omnipresence of ideas in people's daily lives, and ultimately (D) enhance desire amongst others to get to know or even further learn about new as well as established management ideas, and (E) encourage others to signal their personal attachment to ideas or stars, their embeddedness in a management community and their purported status as innovative knowledge entrepreneur. With regard to the latter, it can be assumed that increased visibility of audience members may strengthen the performances' desired outcomes which may likely fuel some form of narcissism (Abercrombie and Longhurst, 1998) amongst management practitioners. Indeed, positive (and perhaps also negative) responses to audience members' textual production related to management ideas and management gurus such as via various social and other media may very well encourage new performances. Overall, both (D) the desire to learn about management ideas, and (E) the management practitioners' performances including these ideas can be expected to (A) stimulate media attention and (C) the social construction of management ideas as an inherent part of management practitioners' working life. Yet, as indicated, management ideas may not only be used in deploying and reconstituting audience members' positions in organisational settings but also in relation to different imaginary communities. The findings suggest that the skills and practices used to construct management ideas cannot be seen as limited to 'traditional' knowledge entrepreneurs. It is these multifaceted patterns of media use, which both shapes and is shaped by contemporary managerial audiences, that constitutes a critical aspect of today's accepted managerial roles.

9 Conclusion

Understanding the impact of management ideas has become widely recognised as an important issue in, and motive for social research that, at present, can be witnessed in many scholarly disciplines and comprises a large variety of research approaches (cf. Piazza and Abrahamson, 2020; Sturdy et al., 2019). Since Clark's (2004a) broad review and critique on the literature, a substantial and still growing number of studies have further and significantly advanced our view on how ideas may diffuse and can be implemented in particular organisations (see Chapter 1 for an overview). Indeed, these studies have provided concrete evidence that some management ideas have had a large impact such as indicated by book sales, business media attention, guru lecture attendances, consulting service offerings and formal change programs labeling. In addition, research has also provided important evidence that, once formally adopted in an organisational context, these management ideas have played an important role in (re)shaping management and organisational practice – even though these intra-organisational consequences may not necessarily be considered as favorable.

Yet, although these long-standing, broad and varied approaches to studying the impact of management ideas have provided important theoretical and empirical advancements in relation to diffusion and implementation, their accounts on how these ideas flow between different relevant contexts remain fragmented and have left our understanding of impact incomplete. Seen in the light of the broader flow of ideas, we found that these literatures both apply relatively narrow scopes with respect to the local-extra-local relationships involved in the adoption decision, and have each paid limited attention to the agentic meaning making related to the adoption dynamics (see Figure 1.1). In brief, whereas macro-level approaches to diffusion end their analyses with adoption, micro-level work on organisational implementation takes adoption as its starting point. The former tends to view impact as largely coinciding with adoption, the latter typically considers adoption as merely a condition for impact, yet not a guarantee as such. In this book we considered adoption as a 'hinge' – a pivot point of potential exchange between seemingly disconnected literatures on diffusion and implementation – and, as such, a starting point to examine: *how management practitioners come to use management ideas in relation to different relevant contexts of their working lives*.

Rethinking Management Practitioners as Audience Members

In response to these challenges, our focus was on exploring management practitioners as audience members, not the least because they are likely to play a critical role in how ideas flow between different relevant contexts. As detailed in the introductory chapter, we started from the assumption that in the light of the expansion of management, and related knowledge and institutions (Engwall et al., 2016), managers are increasingly being put in the role of *audience member*. The practice of management and managerial work has traditionally been considered in terms of the organisational role-related expectations and the way these roles are enacted (cf. Mintzberg, 1971; Tengblad, 2006). However, at present, many people in this role show a continuous engagement in management education, traditional business media such as management books, management magazines, and newsletters but also in new social media platforms such as YouTube and the TED Talks channel (Barros and Ruling, 2019; Madsen, 2020; Piazza and Abrahamson, 2020). These management practitioners are not only involved in contexts within which management ideas are typically promoted, but are also systematically associated with the implementation of these ideas within organisational contexts. Moreover, in the light of the possibilities of the 'digital era' (Madsen, 2020), managers can also be expected to draw on various forms of new media (LinkedIn, Twitter, Facebook) to signal their attitudes towards these ideas, legitimate their adoption, and demonstrate their specific use. Given the omnipresence of these media targeted at and produced by management practitioners and management intellectuals (Guillén, 1994), we posited that *being an audience member is an essential part of the contemporary managerial role*. Accordingly, by examining managerial audiences both within and beyond mass communication settings, this book not only seeks to challenge the current views of the nature of contemporary managerial work, but also contributes to bridging and extending the currently disconnected approaches to studying the impact of ideas.

Rethinking the Impact of Management Ideas

In Chapter 1, we detailed how extant approaches to studying the impact of management ideas have considered only parts of the broader flow of these ideas, leaving under-conceptualised critical aspects concerning *scope and agentic meaning making.* Our empirical focus is on analysing managerial audience members' activities and related meaning making prior to, during and after guru events. The findings discussed in the chapters that follow indicate the significance of a broader, more differentiated and dynamic view of how managerial audience members come to use management ideas throughout different relevant contexts of their working lives. On the basis of these findings, the book argues that current approaches to studying the impact of management ideas need a much deeper and broader view by further integrating important aspects of flow concerning scope and agentic meaning making, particularly in relation to (A) the dynamics of managerial audience activities, (B) the protracted involvement of managerial audiences, (C) the managerial audience members' social uses of ideas and (D) the managerial audience members textual productivity (see Figure 9.1).

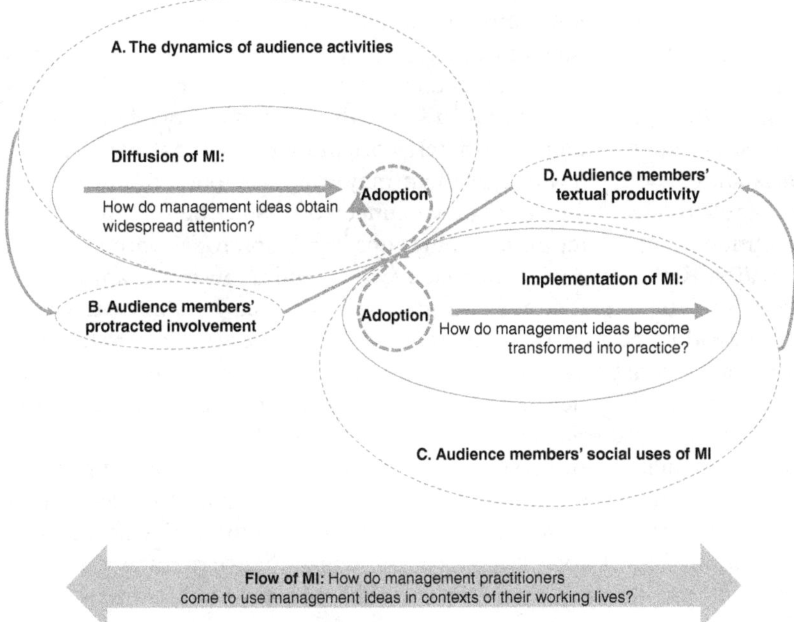

Figure 9.1 Proposed areas for research in relation to flow

The Dynamics of Managerial Audience Activities (A)

Whilst prior diffusion studies have given much attention to the role of various rhetorical practices of those associated with creating and fashioning ideas amongst a mass audience of management practitioners (e.g. Giroux, 2006; Kieser, 1997; Røvik, 2002), our findings suggested that *much broader and more nuanced analyses* are needed to gain adequate insight into how the managerial audience members' activities may actually work in the light of the broader flow of management ideas. For instance, we found in the lectures of successful management gurus that it is not solely a matter of drawing on these rhetorical practices to win and retain converts to their ideas. A much more fundamental issue entails how audience members may actively or passively contribute to the ongoing development of a favourable atmosphere that may enhance the development of positive associations amongst audience members during the management guru performance (Chapter 3). Yet, and as indicated in Chapters 3 and 4, audience members' independent decision-making and related activities are critical in shaping such an atmosphere during management guru lectures. Thus ultimately, managerial audience members' activities during guru lectures need to be considered as important elements in the processes through which management practitioners come to use management ideas throughout different relevant contexts.

In a similar way, much more attention needs to be given to the activities of individual audience members themselves in shaping their orientations to ideas. In exploring potential audience differentiation, our findings not only show how audience members' orientation towards management ideas and the ones promoting them may vary (Chapters 5 and 6), but also explain how this is intimately connected to how these management practitioners construct these orientations in relation to relevant audience activities. Rather than viewing managers' attitudes towards management ideas as relatively static, our findings stress the need for a more dynamic understanding of audience orientations that can better account for individual-level variability. The analyses indicate that the managerial audience members' broader pattern of management knowledge consumption – accumulated experiences generated from prior business media-related audience activities – are systematically associated with a range of possible orientations towards particular ideas. Indeed, we found evidence that experienced audience members are more inclined to display an engaged orientation. This means that whilst fulfilling audience members' expectations is generally seen as critical in developing favourable orientations, the analysis in Chapters 5 and 6 shows that these expectations are largely shaped by the audience members' experiences obtained prior to a guru lecture and thus beyond the direct and immediate efforts of those involved in promoting ideas. Overall, more work is needed to understand audience members' ongoing meaning making prior to and during events such as via processual accounts of thoughts, impressions and conversations.

The findings do not only have implications for current explanations of managerial audiences' orientations in processes of flow, but also open up new possibilities for future studies. Indeed, there is a need to see management practitioners' orientations to particular management ideas not as more or less constant, but as dynamic and related to audience members' activities in time and space (cf. Sonenshein, 2010). A critical issue is to better understand the potential variety of different orientations that is drawn upon by individual audience members in different interactional contexts – to whom and at what stage do particular orientations become part of the management practitioners' discourse? For instance, in relation to the guru lectures (see Chapters 3 and 4), research is needed to get a better understanding of how the orientations of audience members may change during the course of lectures. Also beyond the setting of a lecture – such as within and outside organisations (see Chapters 7 and 8) – further research is needed to know more about the conditions under which these audience members engage in activities that may (de)activate particular orientations in their interactions with others.

The Protracted Involvement of Managerial Audiences (B)

The findings also indicate that we need *a much broader and integrated view* on the factors that contribute to the potential protracted involvement of managerial audience members in processes of diffusion that may further amplify or inhibit management practitioners to use management ideas in other relevant contexts. Whilst studies on the diffusion of management ideas have habitually focused on settings closely related to the traditional knowledge entrepreneurs such as management gurus, business media organisations and management consultants (see Chapter 1), we found that important forms of ideas diffusion occurr outside these typical settings such as via various forms of networked involvement (Chapter 8).

Following Huising (2016) who explored the role of extra-organisational communities in processes of organisational implementation, we found various forms of fan involvement that extend the processes that have been typically associated with diffusion. Importantly these forms of fan involvement are ultimately expected to have a bearing on management practitioners' use of ideas. For instance, we found accounts of managers who recommend others in their network to attend a guru lecture or deliberately advise against it; consultants that stimulate their clients to read about particular ideas; and managers that are encouraged to use ideas based on others' experiences. These forms of extended involvement are seen by audience members as mainly driven by exploring one's taste concerning preferred approaches to management, signalling some form of belonging to a management community or generating business. Yet, whatever the main motivation, these forms of involvement may have notable implications in shaping the possibilities of idea diffusion. As such, our analyses contribute not only to the development of a broader and more differentiated view of idea diffusion, but also signal the need to further explore this area.

Audience Members and the Social Uses of Ideas (C)

The findings presented in our book emphasise the need to consider a much broader view on the *nature and direction of agency* that plays a role shaping the organisational use of management ideas (Chapter 7). In particular, these findings have the potential to push future analyses of the impact of these ideas beyond the assumption that management idea use is primarily connected to systemic forms of power. Rather than considering agency in the organisational use of management ideas mainly in terms of such a top-down direction, our analysis suggests the importance of accounting for multiple directions – audience members' accounts reveal how forms of power are deployed and reconstituted in relational interactions of a downward, lateral or upward fashion.

Our analysis also provides important evidence for the development of a more *differentiated view of the background and attitudes of the key agents* that play a role in the organisational use of management ideas (Chapter 7). The findings indicate that management ideas not only arrive in an organisation via those in (top) management positions, nor did we find evidence that those agents could be considered unambiguously positive about the ideas they bring into an organisation. Overall these findings suggest that more research is required to enhance our understanding of the nature, background and perceptions of those who use management ideas, but also more research is required into the consequences of the variety of ways in which ideas can be used. In Chapter 4, for instance, we found that the efforts of those promoting management ideas may not only relate to the adoption of ideas but also to their application, and, as such, may even constitute an important starting point for the possible alternative interpretations in the usage of ideas. Accordingly, more attention needs to be paid to the intra-organisational interactions between agents carrying different management ideas or interpretations thereof, especially in relation to the influence they may exercise as a way to affect the broader perception and interpretation of these ideas.

The Textual Productivity of Managerial Audiences (D)

In prior diffusion studies adoption has been primarily related to distinct factors that are associated with individual- and organisational-level positive responses to particular ideas such as socio-psychological pressures, and the rhetoric used by various knowledge entrepreneurs. Yet, our research shows that a *much deeper and broader view* is needed to understand how these positive responses are evoked as well as their relative importance in relation to other factors. With regard to the latter, our analyses show how other channels than the traditional ones may contribute substantially to the diffusion of management ideas (Chapter 8). In particular, the results show that, as an extended form of audience members' social uses of management ideas, these ideas are being discussed and even further promoted via audience members' textual productivity, conveyed particularly through traditional business media such as business magazines, but also via new social media such as company websites and LinkedIn. This textual productivity has been considered as part of practitioners' efforts to signal their social position as members of a management community, to enlarge the community or to generate business. Moreover, the analysis also indicates that these efforts are systematically connected to distinct identifications either as members of a broader community or in relation to an imagined consumer. This indeed confirms the performance of a management guru as critical in enhancing the willingness of managerial audience members to use management ideas, but at the same time shows how these gurus need to be considered as 'only' one amongst many influences, not least given the potential influence of audience members' own textual productivity.

So, while particularly in the earlier literature on management ideas, studies focused on the efforts of those knowledge entrepreneurs typically involved in creating and promoting management ideas to mass audiences, we argue that our understanding of these dynamics is still in its infancy. Rather than considering management idea use as primarily driven by guru performances, or by socio-psychological forces attached to particular ideas or gurus, there is a need to broaden our view on these potential areas of influence. In particular, our findings show the significance of specifying the relative importance of different types of textual productivity of audience members – as stemming from their social uses of ideas – via a variety of different media (cf. Barros and Ruling, 2019; Madsen, 2020; Piazza and Abrahamson, 2020). Further research is needed not only to understand the nature and development of managerial audience members' textual productivity (cf. Abercrombie and Longhurst, 1998; Jenkins, 2013), but also how this may play a role both in how management practitioners come to use an idea and how this may simultaneously constrain possible forms of use.

Closing Remarks

By developing a critical understanding of what it means to be an audience member in the context of management we have sought to shed more light on how and why management practitioners are open to particular management ideas in the contexts of mass communication settings, how these ideas are filtered and critically appraised via a primarily differentiated and volatile audience, and how this may subsequently become apparent in the use of ideas in different social and situational contexts. Such a focus on audience members' activities and meaning making allows us to see knowledge entrepreneurs and the management ideas they seek to communicate as having some influence in management practitioners' orientations towards these ideas, albeit one amongst many factors. It also highlights that the social use of management ideas may entail much more than implementing some kind of change program in an organisation, and that the ones who are typically considered as championing this organisational use are not only (top) managers, nor are they limited to audience members who clearly and consistently affiliate with particular management ideas. Overall, our current research establishes the need to consider the broader flow of management ideas as critical to rethink our view of management occupations – and the nature of contemporary managerial work – to one that includes a conceptualisation of management practitioners as audience members both within and beyond mass communication Settings. It also requires us to rethink the complexities concerning how the impact of management ideas becomes apparent and is mediated throughout the different relevant contexts of management practitioners' working lives (cf. Sturdy, 2011).

Appendix A Overview of Informants

Guru A Lecture

No.	Informant			Organisation		Espoused main orientations	Espoused fan involvement
	Background	Function	Gender	Sector	Size		
A1	Medicine	MM	Male	Healthcare	Large	*Engaged*: guru as medium; efficient idea absorption *Non-committal*: guru as entertainer; day off; joining colleague	*Socialisation*: using meetings around gurus to network and enjoy membership of community
A2 (2x)*	Chemistry	TM	Male	IT	Small	*Engaged*: guru as re-invigorator of ideas; need to make ideas valuable by yourself *Critical*: guru as salesperson; being palmed off; simplistic ideas	*Socialisation*: using guru lectures to connect to community of entrepreneurs and circulate experiences in network
A3	Engineering	SE	Male	MC	Small	*Engaged*: guru as re-invigorator; some ideas useful to apply	*Socialisation*: using guru lectures to re-connect to management community *Marketisation*: recommending and translating guru ideas to promote management thinking towards clients
A4	Public mgt.	MM	Female	Government	Med.	*Devoted*: guru as knowledge expert; improves insight; intention to apply and further study	*Exaltation*: enhancing and extending proximity by obtaining guru-related artefacts; identification with guru ideas

A5	Business	STAFF	Female	Bank	Large	*Non-committal*: guru as entertainer; well-organised performance; enjoyable experience *Engaged*: guru has interesting ideas that might be partially useful *Critical*: superficial one-liners that do not stick; no real learning; too expensive; too much show	*Socialisation*: using management gurus to enhance social status and one's career
A6	IT	SE	Male	IT	Small	*Engaged*: guru as messenger; ideas insightful and useful framework for marketing	*Marketisation*: collecting and translating guru ideas and language to promote own service offerings
A7	Business	SE	Male	Trade	Small	*Non-committal*: guru as entertainer; relaxing day off *Critical*: guru as smart entrepreneur; commercial event; too expensive	*Exaltation*: valuation of proximity to guru
A8	Communication	MM	Male	IT	Small	*Non-committal*: guru as performer; day off; recognisable but superficial knowledge	*n/a*
A9	Public mgt.	TM	Male	Government	Med.	*Devoted*: guru inspirer; insightful and useful knowledge; intention to apply directly	*Exaltation*: enhancing proximity to gurus to gain deeper insight and amplify positive experiences *Socialisation*: using guru lectures to connect to management community

(cont.)

No.	Informant			Organisation		Espoused main orientations	Espoused fan involvement
	Background	Function	Gender	Sector	Size		
A10	Business	TM	Female	Bank	Large	*Non-committal*: guru as entertainer; relaxing day off *Critical*: guru as fake coach; ideas superficial, not new, not true; seminar too expensive and too much show	*Exaltation*: enhancing and extending proximity by obtaining guru-related artefacts
A11	IT	STAFF	Female	Telecom	Large	*Engaged*: guru offers knowledge *Non-committal*: guru as storyteller/ entertainer; being inspired during seminar without applying ideas afterwards *Critical*: ideas too superficial; ideas do not change way of working	*n/a*
A12	Shipping, IT	MM	Male	Telecom	Large	*Devoted*: guru as knowledge provider; efficient form of learning *Engaged*: guru as stimulator; offers several tools to select from; transfer of certain elements to own situation	*n/a*
A13	Engineering	MM	Male	Telecom	Large	*Devoted*: guru inspirer; ideas are new; offers eye-openers *Non-committal*: guru as performer; too large and too much a play; ideas too distanced from daily practice	*Socialisation*: using guru lectures to connect to management community

A14	Engineering	MM	Male	Telecom	Large	*Devoted*: guru as well-founded idea provider; eye-openers *Non-committal*: fascinating, energising show; day off; insights forgotten	*Socialisation*: using guru lectures to connect to management community
A15	Business	MM	Male	Telecom	Large	*Non-committal*: guru as impassionate; nice day off; entertaining; joining colleagues *Critical*: seminar as wasted money; ideas have no added value; too general; lack of depth	*n/a*
A16	Business	STAFF	Male	Telecom	Large	*Devoted*: guru inspirer; ideas are eye-openers; intention to apply ideas	*Exaltation*: enhancing proximity to guru to better experience the message; recognise own aspirational identity *Socialisation*: using guru lectures to connect to management community
A17	Graphic design	TM	Male	Telecom	Large	*Engaged*: guru as motivator; refreshment of knowledge; stimulates application of ideas to own situation *Non-committal*: guru as charismatic presenter; well-organised day off	*Exaltation*: enhancing proximity to guru to better experience the message; better define one's identity *Socialisation*: using guru lectures to connect to management community

(cont.)

	Informant			Organisation			
No.	Background	Function	Gender	Sector	Size	Espoused main orientations	Espoused fan involvement
A18	Business	MM	Female	Telecom	Large	*Devoted*: guru as knowledge expert; inspirational and recognisable ideas; intention to apply knowledge	*Exaltation*: extending proximity to guru to further experiencing the guru and the message *Socialisation*: using guru lectures to connect to management community
A19	Business	MM	Male	Telecom	Large	*Critical*: guru as superficial speaker; ideas not new, no added value and not applicable; mainly impression management	*Socialisation*: using guru lectures to connect to management community
A20	Economics	STAFF	Male	Telecom	Large	*Devoted*: guru as trustworthy master of knowledge; useful ideas already applied and intention to apply more *Non-committal*: day off paid by company; guru as entertainer; show elements motivating but of little value	*Exaltation*: using guru lectures to enhance proximity and reinvigorate the message *Socialisation*: using guru lectures to enhance one's career
A21	Public mgt.	STAFF	Male	Telecom	Large	*Devoted*: guru as knowledge provider; ideas are eye-openers; deliberately and consciously applied ideas	*Exaltation*: extending proximity to guru *Socialisation*: using guru lectures to remain up to date in a community

A22	Engineering	MM	Male	Telecom	Large	*Non-committal*: guru as entertainer; high-level entertainment; enjoyable day off *Critical*: guru as charlatan and untrustworthy; ideas not applicable and no added value; not recommendable	*Socialisation*: displaying knowledgeability by comparing and signalling misinterpretations by gurus; promoting guru ideas to community
A23	Sports Academy	TM	Female	IT	Small	*Devoted*: guru as knowledgeable; learning and knowledge motives; direct application	*Exaltation*: recognise aspirational characteristics of guru *Socialisation*: using guru lectures to connect to management community
A24	Biotech, Business	MM	Female	Biotech	Small	*Engaged*: guru as credible motivator; stimulus for further reading	*n/a*
A25	Communication	STAFF	Male	Aid	Med.	*Engaged*: guru inspirer and motivator; stimulus for further reading and application	*Exaltation*: experiencing guru and ideas as in line with one's own identity; desire to be similar; maintain connection to insights from management genre *Marketisation*: using ideas from guru lectures to enhance service offerings

(cont.)

	Informant			Organisation			
No.	Background	Function	Gender	Sector	Size	Espoused main orientations	Espoused fan involvement
A26	Engineering	MM	Male	Airlines	Large	*Engaged*: seminars as means to reflect; guru as motivator; enthusiasm and starting point for further reading and application *Non-committal*: no particular expectations; guru as entertainer	*Exaltation*: enhancing and extending proximity to guru to further experiencing the guru and the message
A27	Engineering	MM	Male	Consultancy	Large	*Engaged*: guru as storyteller; contributes to refreshment of knowledge and development of repertoire; discussion with colleagues; selective application	*Exaltation*: maintain connection to insights from management genre
A28	Education	TM	Male	Consultancy	Med.	*Engaged*: guru as creator of drive/ enthusiasm; inspirer development of repertoire and symbolic application	*Exaltation*: using guru language to frame one's working life; experiencing guru and ideas as in line with one's own identity; desire to be similar; using guru seminar to connect to management genre

* Respondent was interviewed twice.

Guru B Lecture

No	Informant			Organisation		Espoused main orientations	Espoused fan involvement
	Background	Function	Gender	Sector	Size		
B1	Economics	SE	Male	Consultancy	Small	*Engaged*: guru as stimulator; triggered to make sense of general ideas and contextualise them *Critical*: guru as performer with oversized ego	*Exaltation*: enhancing proximity to guru to amplify valuable experiences
B2	Biology	TM	Male	Government	Large	*Non-committal*: guru as entertainer; ideas not new; enthusiastic stories; enjoyable day off	*n/a*
B3	Business	TM	Female	Healthcare	Large	*Engaged*: guru as powerful messenger; useful addition to repertoire of ideas; stimulates further learning; need to contextualise	*Exaltation*: enhancing proximity to guru to better experience the message *Socialisation*: using management gurus to enhance social status and networking
B4	Business	TM	Male	Bank	Large	*Engaged*: guru as high-level energiser; offers motivation and toolbox which needs to be adapted	*Exaltation*: enhancing proximity to guru to amplify valuable experiences *Socialisation*: attending guru lectures to signal knowledgeability
B5 (2x)*	Chemistry	TM	Male	Education	Large	*Devoted*: guru as authority/expert; offers eye-openers and highly relevant ideas; applied in practice *Critical*: guru as charlatan; hot air	*Exaltation*: enhancing proximity to guru to better experience the message *Socialisation*: recommending and translating guru ideas to promote management thinking in a community

(cont.)

No	Informant			Organisation			
	Background	Function	Gender	Sector	Size	Espoused main orientations	Espoused fan involvement
B6 (2x)*	Business	STAFF	Male	Consultancy	Large	*Engaged*: guru as awareness creator; offers useful ideas as starting point for application *Non-committal*: guru as an enjoyable speaker; nothing new; entertaining sessions; no adaptation to practices	*Exaltation*: experiencing guru ideas as in line with one's own identity *Marketisation*: collecting, promoting and translating guru ideas to enhance market position
B7	Accounting	MM	Male	Education	Large	*Devoted*: guru as master of knowledge; offers insight and useful solutions; intention to apply	*Socialisation*: recommending and translating guru ideas to promote management thinking in a community
B8	Business	MM	Female	Animal Health	Large	*Devoted*: guru inspirer; new ideas and eye-openers; food for thought; intention to buy book and apply ideas *Non-committal*: guru as entertainer; offers humoristic but recognisable stories of daily problems; enjoyable to listen to but no effect on work	*Exaltation*: enhancing proximity to guru to better experience the message; recognise own aspirational identity; collecting and using guru language in one's working life
B9 (2x)*	English Language	TM	Female	Education	Small	*Engaged*: guru as awareness maker; enhances enthusiasm for ideas, their relevance and their application	*Exaltation*: enhancing proximity to guru to better experience the message; using guru language in

							one's working life; recognise own aspirational identity *Socialisation*: using guru lectures to connect to management community
B10	Business	SE	Female	Education	Med.	*Devoted*: guru inspirer	*Exaltation*: enhancing and extending proximity to guru to further experiencing the guru and the message
B11	IT	MM	Male	Consultancy	Med.	*Devoted*: guru as highly knowledgeable; offers inspiring ideas and eye-openers; intention to apply *Engaged*: guru as motivator; ideas useful to incorporate in repertoire	*Socialisation*: using guru lectures to enhance status in community; engaging in comparisons between gurus
B12	Accounting	STAFF	Male	Government	Large	*Non-committal*: guru as skillful storyteller; ideas not directly applicable and not to follow blindly; enjoyable performance	*n/a*
B13	Finance	MM	Female	Bank	Large	*Devoted*: guru as inspiring knowledge provider; offers proven ideas; intention to apply *Engaged*: guru as enthusiast knowledge provider; provides energy and drive to learn and to contextualise *Non-committal*: guru as skillful speaker; few new ideas; enjoyable performance; too much show	*Exaltation*: enhancing proximity to guru to amplify valuable experiences

(cont.)

No	Informant			Organisation		Espoused main orientations	Espoused fan involvement
	Background	Function	Gender	Sector	Size		
B14	Psychology	TM	Male	Bank	Large	*Devoted*: guru as independent and respectful authority; offers eye-openers; direct application	*Exaltation*: enhancing proximity to guru to better experience the message; recognise own aspirational identity; collecting and using guru language as in one's working life
B15	Business	STAFF	Female	Bank	Large	*Engaged*: guru as impassionate speaker; mainly symbolic uses	*Exaltation*: enhancing proximity to guru to better experience the message
B16	HRM	TM	Female	Education	Large	*Engaged*: guru as offering stimulating programme, awareness and refreshing ideas; intention to further reading	*Socialisation*: using guru lectures to remain up to date in a community
B17	Psychology	MM	Male	Healthcare	Small	*Devoted*: guru as authority; address need for knowledge; application and discussion with colleagues	*Exaltation*: enhancing proximity to guru to amplify valuable experiences
B18	Business	TM	Male	Mechanical engineering	Large	*Devoted*: guru as expert and management thinker; possibility to learn; direct application by changes in style and organisation	*Exaltation*: constructing guru ideas as part of one's aspirational identity
B19	Economics	TM	Male	Consultancy	Med.	*Engaged*: guru as motivating storyteller; seminar as stimulating form of learning; useful addition to repertoire; intention to apply	*Exaltation*: enhancing proximity to guru to amplify valuable experiences *Marketisation*: collecting, promoting and translating guru ideas to help potential clients

* Respondent was interviewed twice.

Gurus C Lecture series

	Informant			Organisation			
No	Background	Level	Gender	Sector	Size	Espoused main orientations	Espoused fan involvement
C1	Economics	STAFF	Male	Bank	Large	*Engaged*: guru as renowned motivator; offers inspiration; intention to improve organisation *Non-committal*: day-off; sneaking out of daily routine	*Exaltation*: using guru language as normal part of one's working life *Socialisation*: promoting a guru's ideas in a specific network of people
C2	Business	STAFF	Male	Automotive	Large	*Devoted*: guru as specialist in particular area; provides focused knowledge and learning; knowledge adapted *Engaged*: guru as stimulator; inspiration for self-development and legitimation; intention to selectively re-distribute to others	*Exaltation*: prolong proximity to guru to extend possibility of gaining knowledge and insights *Marketisation*: collecting, promoting and translating guru ideas to help potential clients
C3	Business	MM	Male	Chemicals	Large	*Devoted*: guru as specialist; learning new ideas; application of knowledge *Engaged*: guru as awareness creator; explicates latent knowledge; inspiration for own work	*Exaltation*: maintaining strong relation with guru; acknowledge being a fan
C4	Business	SE	Male	Consultancy	Small	*Engaged*: guru as expert; offers inspiration for self-development; intention to apply	*Exaltation*: attending guru lectures and books as part of one's passion *Marketisation*: using guru lectures to enhance one's market value towards potential clients

(cont.)

	Informant			Organisation			
No	Background	Level	Gender	Sector	Size	Espoused main orientations	Espoused fan involvement
C5	Business	MM	Male	Consultancy	Large	*Engaged*: guru as respected knowledge stimulator; offers status and useful ideas for agenda setting *Critical*: seminar as commercial activity; guru offers stylised pictures and dramatic rhetoric; limited use in Dutch context	*Socialisation*: use proximity to gurus to enhance status *Marketisation*: using gurus to maintain strong market position and enhance demand
C6	Business	MM	Male	Bank	Large	*Engaged*: guru as renowned inspirator; offers stimulus to assess and complement own ideas and further agenda setting *Critical*: guru seminar as money-maker; US ideas difficult to apply in Dutch context and low relevance for low-level management	*Exaltation*: enhancing proximity to gurus to gain deeper insight *Socialisation*: engaging in comparisons between gurus to signal knowledgeability

Diverse guru lectures

No	Informant			Organisation		Espoused main orientations	Espoused fan involvement
	Background	Level	Gender	Sector	Size		
D1	Economics	MM	Male	Education	Large	*Engaged*: guru as inspirer; offers useful tools and enthusiasm which motivates to use them; seminar visit provides status *Non-committal*: forgetting input *Critical*: guru as charlatan; ideas without sound (scientific) basis; lack credibility; too expensive	*Socialisation*: using guru lecture attendances to maintain social status and engage in networking *Marketisation*: using guru lectures to enhance one's market value towards potential clients
D2	Chemistry	MM	Male	Utilities	Large	*Devoted*: guru as experienced knowledge master; immediate fit with daily practice; direct application *Engaged*: broad interest in ideas; own transfer to context needed *Critical*: difference between motivating experts and money-makers; sometimes too much show	*Exaltation*: maintaining strong relation with guru; seeking proximity to new gurus; acknowledge being a fan
D3	Hotel mgt.	STAFF	Female	Consultancy	Large	*Engaged*: guru as charismatic speaker; offers insight and new energy for further study and putting ideas into practice *Critical*: guru as pop star; offers nothing new or useful tools; too expensive	*Exaltation*: enhancing proximity to guru to amplify valuable experiences *Socialisation*: using meetings around gurus to network and enjoy membership of community

(cont.)

No	Informant			Organisation		Espoused main orientations	Espoused fan involvement
	Background	Level	Gender	Sector	Size		
D4	Nursing school	MM	Male	Healthcare	Large	*Engaged*: guru as excellent knowledge provider; enriching ideas/eye-openers; stimulates thinking	*Exaltation*: using guru language as normal part of one's working life
D5	Mgt.	MM	Female	Education	Large	*Critical*: guru as hype creator; ideas are superficial and highly repetitive; no consumption of seminars	*n/a*
D6	Mgt.	MM	Male	Government	Large	*Engaged*: guru as expert; offers knowledge that needs to be transferred to own situation; contributes to own development *Critical*: guru as businessperson; too expensive simplistic and no added value; little possibilities to transfer to own context	*Exaltation*: enhancing proximity to guru to deepen background knowledge
D7	Economics	MM	Male	Cultural industry	Med.	*Non-committal*: guru as commercial preacher; offers fascinating and entertaining show; popular but weak contents	*Socialisation*: using meetings around gurus to network and enjoy membership of community
D8	Mgt.	SE	Female	Consultancy	Small	*Engaged*: guru as charismatic personality; offers strong stories and awareness; encourages enthusiasm for application	*Socialisation*: using guru lectures to enhance status in a specific community

D9	Mgt.	SE	Female	Consultancy	Small	*Engaged*: guru as likeable personality; offers vision and energy; contributes to creating awareness	*Exaltation*: enhancing proximity by obtaining guru-related artefacts
D10	Mgt.	MM	Female	Healthcare	Large	*Devoted*: guru as authority; ideas as sound and established theories; application on continuous basis *Engaged*: guru as exciting inspirator; offers awareness and food for thought; ideas need to be carefully adopted *Critical*: guru as non-credible storyteller; ideas lack credibility; no added value, too expensive	*Marketisation*: Using guru lectures to better understand potential client demands and establish market relationships
D11	Engineering	SE	Male	Education	Small	*Critical*: guru as pop star; seminar as money-making; ideas not new, not useful, transient; seminar too much buzz and show	*n/a*
D12	Mgt.	STAFF	Male	Education	Large	*Engaged*: guru as charismatic speaker; well-founded knowledge that adds to own knowledge; ideas are potentially useful after selecting *Critical*: guru as commodifier with large ego; knowledge simplistic and hot air	*Socialisation*: using guru lectures to enhance one's career *Marketisation*: using guru lectures to commercial ends

(cont.)

	Informant			Organisation			
No	Background	Level	Gender	Sector	Size	Espoused main orientations	Espoused fan involvement
D13	Accounting	MM	Female	Corporate Services	Small	*Engaged*: guru as stimulator; provides ideas, some well-known, and stimulates to apply them to practice	
D14	HRM	MM	Female	Corporate Services	Small	*Engaged*: guru as knowledge provider; provides terms and concepts that are useful for and easy to apply to own practice	*Socialisation*: circulating experiences of the guru lecture to share and promote enthusiasm in a community
D15	Entrepreneur	TM	Male	Corporate Services	Small	*Engaged*: guru as energiser and powerful messenger; provides food for thought for oneself and for sharing with others	*Socialisation*: circulating experiences of the guru lecture to share and promote enthusiasm in a community of entrepreneurs

Appendix B Glossary of Transcription Symbols

The transcription symbols used in the extracts from management guru lectures in Chapters 3 and 4 are drawn from the transcription notation used in conversation analysis, which was developed by Gail Jefferson. For details on this notation, see Atkinson and Heritage (1984).

[	A left bracket between adjacent lines indicates where overlapping talk begins
]	A right bracket indicates where overlapping talk ends
(0.4)	Numbers in parentheses indicates the length of a silences in tenths of a second
=	Equals signs indicate that different speakers' utterances are 'latched'. They also link continuous talk by a single speaker that has been distributed across nonadjacent lines because of another speaker's overlapping utterance
(.)	A dot in parentheses indicates a silence of less than two tenths of a second
-	A dash indicates a cut off sound like a guttural stop
<u>Word</u>	Underlining indicates some form of stress via pitch and/or amplitude
WORD	Capital letters indicate talk that is spoken louder than the surrounding talk
Wo::rd	Colons indicate elongation of the immediately preceding sound
., ?	Period, commas, and question marks are used respectively to indicate falling, non-terminal and rising intonation
(Word)	Parenthesised words indicate that the transcriber was not sure of what was said
()	Empty parentheses indicate that the transcriber could not hear what was said
(())	Double parentheses contain transcriber's comments and/or descriptions
.hhh	hs preceded by a period represent discernible inhalations

hhhh	hs without a preceding period represent discernible aspiration
LLLL	A string of l's are used to indicate laughter
L-L-L	Spasmodic laughter is indicated by a chain punctuated by dashes

References

Abercrombie, N. and Longhurst, B. J. (1998). *Audiences: A Sociological Theory of Performance and Imagination*. London: Sage.

Abrahamson, E. (1996). Management fashion. *Academy of Management Review*, 21(1): 254–85.

Abrahamson, E. and Eisenman, M. (2008). Employee-management techniques: transient fads or trending fashions? *Administrative Science Quarterly*, 53(4): 719–44.

Abrahamson, E. and Fairchild, G. (1999). Management fashion: lifecycles, triggers and collective learning processes. *Administrative Science Quarterly*, 44(4): 708–40.

Ansari, S. M., Fiss, P. C. and Zajac, E. J. (2010). Made to fit: how practices vary as they diffuse. *Academy of Management Review*, 35(1): 67–92.

Ansari, S., Reinecke, J. and Spaan, A. (2014). How are practices made to vary? Managing practice adaptation in a multinational corporation. *Organisation Studies*, 35(9): 1313–41.

Asch, S. E. (1951). Effects of group pressure upon the modification and distortion of judgments. In H. Guetzkow (ed.), *Groups, leadership and men; research in human relations*, pp. 177–90. Pittsburgh, PA: Carnegie Press.

Asmuß, B. (2008). Performance appraisal interviews: preference organization in assessment sequences. *Journal of Business Communication*, 45(4): 408–29.

Asmuß, B. (2013). The emergence of symmetries and asymmetries in performance appraisal interviews: an interactional perspective. *Economic and Industrial Democracy*, 34(2): 1–18.

Asmuß, B. and Svennevig, J. (2009). Meeting talk: an introduction. *Journal of Business Communication*, 46(1): 3–22.

Astley, W. G. and Zammuto, R. F. (1992). Organization science, managers, and language games. *Organization Science*, 3(4): 443–60.

Atkinson, J. M. (1984a). *Our Masters' Voices: The Language and Body Language of Politics*. London: Methuen.

Atkinson, J. M. (1984b). Public speaking and audience response: some techniques for inviting applause. In J. M. Atkinson and J. Heritage (eds.), *Structures of Social Action*, pp. 370–410. Cambridge: Cambridge University Press.

Atkinson, J. M. and Heritage, J. (eds.) (1984). *Structures of Social Action: Studies in Conversation Analysis*. Cambridge: Cambridge University Press.

Barley, S. and Kunda, G. (1992). Design and devotion: surges of rational and normative ideologies of control in managerial discourse. *Administrative Science Quarterly*, 37(3): 363–99.

Barnes, R. (2007). Formulations and the facilitation of common agreement in meetings talk. *Text & Talk: An Interdisciplinary Journal of Language, Discourse & Communication Studies*, 27(3): 273–96.

Barros, M. and Rüling, C. C. (2019). Business media: from gatekeeping to transmediality. In A. Sturdy, S. Heusinkveld, T. Reay and D. Strang (eds.), *The Oxford Handbook of Management Ideas*, pp. 195–215. Oxford: Oxford University Press.

Bauer, R. A. (1964). The obstinate audience: the influence process from the point of view of social communication. *American Psychologist*, 19(5): 319.

Baur, C. (1994). Management evangelists in showbiz arena. *Sunday Times*, 19 June.

Beaven, Z. and Laws, C. (2007). 'Never let me down again': loyal customer attitudes towards ticket distribution channels for live music events: a netnographic exploration of the US leg of the Depeche Mode 2005–2006 world tour. *Managing Leisure*, 12(2–3): 120–42.

Benders, J. (1999). Tricks and trucks: a case study of organization concepts at work. *International Journal of Human Resource Management*, 10(4): 624–37.

Benders, J. and van Veen, K. (2001). What's in a fashion? Interpretative viability and management fashions. *Organization*, 8(1): 33–53.

Benders, J. and Verlaar, S. (2003). Lifting parts: putting conceptual insights into practice. *International Journal of Operations & Production Management*, 23(7): 757–74.

Benders, J., van Grinsven, M. and Ingvaldsen, J. (2019). The persistence of management ideas. In A. Sturdy, S. Heusinkveld, T. Reay and D. Strang (eds.), *The Oxford Handbook of Management Ideas*, pp. 271–85. Oxford: Oxford University Press.

Bhatanacharoen, P., Clark, T. and Greatbatch, D. (2013). Managing boundaries through talk: epiphanal stories in management guru lectures. Paper presented at 29th EGOS Colloquium 2013, Montreal, 4–6 July in Subtheme 33: Management Occupations – 'Exploring Boundaries and Knowledge Flows'.

Bikhchandani, S., Hirshleifer, D. and Welch, I. (1998). Learning from the behavior of others: conformity, fads, and informational cascades. *Journal of Economic Perspectives*, 12(3): 151–70.

Biocca, F. (1988). Opposing conceptions of the audience: the active and passive hemispheres of mass communication theory. *Annals of the International Communication Association*, 11(1): 51–80.

Bloom, N. and van Reenen, J. (2007). Measuring and explaining management practices across firms and countries. *The Quarterly Journal of Economics*, 122(4): 1351–408.

Bloomfield, B. P. and Danieli, A. (1995). The role of management consultants in the development of information technology: the indissoluble nature of socio-political and technical skills. *Journal of Management Studies*, 32(1): 23–46.

Blumler, J. G. (1979). The role of theory in uses and gratifications studies. *Communication Research*, 6(1): 9–36.

Boaden, R. J. (1997). What is total quality management ... and does it matter? *Total Quality Management*, 8(4): 153–71.

Bodrožić, Z. and Adler, P. S. (2018). The evolution of management models: a neo-Schumpeterian theory. *Administrative Science Quarterly*, 63(1): 85–129.

Bogart, D. (ed.) (1998). *The Bowker Annual: Library and Trade Book Almanac* (Vol. 43). New Providence, NJ: R. R. Bowker LLC.

Bogart, D. (ed.) (2005). *The Bowker Annual. Library and Book Trade Almanac* (Vol. 50). Medford, NJ: Information Today.

Bogart, D. (ed.) (2008). *Library and Book Trade Almanac* (Vol. 53). Medford, NJ: Information Today.

Bogart, D. (ed.) (2010). *Library and Book Trade Almanac* (Vol. 55). Medford, NJ Information Today.

Bogart, D. (ed.) (2013). *Library and Book Trade Almanac* (Vol. 58). Medford, NJ: Information Today.

Bogart, D. (ed.) (2015). *Library and Book Trade Almanac* (Vol. 60). Medford, NJ: Information Today.

Bogart, D. (ed.) (2018). *Library and Book Trade Almanac* (Vol. 63). Medford, NJ: Information Today.

Boiral, O. (2003). ISO 9000: outside the iron cage. *Organization Science*, 14(6): 720–37.

Bort, S. (2015). Turning a management innovation into a management panacea: management ideas, concepts, fashions, practices and theoretical concepts. In A. Örtenblad (ed.), *Handbook of Research on Management Ideas and Panaceas*, pp. 35–52. Cheltenham: Edward Elgar.

Bort, S. and Kieser, A. (2019). The consumers and co-producers of management ideas. In A. Sturdy, S. Heusinkveld, T. Reay and D. Strang (eds.), *The Oxford Handbook of Management Ideas*, pp. 232–48. Oxford: Oxford University Press.

Brodine, R. (1986). Getting the applause. In R. M. B. Bosinelli (ed.), *US presidential election 1984: an interdisciplinary approach to the analysis of political discourse*. Bologna: Pitagoria Editrice.

Brunsson, N. and Olsen, J. (1997). *The Reforming Organization*. Bergen/Sandviken: Fagbokforlaget.

Busse, K. and Gray, J. (2014). Fan cultures and fan communities. In V. Nightingale (ed.), *The Handbook of Media Audiences*, pp. 425–43. Chichester: John Wiley.

Butsch, R. (2008). *The Citizen Audience: Crowds, Publics, and Individuals*. New York: Routledge.

Canato, A., Ravasi, D. and Phillips, N. (2013). Coerced practice implementation in cases of low cultural fit: cultural change and practice adaptation during the implementation of Six Sigma at 3M. *Academy of Management Journal*, 56(6): 1724–53.

Carlone, D. (2006). The ambiguous nature of a management guru lecture: providing answers while deepening uncertainty. *The Journal of Business Communication*, 43(2): 89–112.

Carson, P. P., Lanier, P. A., Carson, K. D. and Guidry, B. N. (2000). Clearing a path through the management fashion jungle: some preliminary trailblazing. *Academy of Management Journal*, 43(6): 1143–58.

Cassell, C. and Lee, B. (2017). Understanding translation work: the evolving interpretation of a trade union idea. *Organization Studies*, 38(8): 1085–106.

Caulkin, S. (1997). Quirky commonsense at $95,000 a day. *Observer* (Business section), 13 April, 14.

Clark, T. (2004a). The fashion of management fashion: a surge too far? *Organization*, 11(2): 297–306.

Clark, T. (2004b). Strategy viewed from a management fashion perspective. *European Management Review*, 1(1): 105–11.

Clark, T. and Greatbatch, D. (2004). Management fashion as image-spectacle: the production of best-selling management books. *Management Communication Quarterly*, 17(3): 396–424.

Clark, T. and Greatbatch, D. (2011). Audience perceptions of charismatic and non-charismatic oratory: the case of management gurus. *The Leadership Quarterly*, 22(1): 22–32.

Clark, T. and Salaman, G. (1996). The management guru as organizational witchdoctor. *Organization*, 3(1): 85–107.

Clark, T. and Salaman, G. (1998). Telling tales: management gurus' narratives and the construction of managerial identity. *Journal of Management Studies*, 35 (2): 137–61.

Clark, T., Bhatanacharoen, P. and Greatbatch, D. (2015). Conveying the adaptation of management panaceas: the case of management gurus. In A. Örtenblad (ed.), *Handbook of Research on Management Ideas and Panaceas*, pp. 223–42. Cheltenham: Edward Elgar.

Clayman, S. E. (1992). Caveat orator: audience disaffiliation in the 1988 presidential debates. *Quarterly Journal of Speech*, 78(1): 33–60.

Clayman, S. E. (1993). Booing: the anatomy of a disaffiliative response. *American Sociological Review*, 58(1): 110–30.

Clifton, J. (2006). A conversation analytical approach to business communication. *Journal of Business Communication*, 43(3): 202–19.

Clifton, J. (2009). Beyond taxonomies of influence: 'doing' influence and making decisions in management team meetings. *Journal of Business Communication*, 46 (1): 57–79.

Collins, D. (2007). *Narrating the Management Guru: In Search of Tom Peters*. London: Routledge.

Collins, D. (2012). Women roar: 'the women's thing' in the storywork of Tom Peters. *Organization*, 19(4): 405–24.

Cooper, R. and Tang, T. (2009). Predicting audience exposure to television in today's media environment: an empirical integration of active-audience and structural theories. *Journal of Broadcasting and Electronic Media*, 53(3): 400–18.

Corbin, J. M. and Strauss, A. (1990). Grounded theory research: procedures, canons, and evaluative criteria. *Qualitative Sociology*, 13(1): 3–21.

Corrigan, P. (1995). *The Sociology of Consumption*. London: Sage.

Cullen, J. G. (2009). How to sell your soul and still get into heaven: Steven Covey's epiphany-inducing technology of effective selfhood. *Human Relations*, 62(8): 1231–54.

David, R. J. and Strang, D. (2006). When fashion is fleeting: transitory collective beliefs and the dynamics of TQM consulting. *Academy of Management Journal*, 49(2): 215–33.

Davis, A. (2005). Media effects and the active elite audience: a study of communications in the London Stock Exchange. *European Journal of Communication*, 20(3): 303–26.

De Cock, C. and Hipkin, I. (1997). TQM and BPR: beyond the beyond myth. *Journal of Management Studies*, 34(5): 659–75.

Du Gay, P. (1996). *Consumption and Identity at Work*. London: Sage.

Emrich, C. G., Brower, H. H., Feldman, J. M. and Garland, H. (2001). Images in words: presidential rhetoric, charisma, and greatness. *Administrative Science Quarterly*, 46(3): 527–57.

Engwall, L. and Wedlin, L. (2019). Business studies and management ideas. In A. Sturdy, S. Heusinkveld, T. Reay and D. Strang (eds.), *The Oxford Handbook of Management Ideas*, pp. 159–76. Oxford: Oxford University Press.

Engwall, L., Kipping, M. and Üsdiken, B. (2016). *Defining Management: Business Schools, Consultants, Media*. New York: Routledge.

Ernst, B. and A. Kieser (2002). In search of explanations for the consulting explosion. In K. Sahlin-Andersson and L. Engwall (eds.), *The Expansion of Management Knowledge: Carriers, Flows, and Sources*, pp. 47–73. Stanford, CA: Stanford University Press.

Fishbein, M. and Ajzen, I. (1975). *Belief, Attitude, Intention, and Behavior*. Reading, MA: Addison-Wesley.

Fiske, J. (1992a). Audiencing: a cultural studies approach to watching television. *Poetics*, 21(4): 345–59.

Fiske, J. (1992b). The cultural economy of fandom. In *The Adoring Audience: Fan Culture and Popular Media*, pp. 30–49. London: Routledge.

Fiss, P. C. and Zajac, E. J. (2006). The symbolic management of strategic change: sensegiving via framing and decoupling. *Academy of Management Journal*, 49 (6): 1173–93.

Fiss, P. C., Kennedy, M. T. and Davis, G. F. (2012). How golden parachutes unfolded: diffusion and variation of a controversial practice. *Organization Science*, 23(4): 1077–99.

Fligstein, N. (1997). Social skill and institutional theory. *American Behavioral Scientist*, 40(4): 397–405.

Furusten, S. (1999). *Popular Management Books: How They Are Made and What They Mean for Organisations*. London: Routledge.

Gabriel, Y. (2016). The essay as an endangered species: should we care? *Journal of Management Studies*, 53(2): 244–9.

Gabriel, Y. and Lang, T. (1995). *The Unmanageable Consumer: Contemporary Consumption and Its Fragmentations*. London: Sage.

Garfinkel, H. (1967). *Studies in Ethnomethodology*. Cambridge: Polity Press.

Gill, J. and Whittle, S. (1993). Management by panacea: accounting for transience. *Journal of Management Studies*, 30(2): 281–95.

Giroux, H. (2006). It was such a handy term: management fashions and pragmatic ambiguity. *Journal of Management Studies*, 43(6): 1227–60.

Giroux, H. (2019). Popular management ideas. In A. Sturdy, S. Heusinkveld, T. Reay and D. Strang (eds.), *The Oxford Handbook of Management Ideas*, pp. 303–33. Oxford: Oxford University Press.

Glaser, B. G. and Strauss, A. L. (1967). *The Discovery of Grounded Theory: Strategies for Qualitative Research*. Chicago, IL: Aldine de Gruyter.

Glenn, P. J. (1989). Initiating shared laughter in multi-party conversations. *Western Journal of Communication (includes Communication Reports)*, 53(2): 127–49.

Godlewski, L. R. and Perse, E. M. (2010). Audience activity and reality television: identification, online activity, and satisfaction. *Communication Quarterly*, 58(2): 148–69.

Goffman, E. (1983). The interaction order. *American Sociological Review*, 48 (1): 1–17.

Gondo, M. B. and Amis, J. M. (2013). Variations in practice adoption: the roles of conscious reflection and discourse. *Academy of Management Review*, 38(2): 229–47.

Grady, K. and Potter, J. (1985). Speaking and clapping: a comparison of Foot and Thatcher's oratory. *Language and Communication*, 5(3): 173–83.

Gray, B., Purdy, J. M. and Ansari, S. (2015). From interactions to institutions: microprocesses of framing and mechanisms for the structuring of institutional fields. *Academy of Management Review*, 40(1): 115–43.

Gray, J., Sandvoss, C. and Harrington, C. L. (eds.). (2017). *Fandom: Identities and Communities in a Mediated World*. New York: NYU Press.

Greatbatch, D. and Clark, T. (2003). Displaying group cohesion: humour and laughter in the public lectures of management gurus. *Human Relations*, 56(12): 1515–44.

Greatbatch, D. and Clark, T. (2005). *Management Speak: Why We Listen to What Management Gurus Tell Us*. London: Routledge.

Greatbatch, D. and Clark, T. (2010). The situated production of stories. In N. Llewllyn and J. Hindmarsh (eds.), *Organisations, Interaction and Practice: Studies in Real Time Work and Organising*, pp. 96–118. Cambridge: Cambridge University Press.

Greatbatch, D. and Clark, T. (2018). *Using Conversation Analysis for Business and Management Students*. London: Sage.

Green, S. D. and May, S. C. (2005). Lean construction: arenas of enactment, models of diffusion and the meaning of 'leanness'. *Building Research & Information*, 33(6): 498–511.

Greenberg, B. S. (1974). Gratifications of television viewing and their correlates for British children. In J. G. Blumler and E. Katz (eds.), *The Uses of Mass Communications: Current Perspectives on Gratifications Research*. Beverly Hills, CA: Sage.

Grey, C. (1999). 'We are all managers now'; 'we always were': on the development and demise of management. *Journal of Management Studies*, 36(5): 561–85.

Grint, K. (1994). Reengineering history: social resonances and business process reengineering. *Organization*, 1(1): 179–202.

Grint, K. and Case, P. (1998). The violent rhetoric of re-engineering: management consultancy on the offensive. *Journal of Management Studies*, 35(5): 557–77.

Groß, C., Heusinkveld, S. and Clark, T. (2015). The active audience? Gurus, management ideas and consumer variability. *British Journal of Management*, 26 (2): 273–91.

Guerrier, Y. and Gilbert, D. (1995). The role of presentation techniques in selling management ideas through the 'heart' not the mind. Paper presented at 12th EGOS Colloquium, Istanbul.

Guillén, M. (1994). *Models of Management: Work, authority, and Organization in a Comparative Perspective*. Chicago: University of Chicago Press.

Gunter, B. (1988). Finding the limits of audience activity. *Annals of the International Communication Association*, 11(1): 108–216.

Gunter, B. (2000). *Media Research Methods*. London: Sage.

Guthey, E., Clark, T. and Jackson, B. (2009). *Demystifying Business Celebrity*. London: Routledge.

Haijtema, D. (2011). *De goeroegids. De beste Nederlandse managementdenkers*. Amsterdam: Business Contact.

Hall, S. (1980). Encoding/decoding. Centre for Contemporary Cultural Studies (ed.) Culture, Media, Language: Working Papers in Cultural Studies, 79, 128–38.

Hancock, P. and Tyler, M. (2019). Management Ideas in Everyday Life. In A. Sturdy, S. Heusinkveld, T. Reay and D. Strang (eds.), *The Oxford Handbook of Management Ideas*, pp. 458–72. Oxford: Oxford University Press.

Harrington, C. L. and Bielby, D. D. (1995). *Soap Fans: Pursuing Pleasure and Making Meaning in Everyday Life*. Philadelphia: Templeton University Press.

Heritage, J. (1984). *Garfinkel and Ethnomethodology*. Cambridge: Polity Press.

Heritage, J. and Greatbatch, D. (1986). Generating applause: a study of rhetoric and response at party political conferences. *American Journal of Sociology*, 92(1): 110–57.

Heusinkveld, S. and Benders, J. (2005). Contested commodification: consultancies and their struggle with new concept development. *Human Relations*, 58(3): 283–310.

Heusinkveld, S., Sturdy, A. and Werr, A. (2011). The co-consumption of management ideas and practices. *Management Learning*, 42(2): 139–47.

Heyden, M. L., Fourné, S. P., Koene, B. A., Werkman, R. and Ansari, S. (2017). Rethinking 'top-down' and 'bottom-up' roles of top and middle managers in organizational change: implications for employee support. *Journal of Management Studies*, 54(7): 961–85.

Hill, A. (2018). Media audiences and reception studies. In E. Di Giovanni and Y. Gambier (eds.), *Reception Studies and Audiovisual Translation*, pp. 3–19. Amsterdam/Philadelphia: John Benjamins.

Huczynski, A. (1993). *Management Gurus: What Makes Them and How to Become One*. London: Routledge.

Huising, R. (2016). From adapting practices to inhabiting ideas: how managers restructure work across organizations. In L. E. Cohen, M. D. Burton and M. Lounsbury (eds.), *Research in the Sociology of Organizations*, vol. 47, pp. 383–413.

Huisman, M. (2001). Decision-making in meetings as talk-in-interaction. *International Studies of Management and Organization*, 31(3): 69–90.

Jackall, R. (1988). *Moral Mazes: The World of Corporate Managers*. New York: Oxford University Press.

Jackson, B. (1996). Re-engineering the sense of self: the manager and the management guru. *Journal of Management Studies*, 33(5): 571–590.

Jackson, B. (2001). *Management Gurus and Management Fashions: A Dramatistic Inquiry*. London: Routledge.

Jackson, B. (2002). A fantasy theme analysis of three guru-led management fashions. In T. Clark and R. Fincham (eds.), *Critical Consulting: New Perspectives on the Management Advice Industry* (pp. 172–88). Oxford: Basil Blackwell.

Jenkins, H. (2013). *Textual Poachers: Television Fans and Participatory Culture.* New York: Routledge.

Jensen, K. B. (1988). News as social resource: a qualitative empirical study of the reception of Danish television news. *European Journal of Communication*, 3(3): 275–301.

Kangasharju, H. and Nikko, T. (2009). Emotions in organizations: joint laughter in workplace meetings. *Journal of Business Communication*, 46(1): 100–19.

Katz, E. (1959). Mass communications research and the study of popular culture: an editorial note on a possible future for this journal. *Studies in Public Communication*, 2(1): 1–6.

Katz, E., Blumler, J. G. and Gurevitch, M. (1974). Uses and gratification research. *Public Opinion Quarterly*, 37(4): 509–23.

Kelemen, M. (2000). Too much or too little ambiguity: the language of total quality management. *Journal of Management Studies*, 37(4): 483–98.

Kieser, A. (1997). Rhetoric and myth in management fashion. *Organization*, 4(1): 49–74.

Kikoski, J. F. (1998). Effective communication in the performance appraisal interview: face-to-face communication for public managers in the culturally diverse workplace. *Public Personnel Management*, 27(4): 491–513.

Kikoski, J. F. and Litterer, J. A. (1983). Effective communication in the performance appraisal interview. *Public Personnel Management*, 12(1): 33–42.

Kim, J., and Rubin, A. M. (1997). The variable influence of audience activity on media effects. *Communication Research*, 24(2): 107–35.

Kim, S. (2004). Rereading David Morley's the 'nationwide' audience. *Cultural Studies*, 18(1): 84–108.

Kipnis, D., Schmidt, S. M. and Wilkinson, I. (1980). Intraorganizational influence tactics: explorations in getting one's way. *Journal of Applied Psychology*, 65 (4): 440–52.

Klapper, J. T. (1960). *The Effects of Mass Communication.* New York: The Free Press.

Knight, E. and Paroutis, S. (2016). Becoming salient: the TMT leader's role in shaping the interpretive context of paradoxical tensions. *Organization Studies*, 38(3–4): 403–32.

Knights, D. and McCabe, D. (1998). 'What happens when the phone goes wild?': staff, stress and spaces for escape in a BPR telephone banking work regime. *Journal of Management Studies*, 35(2): 163–94.

Kortti, J. (2011). Multidimensional social history of television: social uses of Finnish television from the 1950s to the 2000s. *Television & New Media*, 12 (4): 293–313.

Kostova, T. and Roth, K. (2002). Adoption of an organizational practice by subsidiaries of multinational corporations: institutional and relational effects. *Academy of Management Journal*, 45(1): 215–33.

Krohe, J. (2004). Look who's talking. *Across the Board*, 41(4): 1–7.

Lammers, C. (1988). Transience and persistence of ideal types in organization theory. In N. DiTomaso and S. Bacharach (eds.), *Research in the Sociology of Organizations*, pp. 203–24. Greenwich, CT: JAI Press.

Larsson, M. and Lundholm, S. E. (2013). Talking work in a bank: a study of organizing properties of leadership in work interactions. *Human Relations*, 66 (8): 1101–29.

Lawrence, T. B., Winn, M. I. and Jennings, P. D. (2001). The temporal dynamics of institutionalization. *Academy of Management Review*, 26(4): 624–44.

Lawrence, T., Mauws M., Dyck, B. and Kleysen, R. (2005). The politics of organizational learning: integrating power into the 4I framework. *Academy of Management Review*, 20(1): 180–91.

Levy, M. R. and Windahl, S. (1984). Audience activity and gratifications: a conceptual clarification and exploration. *Communication Research*, 11(1): 51–78.

Levy, M. R. and Windahl, S. (1985). The concept of audience activity. In K. E. Rosengren, L. A. Wenner and P. Palmgreen (eds.), *Media Gratifications Research: Current Perspectives*, pp. 109–22. Newbury Park, CA: Sage.

Lischinsky, A. (2008). Examples as persuasive argument in popular management literature. *Discourse & Communication*, 2(3): 243–69.

Liu, W. (2015). A historical overview of uses and gratifications theory. *Cross-Cultural Communication*, 11(9): 71–8.

Llewellyn, N. and Hindmarsh, J. (2013). The order problem: inference and interaction in interactive service work. *Human Relations*, 66(11): 1401–26.

Lull, J. (1980). The social uses of television. *Human Communication Research*, 6 (3): 197–209.

Lull, J. (1982). How families select television programs: a mass-observational study. *Journal of Broadcasting & Electronic Media*, 26(4): 801–11.

Lull, J. (2014). *Inside Family Viewing: Ethnographic Research on Television's Audiences*. Abingdon: Routledge.

Madsen, D. Ø. (2020). Book Review: The Oxford Handbook of Management Ideas. *Organization Studies*, https://journals.sagepub.com/doi/full/10.1177/0170840620943131.

Mazza, C. and Alvarez, J. L. (2000). Haute couture and prêt-à-porter: the popular press and the diffusion of management practices. *Organization Studies*, 21(3): 567–88.

McCabe, D. (2011). Opening Pandora's box: the unintended consequences of Stephen Covey's effectiveness movement. *Management Learning*, 42(2): 183–97.

McCabe, D. and Russell, S. (2017). 'The costumes don't do it for me': obstacles to the translation of 'new' management ideas. *Management Learning*, 48(5): 566–81.

McCann, L., Hassard, J. S., Granter, E. and Hyde, P. J. (2015). Casting the lean spell: the promotion, dilution and erosion of lean management in the NHS. *Human Relations*, 68(10): 1557–77.

McDermott, A. M., Fitzgerald, L. and Buchanan, D. A. (2013). Beyond acceptance and resistance: entrepreneurial change agency responses in policy implementation. *British Journal of Management*, 24, S93–S115.

McIlvenny, P. (1996). Heckling in Hyde Park: verbal audience participation in popular public discourse. *Language in Society*, 25(1): 27–60.

McQuail, D. (2010). *Mass Communication Theory*. London: Sage.

McQuail, D., Blumler, J. G. and J. Brown (1972). The television audience: a revised perspective. In D. McQuail (ed.), *Sociology of Mass Communication*, pp. 135–65. Harmondsworth: Penguin.

Meyer, J. C. (2000). Humor as a double-edged sword: four functions of humor in communication. *Communication Theory*, 10(3): 310–31.

Micklethwait, J. and A. Wooldridge (1996). *The Witch Doctors: What Management Gurus Are Saying, Why It Matters and How to Make Sense of It.* London: Heinemann.

Miles, M. B. and Huberman, M. A. (1994). *Qualitative Data Analysis: An Expanded Sourcebook.* Thousand Oaks, CA: Sage.

Miller, W. and C'de Baca, J. (2001). *Quantum Change: When Epiphanies and Sudden Insights Transform Ordinary Lives.* New York: Guilford Press.

Mintzberg, H. (1971). Managerial work: analysis from observation. *Management Science*, 18(2): B97–B110.

Mol, M., Birkinshaw, J. and Foss, N. J. (2019). The system of management ideas. In A. Sturdy, S. Heusinkveld, T. Reay and D. Strang (eds.), *The Oxford Handbook of Management Ideas*, pp. 25–41. Oxford: Oxford University Press.

Moores, S. (1993). *Interpreting Audiences: The Ethnography of Media Consumption.* London: Sage.

Morley, D. (2003). *Television, Audiences and Cultural Studies*. London: Routledge.

Morley, D. (2005). *Family Television: Cultural Power and Domestic Leisure.* London: Routledge.

Morley, D. and Silverstone, R. (1990). Domestic Communication: Technologies and Meanings. *Media, Culture & Society*, 12(1): 31–55.

Morris, T. and Lancaster, Z. (2006). Translating management ideas. *Organization Studies*, 27(2): 207–33.

Mueller, F. and Carter, C. (2005). The scripting of total quality management within its organizational biography. *Organization Studies*, 26(2): 221–47.

Mueller, F. and Whittle, A. (2011). Translating management ideas: a discursive devices analysis. *Organization Studies*, 32(2): 187–210.

Nicolai, A. T. and Dautwiz, J. M. (2010). Fuzziness in action: what consequences has the linguistic ambiguity of the core competence concept for organizational usage? *British Journal of Management*, 21(4): 874–88.

Nicolai, A. T., Schulz, A. C. and Thomas, T. W. (2010). What Wall Street wants: exploring the role of security analysts in the evolution and spread of management concepts. *Journal of Management Studies*, 47(1): 162–89.

Nielsen, M. F. (2009). Interpretative management in business meetings: understanding managers' interactional strategies through conversation analysis. *Journal of Business Communication*, 46(1): 23–56.

Nijholt, J. J., Bezemer, P. J. and Reinmoeller, P. (2016). Following fashion: visible progressiveness and the social construction of firm value. *Strategic Organization*, 14(3): 220–47.

O'Mahoney, J., Heusinkveld, S. and Wright, C. (2013). Commodifying the commodifiers: the impact of procurement on management knowledge. *Journal of Management Studies*, 50(2): 204–35.

Örtenblad, A. (2007). Senge's many faces: problem or opportunity? *The Learning Organization*, 14(2): 108–22.

Örtenblad, A. (ed.) (2015). *Handbook of Research on Management Ideas and Panaceas*. Cheltenham: Edward Elgar.

Oshima, S. (2014). Achieving consensus through professionalized head nods: the role of nodding in service encounters in Japan. *Journal of Business Communication*, 51(1): 31–57.

Outila, V., Piekkari, R., Mihailova, I. and Angouri, J. (2020). 'Trust but verify': how middle managers in a multinational use proverbs to translate an imported management concept. *Organization Studies*, https://journals.sagepub.com/doi/full/10.1177/0170840620934065.

Pagel, S. and Westerfelhaus, R. (2005). Charting managerial reading preferences in relation to popular management theory books: a semiotic analysis. *The Journal of Business Communication*, 42(4): 420–448.

Palmgreen, P. and Rayburn, J. D. (1982). Gratifications sought and media exposure: an expectancy value model. *Communication Research*, 9(4): 561–80.

Palmgreen, P., Wenner, L. A. and Rayburn, J. D. (1980). Relations between gratifications sought and obtained: a study of television news. *Communication Research*, 7(2): 161–92.

Peccei, R. and Rosenthal, P. (2000). Front-line responses to customer orientation programmes: a theoretical and empirical analysis. *International Journal of Human Resource Management*, 11(3): 562–90.

Perse, E. M. (1990). Audience selectivity and involvement in the newer media environment. *Communication Research*, 17(5): 675–97.

Peters, P. and Heusinkveld, S. (2010). Institutional explanations for managers' attitudes towards telehomeworking. *Human Relations*, 63(1): 107–35.

Piazza, A. and Abrahamson, E. (2020). Fads and fashions in management practices: taking stock and looking forward. *International Journal of Management Reviews*, 22(3): 264–86.

Psathas, G. (1995). *Conversation Analysis: The Study of Talk-in-Interaction*. Thousand Oaks, CA: Sage.

Radaelli, G. and Sitton-Kent, L. (2016). Middle managers and the translation of new ideas in organizations: a review of micro-practices and contingencies. *International Journal of Management Reviews*, 18(3): 311–32.

Rayburn, J. D. and Palmgreen, P. (1984). Merging uses and gratifications and expectancy-value theory. *Communication Research*, 11(4): 537–62.

Reay, T., Chreim, S., Golden-Biddle, K. et al. (2013). Transforming new ideas into practice: an activity based perspective on the institutionalization of practices. *Journal of Management Studies*, 50(6): 963–90.

Røvik, K. A. (2011). From fashion to virus: an alternative theory of organizations' handling of management ideas. *Organization Studies*, 32(5): 631–53.

Røvik, K. A. (2002). The secrets of the winners: management ideas that flow. In K. Sahlin-Andersson and L. Engwall (eds.), *The Expansion of Management Knowledge: Carriers, Ideas and Sources*, pp. 113–44. Stanford, CA: Stanford University Press.

Rubin, A. M. (2009). Uses-and-gratifications perspective on media effects. In Jennings B. and Oliver, M.B. *Media Effects: Advances in Theory and Research*, pp. 181–200. London: Routledge.

Rubin, A. M. and Perse, E. M. (1987). Audience activity and soap opera involvement: a uses and effects investigation. *Human Communication Research*, 14(2): 246–68.

Rubin, H. J. and I. S. Rubin (1995). *Qualitative Interviewing: The Art of Hearing Data*. Thousand Oaks, CA: Sage.

Ruggiero, T. E. (2000). Uses and gratifications theory in the 21st century. *Mass Communication & Society*, 3(1): 3–37.

Sahlin-Andersson, K. and Engwall, L. (2002). *The Expansion of Management Knowledge: Carriers, Flows, and Sources*. Stanford, CA: Stanford University Press.

Sandvoss, C. (2005). *Fans: The Mirror of Consumption*. Cambridge: Polity.

Sandvoss, C., Gray, J. and Harrington, C. L. (2017). Why still study fans? In J. Gray, C. Sandvoss and C. L. Harrington (eds.), *Fandom: Identities and Communities in a Mediated World*, pp. 1–26. New York: NYU Press.

Scarborough, H. and Swan, J. (2001). Explaining the diffusion of knowledge management: the role of fashion. *British Journal of Management*, 12(1): 3–12.

Scarbrough, H., Robertson, M. and Swan, J. (2015). Diffusion in the face of failure: the evolution of a management innovation. *British Journal of Management*, 26(3): 365–87.

Scardaville, M. C. (2005). Accidental activists: fan activism in the soap opera community. *American Behavioral Scientist*, 48(7): 881–901.

Scheuer, J. (2014). Managing employees' talk about problems in work in performance appraisal interviews. *Discourse Studies*, 16(3): 407–29.

Scott, W. R. (2001). *Institutions and Organizations*. Thousand Oaks, CA: Sage.

Silverstone, R. (1994). *Television and Everyday life*. London: Routledge.

Sims, D., Huxham, C. and Beech, N. (2009). On telling stories but hearing snippets: sense-taking from presentations of practice. *Organization*, 16(3): 371–88.

Sonenshein, S. (2010). We're changing – or are we? Untangling the role of progressive, regressive, and stability narratives during strategic change implementation. *Academy of Management Journal*, 53(3): 477–512.

Sorge, A. and Van Witteloostuijn, A. (2004). The (non) sense of organizational change: An essai about universal management hypes, sick consultancy metaphors, and healthy organization theories. *Organization Studies*, 25(7): 1205–31.

Spell, C. (1999). Where do management fashions come from, and how long do they stay for? *Journal of Management History*, 5(6): 334–48.

Spell, C. S. (2001). Management fashions: where do they come from, and are they old wine in new bottles? *Journal of Management Inquiry*, 10(4): 358–73.

Spyridonidis, D. and Currie, G. (2016). The translational role of hybrid nurse middle managers in implementing clinical guidelines: effect of, and upon, professional and managerial hierarchies. *British Journal of Management*, 27(4): 760–77.

Staw, B. M. and Epstein, L. D. (2000). What bandwagons bring: effects of popular management techniques on corporate performance, reputation, and CEO pay. *Administrative Science Quarterly*, 45(3): 523–56.

Strang, D. (2010). *Learning by example: Imitation and Innovation at a Global Bank*. Princeton, NJ: Princeton University Press.

Strang, D. and Siler, K. (2017). From 'just the facts' to 'more theory and methods, please': the evolution of the research article in *Administrative Science Quarterly*, 1956–2008. *Social Studies of Science*, 47(4): 528–55.

Strang, D., David, R. J. and Akhlaghpour, S. (2014). Coevolution in management fashion: an agent-based model of consultant-driven innovation. *American Journal of Sociology*, 120(1): 226–64.

Sturdy, A. (1997). The consultancy process: an insecure business? *Journal of Management Studies*, 34(3): 389–413.

Sturdy, A. (1998). Customer care in a consumer society: smiling and sometimes meaning it? *Organization*, 5(1): 27–53.

Sturdy, A. (2004). The adoption of management ideas and practices: theoretical perspectives and possibilities. *Management Learning*, 35(2): 155–79.

Sturdy, A. (2011). Consultancy's consequences? A critical assessment of management consultancy's impact on management. *British Journal of Management*, 22(3): 517–30.

Sturdy, A. and Fleming, P. (2003). Talk as technique: a critique of the words and deeds distinction in the diffusion of customer service cultures in call centres. *Journal of Management Studies*, 40(4): 753–73.

Sturdy, A. and Gabriel, Y. (2000). Missionaries, mercenaries or car salesmen? MBA teaching in Malaysia. *Journal of Management Studies*, 37(7): 979–1002.

Sturdy, A., Brocklehurst, M., Winstanley, D. and Littlejohns, M. (2006). Management as a (self) confidence trick: management ideas, education and identity work. *Organization*, 13(6): 841–60.

Sturdy, A., Clark, T., Handley, K. and Fincham, R. (2009). Management Consultancy: Boundaries and Knowledge in Action. Oxford: Oxford University Press.

Sturdy, A., Heusinkveld, S., Reay, T. and Strang, D. (2019). *The Oxford Handbook of Management Ideas*. Oxford: Oxford University Press.

Suddaby, R. (2019). Objectivity and truth: the role of the essay in management scholarship. *Journal of Management Studies*, 56(2): 441–47.

Suddaby, R. and Greenwood, R. (2001). Colonizing knowledge: commodification as a dynamic of jurisdictional expansion in professional service firms. *Human Relations*, 54(7): 933–53.

Sullivan, J. L. (2013). *Media Audiences: Effects, Users, Institutions, and Power*. Thousand Oaks, CA: Sage.

Svennevig J. (2012). Interaction in workplace meetings. *Discourse Studies*, 14 (1): 3–10.

Svennevig, J. (2008). Exploring leadership conversations. *Management Communication Quarterly*, 21(4): 529–36.

TED (2009). Simon Sinek: how great leaders inspire action. Retrieved August 4, 2020, from https://bit.ly/349HOfq.

TED (2011). Tim Harford: trial, error and the God complex. Retrieved August 4, 2020, from https://bit.ly/2Wh65LX.

TED (2013). Rosalinde Torres: what it takes to be a great leader. Retrieved August 4, 2020, from https://bit.ly/3a5htmq.

Tefertiller, A. and Sheehan, K. (2019). TV in the streaming age: motivations, behaviors, and satisfaction of post-network television. *Journal of Broadcasting & Electronic Media*, 63(4): 595–616.

ten Bos, R. and Heusinkveld, S. (2007). The guru's gusto: management fashion, performance and taste. *Journal of Organizational Change Management*, 20(3): 304–25.

Tengblad, S. (2006). Is there a 'new managerial work'? A comparison with Henry Mintzberg's classic study 30 years later. *Journal of Management Studies*, 43(7): 1437–61.

The Economist (1994a). A continent without gurus. *The Economist*, 4 June, p. 90.

The Economist (1994b). Tom Peters, performance artist. *The Economist*, 24 September, p. 101.

Thomas, R., Sargent, L. D. and Hardy, C. (2011). Managing organizational change: negotiating meaning and power-resistance relations. *Organization Science*, 22(1): 22–41.

Thorne, S. and Bruner, G. C. (2006). An exploratory investigation of the characteristics of consumer fanaticism. *Qualitative Market Research*, 9(1): 51–72.

Vaara, E. and Monin, P. (2010). A recursive perspective on discursive legitimation and organizational action in mergers and acquisitions. *Organization Science*, 21(1): 3–22.

Vaara, E., Tienari, J. and Laurila, J. (2006). Pulp and paper fiction: on the discursive legitimation of global industrial restructuring. *Organization Studies*, 27(6): 789–813.

Valenzuela, S., Bachmann, I. and Aguilar, M. (2019). Socialized for news media use: how family communication, information-processing needs, and gratifications determine adolescents' exposure to news. *Communication Research*, 46(8): 1095–118.

van Grinsven, M., Heusinkveld, S. and Cornelissen, J. (2016). Translating management concepts: towards a typology of alternative approaches. *International Journal of Management Reviews*, 18(3): 271–89.

van Grinsven, M., Sturdy, A. and Heusinkveld, S. (2020). Identities in translation: management concepts as means and outcomes of identity work. *Organization Studies*, 41(6): 873–97.

van Rossem, A., Heusinkveld, S. and Buelens, M. (2015). The consumption of management ideas: a cognitive perspective. *Management Decision*, 53(10): 2356–76.

van Veen, K., Bezemer, J. and Karsten, L. (2011). Diffusion, translation and the neglected role of managers in the fashion setting process: the case of MANS. *Management Learning*, 42(2): 149–64.

Visscher, K. , Heusinkveld, S. and O'Mahoney, J. (2018). Bricolage and identity work. *British Journal of Management*, 29(2): 356–72.

Watson, T. (1994). Management flavours of the month: their role in managers' lives. *International Journal of Human Resource Management*, 5(4): 892–909.

Webster, J. G. (1998). The audience. *Journal of Broadcasting & Electronic Media*, 42(2): 190–207.

Westphal, J. D., Gulati, R. and Shortell, S. M. (1997). Customization or conformity? An institutional and network perspective on the content and consequences of TQM adoption. *Administrative Science Quarterly*, 42(2): 366–94.

Wilhelm, H. and Bort, S. (2013). How managers talk about their consumption of popular management concepts: identity, rules and situations. *British Journal of Management*, 24(3): 428–44.

Younkin, P. (2016). Complicating abandonment: how a multi-stage theory of abandonment clarifies the evolution of an adopted practice. *Organization Studies*, 37(7): 1017–53.

Yukl, G. and Falbe, C. M. (1990). Influence tactics and objectives in upward, downward, and lateral influence attempts. *Journal of Applied Psychology*, 75(2): 132–40.

Zeitz, G., Mittal, V. and McAulay, B. (1999). Distinguishing adoption and entrenchment of management practices: a framework for analysis. *Organization Studies*, 20(5): 741–76.

Zbaracki, M. (1998). The rhetoric and reality of Total Quality Management. *Administrative Science Quarterly*, 43(3): 602–36.

Zilber, T. B. (2006). The work of the symbolic in institutional processes: translations of rational myths in Israeli high tech. *Academy of Management Journal*, 49 (2): 281–303.

Index

CPSIA information can be obtained
at www.ICGtesting.com
Printed in the USA
LVHW081308280721
693938LV00002B/35

9 781107 182912